# PHOTOSHOP MOST WANTED

## EFFECTS AND DESIGN TIPS

**AL WARD**
**COLIN SMITH**

D1366946

# PHOTOSHOP MOST WANTED

© 2002 friends of ED

First published March 2002

## Trademark Acknowledgments

friends of ED has endeavored to provide trademark information about all the companies and products mentioned in this book by the appropriate use of capitals. However, friends of ED cannot guarantee the accuracy of this information.

Published by friends of ED
30-32 Lincoln Road, Olton, Birmingham.
B27 6PA. UK.

Printed in USA

ISBN: 1-903450-55-1

## CREDITS

**AUTHORS**
AL WARD
COLIN SMITH

**FOREWORD**
SCOTT KELBY

**COMMISSIONING EDITOR**
LUKE HARVEY

**EDITORS**
VICTORIA BLACKBURN
LIBBY HAYWARD

**AUTHOR AGENT**
MEL JEHS

**PROJECT MANAGER**
SIMON BRAND

**TECHNICAL REVIEWERS**
DARLENE BILLMAIR
GARRETT CARR
JEFFREY DIAMOND
JOSH FALLON
GLAIN MARTIN
PAUL SINCLAIR
JOHN WILLIAMS

**GRAPHIC EDITORS**
KATY FREER
CHANTAL HEPWORTH
DEB MURRAY

**INDEXERS**
SIMON COLLINS
FIONA MURRAY

**PROOF READERS**
SIMON BRAND
JULIE CLOSS
DAN SQUIER

**MANAGING EDITOR**
CHRIS HINDLEY

# CONTENTS

## Colin Smith

**Colin Smith** is an award winning Graphic Designer who has caused a stir in the design community with his stunning photorealistic illustrations composed entirely in Photoshop. He is also founder of the popular PhotoshopCAFE web resource for Photoshop users and web designers. His images have been featured on the National Association of Photohsop Professionals web site.

He has won numerous design contests and awards, including the Guru Award at the 2001 Photoshop World Convention in LA. Colin's work has been recognized by Photoshop User, Mac Design, Dynamic Graphics, and WWW Internet Life magazines. Colin is also listed in the International Who's Who of Professional Management, and is an active member of NAPP. Colin has co-authored 'New Masters of Photoshop' and 'Foundation Photoshop 6.0', he is also a regular columnist for Planet Photoshop.

*I dedicate this book to all my loyal visitors at Photoshopcafe, thanks for helping it become the success it is today.*

*For the late Dr. Jerry Jensen, a scholar and a gentleman. My mentor and friend, thanks for everything.*

*Thanks to my Mom for always supporting my hobbies when I was a child.*

*Thanks to Scott and Jeff Kelby from NAPP. You guys are the best, and you give someone a chance even when they are starting out.*

*To Mauriah, George and Hazel, Mo, Frank, Jason, Nancy, Linda, Dr J. and others. Thanks for your friendship and believing in me.*

*To all the folks over at friends of ED, you rock!*

*Finally to my co-author, Al, thanks for your friendship and constant help.*

**Colin Smith**
**February 2002**

## Al Ward

**Al Ward**, a certified Photoshop Addict and Webmaster of Action FX Photoshop Resources (www.actionfx.com) hails from Missoula, Montana. A former submariner in the U.S. Navy, Al now spends his time creating add-on software for Photoshop and writing on graphics related topics. Al has been a contributor to **Photoshop User Magazine**, a contributing writer for '**Inside Photoshop 6**' and '**Special Edition Inside Photoshop 6**' from New Riders Publishing, has Co-Authored '**Foundation Photoshop 6.0**' from friends of ED Publishing, and writes for several Photoshop related websites. Al was also a panelist at the Photoshop World 2001 Los Angeles Conference, and contributes to the official NAPP website as the Actions area coordinator.

In his time off he enjoys his church, his family, fishing the great Northwestern United States and scouring the Web for Photoshop related topics.

*To begin with, I have to thank my wife Tonia. She defines 'the Other Half', as I'd be half a man were she not traveling with me. Also, my children, Noah and Ali, who round out my life. To Scott Kelby, who gave this guy a shot in the first place and the friendship that continues. Special thanks to everyone at NAPP, with specific mention of Jeff Kelby and Felix Nelson. Great guys both, and exceptional singers to boot! 'The Autumn leaves drift by my window...'*

*To my co-author, Colin Smith: What can I say, Kiwi? It is a joy working with Colin, but even beyond that, I appreciate our friendship more.*

*To the excellent team at friends of ED: Luke, Mel, Libby, Victoria, Simon and all the rest who stuck with it and put in some exceptional hours to make this work possible.*

*To JB, Michael, and the rest of the Alien Skin Software clan. You Rock, green hair and all!*

*To Richard Lynch, Sherry London, Jack Davis, Pete Bauer, and all the other authors/Photoshop Gurus who have not only inspired me with their work but their accessibility and, in some cases, growing friendships.*

*To Mike Maney and the whole Missoula gang at MLMBC. I'm honored to call you friends, family and Brethren.*

*To my parents, my extended family, and all my friends both past and present.*

*Finally, thanks to God the Father who allows this simple soul to do what he loves, love what he does, and to share that meager experience with others. Through His Son I have learned what it is to be 'Truly Blessed'.*

**Al Ward**
**February 2002**

# Foreword

## By Scott Kelby
### Editor-in-Chief, Photoshop User magazine

One of the most powerful features of Photoshop may be the effect it has on people who use it. They become hungry for information; hungry to learn the latest tricks, the hot new techniques, and that common interest has an amazing way of bringing like-minded people together. In fact, it's through that common interest that I met both Al and Colin, at separate times, but both directly related to Photoshop.

I first met Al a few years ago, while digging around some of the most popular Photoshop sites on the Web. His top-flight actions site, ActionFX.com, really caught my attention, and I noticed that he had the logo of the National Association of Photoshop Professionals at the bottom of his home page. As President of that organization, it's always gratifying to see members supporting the group, but in Al's case I was particularly interested because the NAPP also maintains an actions area that is exclusively for its members.

I dropped Al an email, and later that same day we were on the phone trading Photoshop tips, talking about actions, and generally shooting the Photoshop breeze. When you get two Photoshop guys together, you can really rack up some long distance charges, and before long a friendship was formed. By the time I hung up the phone, NAPP had a real pro, a top actions expert, moderating and updating the entire NAPP actions area, which to this day remains one of the most popular areas on the site.

Al's just one of those guys that wants to get involved, wants to share his tips and techniques. He has a love for both Photoshop and the people that use it, and that's what makes him special. That's why I've had Al speaking on "Guru" panels at Photoshop World (NAPP's annual convention) so he can share his experience and knowledge with other NAPP members. That's why I'm also delighted to see Al revealing his techniques in this new book.

I met Colin through a different path: I was one of the judges for the Photoshop World "Guru Awards" for Excellence in Photoshop design. His Photoshop photo-realistic work was so compelling that the panel chose his work as one of the finalists, out of the hundreds of entries competing for the honor. It was just a few weeks later that I met Colin in person for the first time, just off stage at Photoshop World, where he had actually just won the Guru Award for his category, and we posed for a photo, together with his Guru.

It wasn't long after that, that someone on our Web development team said they had found a new columnist for our sister site, PlanetPhotoshop.com and they said this guy was fantastic. His name? Colin Smith. As luck would have it, one of our other Photoshop columnists was Al Ward, and the rest, as they say, is history.

Both Al and Colin have a lot to share with Photoshop users and I can tell you this: you're going to have a lot of fun, you're going to learn an awful lot, and you're going to meet two of the nicest, most sincere guys in the business along the way. Enjoy!

# Welcome

The genesis for this book came from a simple source: you. Well, people like you at any rate.

We created this book as a response to the huge demand for tutorials on creating dynamic Photoshop effects. We see effects all around us: in advertisements, on cereal boxes, in movie splash screens, and junk mail. Take a look at the magazine section in the local grocery store. What do you see? Typography effects. Photographic effects. All generated with a certain program called Photoshop.

The authors, Al Ward and Colin Smith, are both respected gurus in the Photoshop community. They each run popular Photoshop web sites, where they have been inundated by requests for more and more tutorial information.

Throughout this book you will not only learn some inspirational special effects, but you'll also gain a greater insight into Photoshop as a design tool. We'll show you ways to improve your workflow, and become a smarter Photoshop user. We'll also give you design tips from two award-winning designers and "Guru" panelists at the Photoshop World convention.

The book follows a simple format: in the first section Al and Colin walk you through the effects that are most often requested by the visitors to their websites, and the readers of the Photoshop magazines for which they write. If you have already had some experience of using Photoshop then you'll probably cover some familiar territory in the first couple of chapters where the emphasis is on textures and surfaces. If you're a Photoshop newbie then don't worry, Al and Colin have included enough tips for you to come up to speed, and you'll see results in no time.

The book then moves up a gear. We've included a chapter on customizing your toolbox to maximize your efficiency, and we then move on to some sound real-world design techniques; web tricks, colorization effects, and collage techniques.

In the final section of the book Al and Colin have collaborated on three design projects, giving you an insight into how working designers address real design issues, and the creative solutions that they have found.

### A quick word about resolution

Throughout the book you may notice that some of the effects are done in different resolutions, sometimes the designer has created an effect at 100 dpi, at other times at 150 dpi. This is dependent entirely on the designer's preferences. 100-150 dpi is fine for home printing. If an image is for professional print purposes then generally the resolution needs to be at least 300 dpi. Note that when an image has been created for the web, the resolution will be 72 dpi, this is normal screen resolution, some designers chose to work at a slightly higher resolution than is strictly necessary, say 96 dpi when creating web projects, this allows them the freedom to scale their images up, and not lose too much quality.

## All you need to know about this book

This book is designed to be fun, but most importantly it's informative. To keep things as simple as possible we've only used a few layout styles to avoid confusion.

You are going to speed through an awful lot of practical exercises, and these will all appear under headings in this style:

### 1: Cool effect

We've given a number to each individual effect that leads to a finished image, but some effects are 'stepping stones' to a bigger picture, and these have been left without numbers.

In the time-honored fashion we have numbered the steps of each tutorial, like this:

1. Do this
2. Then do this
3. Do this next, etc...

We've packed in lots of helpful hints, which have been highlighted in the following way:

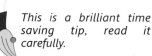

*This is a brilliant time saving tip, read it carefully.*

And we've also provided you with little gems of background information, which you'll see presented like this:

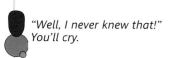

*"Well, I never knew that!" You'll cry.*

Throughout the book we've included all the keyboard shortcuts you'll need, these are written thus. (Windows first, Mac second):

To create a new layer click CTRL/CMD+N

When you come upon an important word or tool for the first time it will be in bold type:

Open the **Gradient Editor**

We've used different fonts to highlight filenames, and URL's too:

`Picture.psd` and friendsofed.com

And finally, all our menu commands are given in the following way:

**Image>Adjust>Hue/Saturation**

## Files for download
To produce the effects as shown, you will need to download the source files required for some of the exercises from our web site at www.friendsofed.com/code.html or you can use similar images of your own.

## Support
If you have any queries about the book, or about friends of ED in general, visit our web site, you'll find a range of contact details there, or you can use feedback@friendsofed.com. The editors and authors will deal with any technical problems quickly and efficiently.

There's a host of other features on the site that may interest you; interviews with top designers, samples from our other books, and a message board where you can post your questions, discussions, and answers. Or you can take a back seat and just see what other designers are talking about. If you have any comments please contact us, we'd love to hear from you.

## Photoshop effects are exciting!
And now, before we dive into the book I'll just hand over to Al Ward for his experience of creating special effects in Photoshop:

Have you ever seen the movie 'Young Frankenstein'? If you have then you will recall the scene in which Dr. Frankenstein (an exceptional Gene Wilder) realizes his experiment has worked. His eyes bugged out, his hair frazzled, he screams at the camera "It's Alive!"

Granted, I could have mentioned the original classic with Boris Karloff, but the Gene Wilder image, especially the hair combined with the scream of insane victory, stand out in my mind as representing the feeling I get when a particular effect in Photoshop comes together.

Al Ward, co-author.

# Chapter 1
# Wood and stone

There is nothing to compete visually with the natural world around us. Though we can try to paint the perfect tree, sunset, or portrait, we will never attain the incredible depth that the physical world contains. In Photoshop, however, we can try to recreate elements of the natural world. Not long ago I saw a demonstration of how a tree could be 'painted' simply using fractals. What was most intriguing was that this underlined the concept that our reality is a complex series of mathematical formulae. For instance, a snowflake is a perfect geometric shape, but no two are alike. Simply by making an infinitesimally small alteration to a single piece of information in the snowflake code brings about infinite results, yet each result is perfect unto itself. Such is the wonder and creativity of Nature.

The math factor is what allows us to visually rebuild aspects of the natural world into an image. Our computers run on ones and zeros, how we stack them up dictates the product on the screen. Break Photoshop down and basically you have a program that applies math into a visual representation. Move a Gaussian Blur slider, and you are simply altering input to the formula that controls the opacity and tonal variation of adjacent pixels in an image.

Let's see what Photoshop allows us to borrow from the physical world for our own work of art.

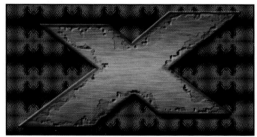

# Wood

There are several ways to render realistic wood textures in your creations. I'll show you a few, and hopefully that will give you enough information to start carving your own creations in no time!

## 1: Basic wood

1. Create a new image of 7x5 inches at 150 pixels per inch, RGB, and fill the background with Black. The black background isn't really important, but that is what I'll be using for this tutorial.

2. Select two wood tones for your foreground and background colors. For this example, the foreground is set to #CF9242 and the background to #904A0B.

3. Create a new layer. Make your selection in whatever manner and shape you like. I'll be using text (**Type Mask** tool, SHIFT+T) as this works for interface parts or picture frames just as easily as a type selection.

>  To use a tool, press the letter on the keyboard to select it, for example, T for the Type tool. In order to get other tools in the same set, hold down SHIFT and press the letter repeatedly to cycle though them, SHIFT+T for the Type Mask tool.

4. Select the Gradient tool (G). In the Options bar, click the Reflected gradient, and make sure the default Foreground to Background gradient is active. If it isn't, click the arrow to the right of the gradient to open the Gradient Picker, and click the Foreground to Background Gradient icon. Starting from the center of the selection and

drawing downwards to the bottom edge of the selection, go ahead and fill the type or shape.

5. Duplicate the filled layer by right-clicking (CTRL-clicking) on the layer in the Layers palette and selecting Duplicate Layer. This is always a good policy, as you have an unaltered template of the original filled shape to go back to if a mistake is made that can't be corrected. Granted, you can always delete steps from the History palette, but it can also be rather tedious. Duplicating this layer is also helpful if we need to activate the original selection again. Also, you may want to name the layers; in this case, I've named them 'wood base' and 'wood working 1'.

6. We are going to add some noise to this layer. Go to **Filter>Noise>Add Noise** and add a Monochromatic Gaussian Noise setting of 10 to 14, depending on the amount of grain you want in the wood. By selecting Monochromatic we are forcing the dots to be two-toned, light or dark. If we don't check this box, the noise will be made up of dots of varying color. We don't need rainbows speckled through our wood effect, so

Monochromatic is the noise of choice!

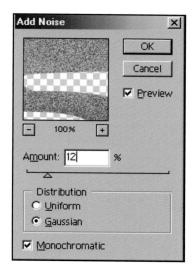

7. Now we want to apply a Motion Blur to give us a wood grain pattern. Go to **Filter>Blur>Motion Blur** and enter a 0 degree motion blur. The amount of blur you apply will dictate the smoothness and length of the grain. For this example I'm using a setting of 20, as that will give a fair contrast for the example image.

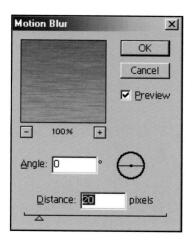

8. If you want to tighten up the effect a bit (increase the contrast of the grain), run the Sharpen filter once (**Filter>Sharpen>Sharpen**).

9. Not all wood is perfect and without blemish, so we are going to add a few imperfections in the grain. Select the **Elliptical Marquee** tool (SHIFT+M). In the Options bar set the Feather radius to 3 pixels. Deselect (CTRL/CMD+D).

10. Make a small circular selection on the wood grain.

11. Go to **Filter>Distort>Twirl** and add some distortion. I've used a setting of 109, but check the viewer and twist the selection to taste.

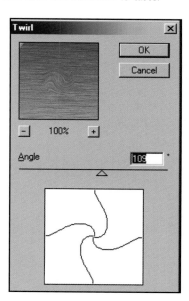

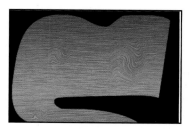

**12.** Repeat the above step in different areas of the image, changing the Twirl settings each time for variation in the knots.

**13.** Now we will apply a few settings from the Layer Styles dialog box. Access the styles for this layer, and start with a Bevel and Emboss with the following settings:

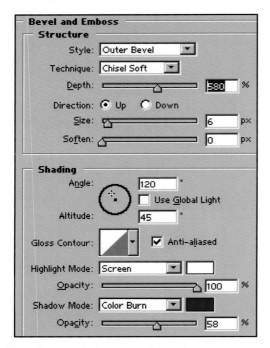

**14.** Since the Bevel Size was set to 6 in the previous step, we'll now apply a 6 pixel Stroke to the outside, with the color set as brown.

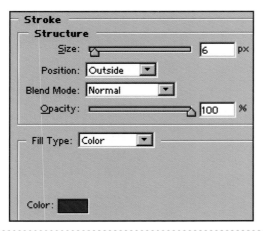

The first image shows the edge of the bevel prior to the stroke being applied. The second is after stroking the layer.

**15.** Next, apply an Inner Shadow. Use the following settings, making sure to change the color to a brownish tint. This will give the edges a 'rustic' feel by blending brown in around the edges of the wood.

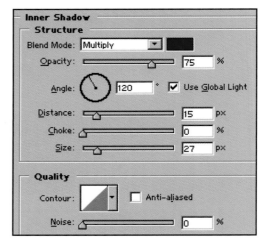

**16.** This time apply an Inner Glow. Be sure to adjust the Noise setting, as this is a great way to further simulate texture on our wood.

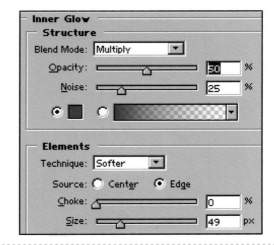

Make sure you save (CTRL/CMD+S) your image before going on to the next exercise.

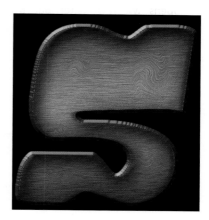

## 2: Wood effect - intermediate

For this next tutorial, we aren't going to change much from the previous one. In just a few steps, we can add some realistic effects that will wow your friends, maybe you won't get the respect of your colleagues, but at least the wood effect will be cool.

1.  To start, go through the tutorial above once again or continue with the image you created. Did you remember to save the layer style? If so, you need only go through the wood grain steps, then apply the style with the bevels and highlights to the text or shape.

2.  Access the Layer Styles, and get rid of the stroke we applied. You can do this by un-checking the Stroke command in the Layer Styles pop up, or click on the Stroke command in the Layers palette and dragging it to the trash can.

3.  CTRL/CMD+click the shape layer in the Layers palette to create a selection.

4.  Create a new layer (SHIFT+CTRL/CMD+N) beneath the shape layer, and fill (**Edit>Fill**) the selection with 50% gray.

SHIFT+BACKSPACE/DELETE *opens the Fill dialog box and you can choose your fill content from there.*

**5.** Select the shape layer. On the bottom of the Layers palette, click the **Add a mask** icon. By applying the mask to the selection, we are setting the image up to chisel and roughen up the edges of the wood.

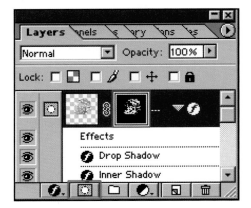

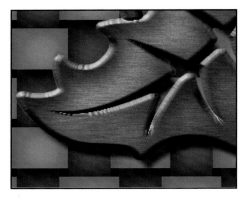

**6.** Go to **Filter>Brush Strokes>Sprayed Strokes** with the following settings. When we apply a distortion-type filter (especially a painting filter) to the mask, the edges of the image/selection conform to the distortions around the edge.

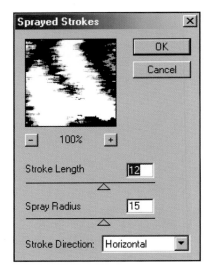

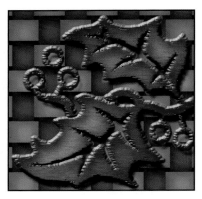

**7.** By altering the Bevel settings, you can draw out finer-tuned edges. For instance, changing the Structure Technique to Chisel Hard and creating or applying different Gloss Contours can give you some interesting results.

*Try applying other filters to your mask to see what effects form. Painting filters are especially useful for this technique.*

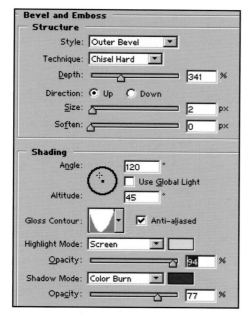

Once you get the effect down, it is fun to apply assorted filters to the layer while the mask is in place. Here is the effect with the Film Grain filter (**Filters>Artistic>Film Grain**):

This shows the Mosaic filter applied to the mask (**Filters>Pixelate>Mosaic**) with a setting of 35:

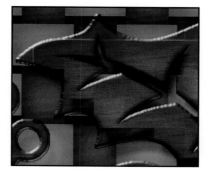

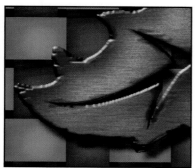

## 3: Termites!

Here's a little effect that gives the wood image the appearance of having become food for some pesky critters.

1.  Create a new image following the first wood tutorial.

2.  CTRL/CMD+click the shape layer in the Layers palette to make your selection.

3. Contract, **Select>Modify>Contract**, your selection by 4 pixels, copy (CTRL/CMD+C) and paste into a new layer (CTRL/CMD+J).

4. Go to the Channels palette and create a new channel by clicking on the **Create new channel** icon. Paste (CTRL/CMD+V) your copy into the new channel also.

5. Fill (SHIFT+BACKSPACE/DELETE) the channel selection with white.

6. Run the Crystalize filter, **Filter>Pixelate> Crystalize**, three times with settings of 32,14, and 9 respectively. This will create the jaggy edges we need for the bug trails.

7. Go to **Select>Deselect**, CTRL/CMD+click the crystallized channel to bring up the jagged selection.

8. Go back to layer 3, copy the selection and paste it into a new layer. Though you can't see it yet, you now have a jagged piece of wood lying on top of the original. The next step will reveal the shape of the jagged layer, and we can start creating the trails. CTRL/CMD+click on your jagged layer to load it.

9. Create a new layer (SHIFT+CTRL/CMD+N). Select a brown tone color (a bit darker than the overall hue of the effect) as your foreground color. Go to **Edit>Stroke**, and stroke the selection by 3 pixels, on the outside. You can now see the trails begin to take shape. Ensure this layer is on top of all the other layers in the Layers palette.

10. Now simply apply a Bevel with the following settings. We are looking for the trail to be embedded into the wood, or at least have the illusion of such.

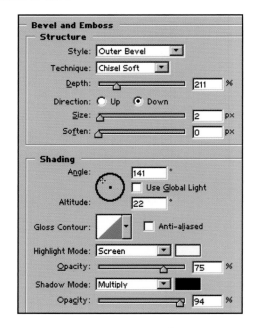

11. See what a little creative beveling can do? We can improve on this though. You can also add depth to the termite tracks simply by applying a Gradient Overlay, Black to White, Blend Mode set to Color Burn.

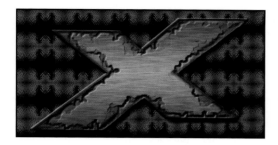

**12.** That's pretty cool! By applying the gradient we have darkened the tracks, furthering the depth illusion of the bevel. But wait, it gets better, CTRL/CMD+click the layer beneath the worm tracks layer to bring up the original jagged selection. Select the worm tracks layer and click the **Add a mask** icon on the bottom of the Layers palette.

**13.** Go to **Filter>Brush Strokes>Sprayed Strokes** and apply a Stroke Length of 19-20, a Spray Radius of 9, and set the Stroke Direction to Horizontal.

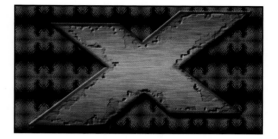

Now that's some buggy wood!

## Quick stone textures

To begin this section on stone, we'll go through a few ways to create the effect from scratch. Later in this chapter I'll show you some ways to adapt an existing stone photo/texture to your work. We are going to look at a really quick and simple method that produces stunning results.

### 4: Rock

**1.** Create a new document of 500X500 at 72dpi and RGB by pressing CTRL/CMD+N.

**2.** Open the Channels palette and create a new Alpha channel.

**3.** Let's create a new bump map: Press CMD/CTRL+A to select all, then use the D key to reset the default foreground and background colors, so that our clouds will be in black and white and have a strong contrast.

**4.** **Filter>Render>Clouds** to apply a cloud pattern to the channel. Click Ctrl/Cmd+ D to deselect.

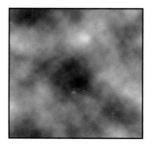

5. Select the RGB composite channel, and then go back to your Layers palette.

6. Now let's run the lighting effect, go to **Filter> Render>Lighting Effects**, select a reddish orange spotlight, with the settings shown below. Load in Alpha 1 as our Texture Channel.

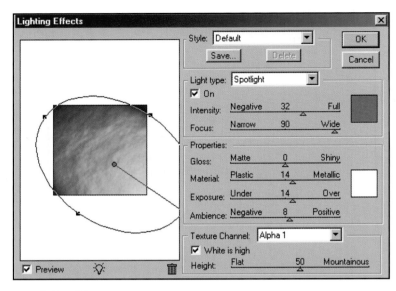

7. Voila! Instant rock that's so realistic it's frightening. This is a great effect for creating backgrounds for product shots, textures for your artwork, planet's surfaces, and even texture maps for 3D imaging.

### 5: Marble

1. To begin with, create a new image.

2. Set your colors to default (hit the 'D' key). The black (default foreground) and white (default background) set up the tones needed for the difference clouds in the next step. Fill the image with the foreground color (black).

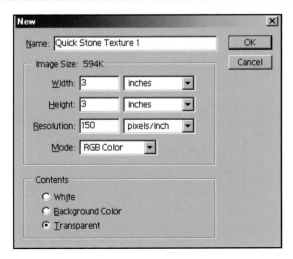

ALT/OPT+BACKSPACE/DELETE *fills a selection with the foreground color while* CTRL/CMD+BACKSPACE+DELETE *fills it with the background color.*

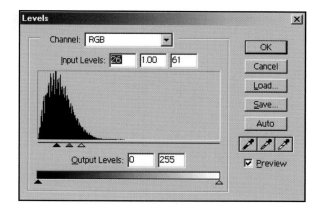

3. Go to **Filters>Render>Difference Clouds**. Hit CTRL/CMD+F 10 times to run the filter over and over again. This will help define lines of contrast in the image.

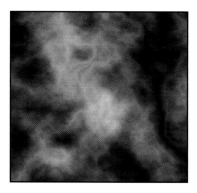

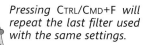
*Pressing* CTRL/CMD+F *will repeat the last filter used with the same settings.*

4. Go to Filter>Stylize>Find Edges. You should see a series of black/dark strings appear, with the overall tone shifting to white.

5. Go to Image>Adjust>Invert, then hit Ctrl/Cmd+L to bring up the Levels dialog box. Move the sliders closer together, staying within the margin of the image range.

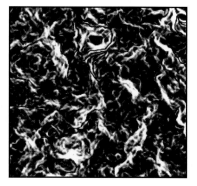

6. We are nearly done with the quick marble. Hit CTRL/CMD+U to bring up the Hue/Saturation dialog box. Check Colorize, and just move the sliders until you find a tone that suits your taste.

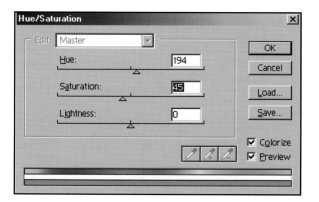

17

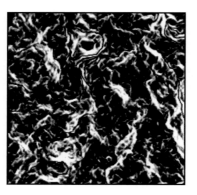

## Variations

If you would like to make the texture seamless, simply go to **Filter>Other>Offset**, and change the values to 50 pixels right, 50 pixels down, and check Wrap Around. Now you can either save the image as a background, or define the completed image as a nice seamless pattern. See Chapter 6 for more on defining and saving patterns.

> Seamless patterns are those that, when duplicates of the image are laid side by side, there is no line apparent between the images.

## 6: Stone from scratch

1. Create a new image (CTRL/CMD+N). I've created one 800x500, 100 dpi, RGB, Transparent.

2. Select a brownish color for the foreground. This will be the base tone of the stone we will create. In this instance I'm using a tone with the RGB settings of R:170, G:129, and B:99 or #AA8163. If you aren't sure about the color, don't worry, we can always change it later. Fill (ALT/OPT+BACKSPACE/DELETE) the image with the color.

3. Create a new layer (SHIFT+CTRL/CMD+N). Choose another color and fill this layer with it. As I've chosen a tan/brown for the foundation color, I'm going to continue the trend and pick another earth tone, somewhat darker than the first.

4. Click the **Add a mask** icon on the bottom of the Layers palette to create a mask for the new layer.

5. In Photoshop 6 when a mask is added to the layer, the foreground defaults to white and background to black. Swap these so that black is the foreground color.

> *To swap the foreground and background colors, press X or click the double-headed arrow shown in the image.*

6. Make sure the mask icon is highlighted in the Layers palette. You can make sure the mask is active by clicking on it, as sometimes the highlight is difficult to see. Select **Filter>Texture>Grain** with the following settings:

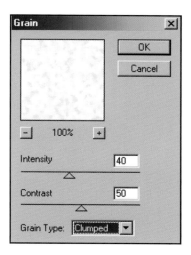

**8.** Select **Filter>Render>Difference Clouds**. Re-apply this filter (CTRL/CMD+F) about 10 times. This builds the complexity and naturalism of the stone.

**7.** Go to **Filter>Noise>Add Noise** and apply a Gaussian setting of 8.

**9.** Choose **Filter>Stylize>Find Edges**.

**10.** Go to **Image>Adjust>Invert**, and then hit CTRL/CMD+L to bring up the Levels dialog box. Move the sliders to increase the contrast.

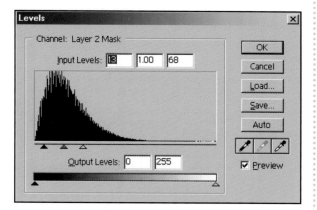

11. Select a new earth tone for your foreground color. This time I'm going for a bit more gray. Create a new layer and fill it with the color.

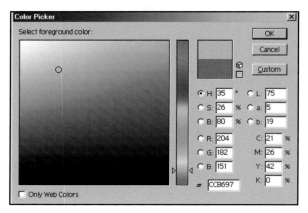

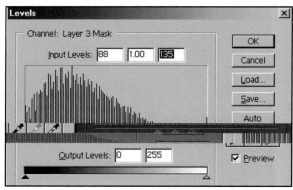

12. Add a layer mask, and again ensure the mask is active. Go to **Filter>Render> Difference Clouds** and apply the filter 20 times (CTRL/CMD+F).

13. Go to **Filter>Stylize>Find Edges**. Again, this filter increases the contrast of the edges, but also inverts the overall color. For this reason, we will:

14. Go to Image>Adjust>Invert, then go to Image>Adjust>Auto Levels. This smoothes out the tone variations a bit.

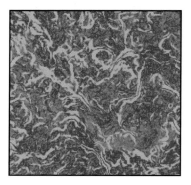

16. Access the Layer Styles for this layer, and apply a Bevel with the following settings:

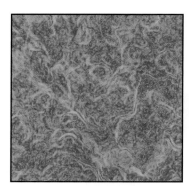

15. Hit CTRL/CMD+L and adjust the levels again manually, moving the sliders toward the center to bring out a bit more contrast and detail.

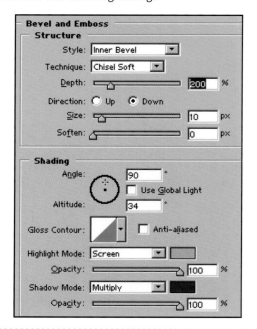

**17.** Repeat Step 11, this time with a brighter color than before.

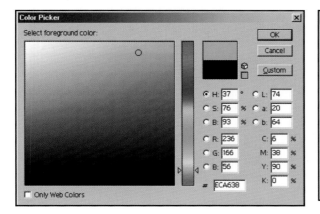

**18.** Click the Add a mask icon and with the layer mask active, select **Filter>Render>Clouds**. Then apply **Filter>Render>Difference Clouds**.

**19.** Choose **Filter>Stylize>Find Edges**.

**20.** Select **Image>Adjust>Invert**.

**21.** Select **Image>Adjust>Levels**. Move the sliders next to each other within the data range.

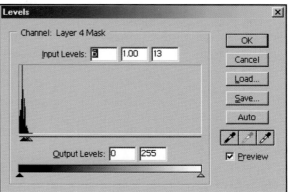

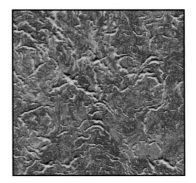

## Variations

Try altering the hues on all the layers. By desaturating layer 1 and adding some noise, you can bring out a gray stone texture. I've done this for the following example, as well as adjusted the hue of the topmost layer to give it a 'mossy' feel.

By applying a Bevel and Drop Shadow to the moss layer, we can really pull out some dimension and realism. Increasing the depth of the Bevel (in this case an increase of 391%) enhances the growth and increases the dimension of the shadow areas.

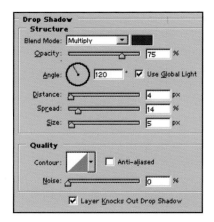

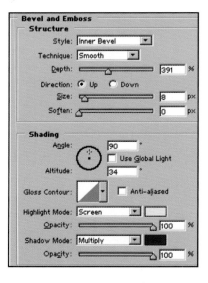

## 7: Chiseling shapes

Now that we have a couple of stone texture tutorials under our collective belts, we can get into the meatier subject of actually chiseling and etching shapes or text into the rock.

To begin, repeat the above tutorial. You can vary the hues to alter the stone colors as you see fit, because 'nothing is written in stone'.

1.   Once you have the stone you are looking for, merge the layers together (**Layer>Merge Visible**).

2.   Go to **Edit>Define Pattern**.

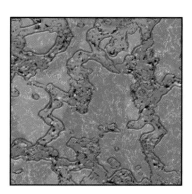

3. Create a new layer. Enter the shape or text into this layer that you would like to see carved in the rock.

4. Access the Layer Styles for the shape layer. Go into Advanced Blending Modes and adjust the settings as follows:

5. Apply a black Color Overlay.

6. Apply a Bevel to the layer. We want to change the Bevel Style to Chisel Hard and adjust the settings as follows:

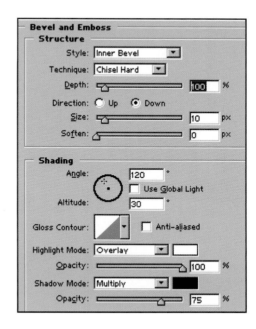

7. Next we are going to apply an Inner Shadow. There are two things we need to note: the color of the shadow should also be an earth tone (R:70, G:21, B:1 or #461501), and the Choke slider controls the depth or intensity of the shadow.

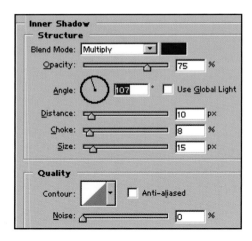

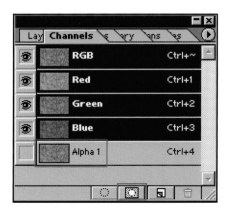

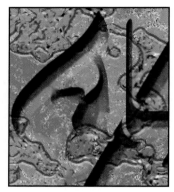

**11.** Select the new channel. Go to **Filter> Blur>Gaussian Blur**, and blur the image by 1.5 pixels.

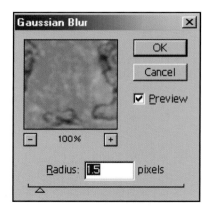

**8.** Make the text/shape layer invisible by clicking the eye icon beside the layer in the Layers palette. Select the original stone layer and go to the Channels palette.

**9.** CTRL/CMD+click the RGB channel to bring up a selection of the highlights.

**10.** Click the **Save selection as channel** icon on the bottom of the palette.

**12.** Now adjust the levels to bring out a bit of contrast between the highlights and shadows.

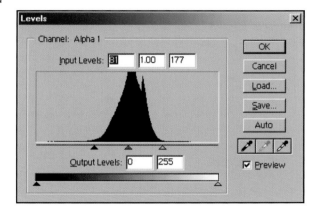

13. We are going to save this channel as a Displacement Map. Right-click/CTRL-click the channel and select Duplicate Channel. Select New from the drop-down menu in the dialog box, name it, and click OK. Save it to a folder on your computer in PSD format, and be sure to remember where you put it. We will need it very soon.

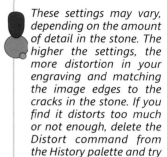

*These settings may vary, depending on the amount of detail in the stone. The higher the settings, the more distortion in your engraving and matching the image edges to the cracks in the stone. If you find it distorts too much or not enough, delete the Distort command from the History palette and try again with new settings.*

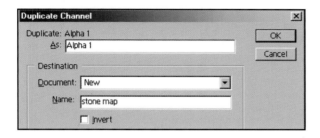

14. Go back to the Layers palette, and make the shape layer visible again.

If you used a custom shape or the standard Type tool, then Rasterize the layer here. If you used a filled selection, you need not worry about rasterizing.

15. Choose **Filter>Distort>Displace**. Choose 3 for the Horizontal setting and –3 for the Vertical setting.

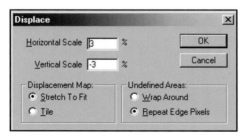

## Variations

I hope that by now you are getting a feel for what Layer Styles do, and that just a few changes to the settings can alter the image with interesting results. Let's go through the tutorial above again, using yet another variation of the texture created in the previous tutorial:

Let's see what happens when we alter our Bevel settings a bit.

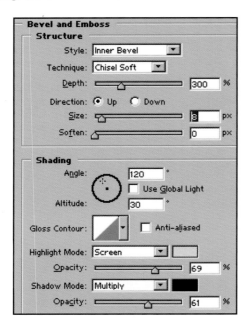

**Stroke:**

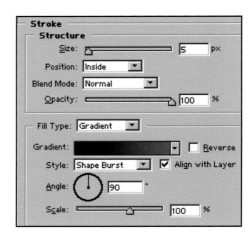

The above setting makes the etched area appear raised from the stone, as opposed to being in relief. We can try a few more setting applications to further draw the rock carving out of the stone face.

**Drop Shadow and Outer Glow:**

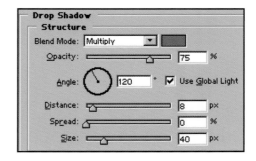

If you have the texture saved as a pattern, uncheck the Color Overlay we applied at the beginning of the etching tutorial and select the Pattern Overlay, applying the same stone texture.

**Inner Shadow:**

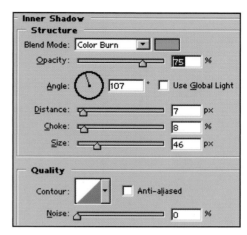

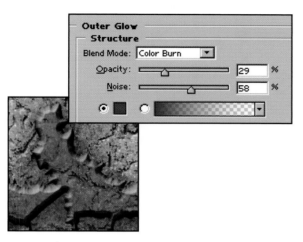

**Pattern Overlay:**

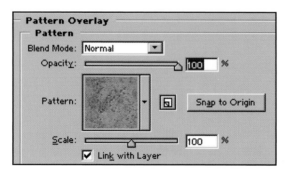

Lastly, we can make it stand out by applying a touch of Inner Shadow:

Try applying the effects we chiseled in a photograph of a stone wall, a sidewalk, or even a picture of a landscape. Once you get the hang of the process, many other doors will be opened as to how you can apply either these exact effects or variations thereof. As always, the buzzword is experiment.

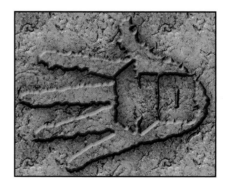

## 7: Concrete

In this section I will demonstrate how to create a concrete effect with cracks. The first thing we are going to do is to create the concrete texture. We will be using channels to create this effect.

1.   Create a new document that is 500X500 at 72ppi and RGB.

2.   Open the Channels palette and click on the **Create new channel** icon to create a new channel called Alpha 1.

3.   We are going to create our bump map for concrete, go to **Filter>Noise>Add Noise** and use a setting of around 17.

**4.** Click RGB to make this channel visible, and return to the Layers palette.

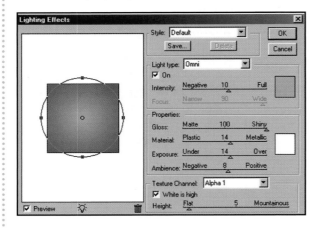

**5.** Ensure that your background layer is active, and then run the lighting effects, **Filters> Render>Lighting Effects**. This time use a gray Omni light and lower the Height to 5. Load in Alpha 1 as our Texture Channel.

We now have a pretty convincing concrete texture.

## 8: Cracking up

To create the random cracks, we will be utilizing the difference clouds and layer blending modes.

**1.** Create a new layer (SHIFT+CTRL/CMD+N) and call it, 'cracks'. Fill with a Black to White Linear gradient using the Gradient tool (G).

**2.** Now go to **Filter>Render>Difference Clouds**. You will now see something that resembles the image here. Of course it will be a little different because this is a random effect.

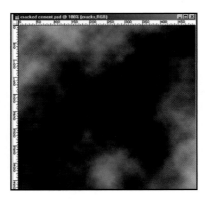

**3.** Now to clean it up we will use Levels. It's amazing what you can achieve by abusing certain tools! Click CTRL/CMD+ L, or go to **Image>Adjust> Levels** in order to open the Levels window.

**4.** Drag the right and middle triangles all the way to the left, to tighten up the image and create sharp edges. Click OK when you are satisfied with the result, this will be our crack.

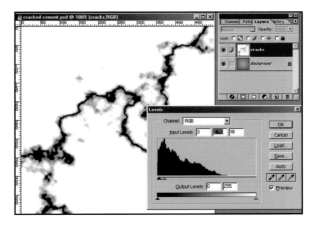

5. Change the layer blending mode to Multiply, and the white will be hidden to reveal the texture underneath with the dark crack showing.

6. To clean up the crack and remove parts of it, choose a white brush and paint over the areas you want to erase.

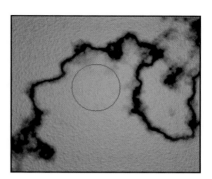

## 9: Adding depth to the cracks

1. To add some 3D depth to the crack, duplicate the 'cracks' layer, and then click CTRL/CMD+I to invert this new duplicated layer. Your screen will turn black.

2. Switch your layer blending mode to Screen to hide the black, and a white crack should be revealed.

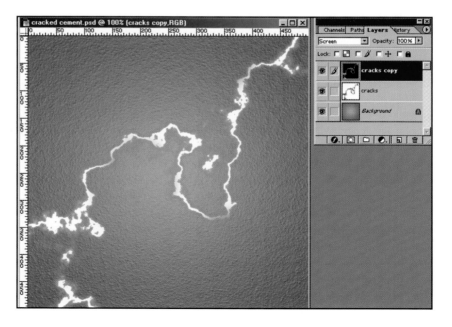

3.  Drag the white crack layer beneath the black one.

4.  Select the **Move** tool, (V), and nudge the layer down and to the right 1 or 2 pixels by tapping the arrow keys on the keyboard. Your cracks will now look embossed and 3D.

As you can see, the possibilities are endless if you experiment with the texture channels and lighting effects. A good tip when using texture in a composite image is to take note of the natural lighting and the direction of the light source and try to match those as closely as possible.

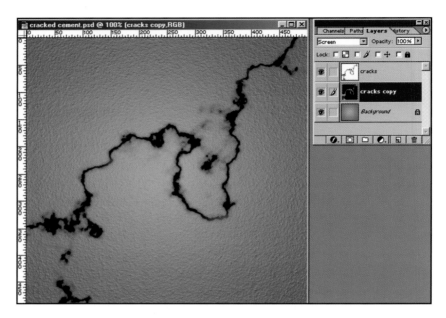

## Café station cracks and cement

Look at the "Photoshop Café Station" image. This image was created entirely in Photoshop. There are three elements to note here: texture, lighting, and color. To achieve the realism we want, it is important to have the balance of these elements. We are not going to look at the steps involved; instead I'll allow you to experiment for yourself. I just wanted to show you how these techniques could be applied to create a cool image.

# Chapter 2
# Metal

In this chapter we will learn how to create a variety of metals, with the aid of Photoshop and a few simple techniques you'll be an alchemist in no time! In fact, due to the relatively simple contrasts metal produces, it is one of the simpler effects we can create. We can achieve quick metallic effects using gradients alone, or get a little crazy with curves to enhance reflections. We can also use channels to further authenticity, and save a layer style with metal settings built in. It all depends on the depth of realism, or surrealism, that you are looking for.

Many of the effects you see in this chapter will pop up again as variations in later chapters, but the metal tutorials serve as a good launching point into more advanced and abstract tutorials we will get into later.

## 1: Sheet metal

1.    Create a new image (Ctrl/Cmd +N).

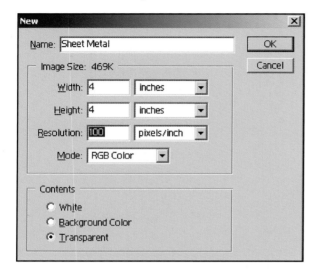

2.    Select the **Gradient** tool from the toolbar.

3.    We have several default gradients to select from, but let's create a custom gradient for the metal effect. Go to the Gradient Options bar and click directly inside the Gradient window.

4.    When we click in the Gradient window, the **Gradient Editor** pops up. We'll create a metal gradient, alternating between light gray and dark gray.

We'll now have a look at how to create a custom gradient, for more information on creating and saving custom gradients, please see Chapter 6.

The default gradients that are already loaded into Photoshop are found in the top portion of the Gradient Editor. In the bottom portion of the Editor is where you create custom gradients.

In this section you will see a larger version of the active gradient. The small arrows along the top and bottom are called **Stops**. It is by adding stops, and changing their colors and opacity that we modify a new gradient. The stops along the top of the bar control the opacity of that portion of the gradient. The lower stops control the color. We won't be playing with opacity this time around, so don't worry about that. We'll only be adding and changing color.

5.    To add stops to the gradient, click on the lower bar. The new stop will have the same color characteristics as the previous stop. You can enter a new color for a stop in the Color Picker below the Gradient Creator. To delete a stop, click on it and hit Delete.

6.    Once you are satisfied with your gradient, give it a suitable name, and Click Save. The new gradient will now appear in the active group.

Now that we have made a gradient, let's proceed with the metal effect.

7. Select the Linear Gradient from the Gradient Options bar.

8. Starting in the upper left corner, draw your gradient through the image to the lower right corner.

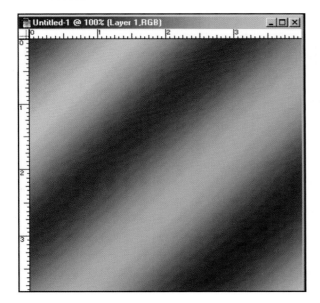

9. Go to **Filter>Add Noise**. Enter something close to the following settings:

10. Again from the Filters menu, go to **Blur>Motion Blur**. Enter a 45-degree blur with a Distance of 25 pixels. Here is our metal thus far:

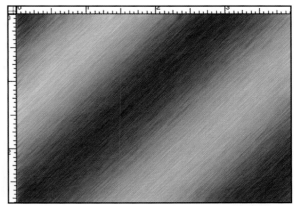

11. The metal may be a bit dark, but we can clean this up with a slight Curve adjustment. Go to **Image>Adjust>Curves** (CTRL/CMD+M) and enter something similar to the capture below.

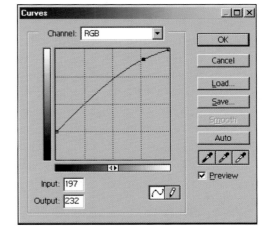

*You may be wondering why the Curves option is such an essential tool when working with metal. Curves are used primarily for contrast, they allow us to adjust the value for individual pixels, rather than making an "across the board" change for all pixel values, which is what happens when we use Brightness/Contrast .The common curve form for metal is generally a sideways 'S'. For more info on Curves go to chapter 6.*

And hey presto! A nice sheet of metal to use as a backdrop!

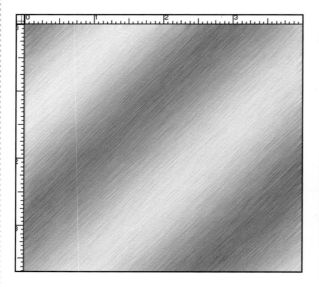

## 2: Bolt heads

**1.** Open a new document (CTRL/CMD+N) and select the **Polygon** tool.

**2.** From the Shape Options bar, enter 6 in the Sides field, so that our shape is a hexagon. Ensure that the **Create new shape layer** icon is depressed.

**3.** To keep the sides of the polygon straight, hold down the SHIFT key. Draw your polygon in the center of your image.

**4.** Rasterize the shape layer, by going to **Layer>Rasterize Layer**. It's good practice to name your layers to avoid later confusion; so let's be imaginative and call it Shape layer.

**5.** Choose a light gray for the foreground, and dark gray for the background colors.

**6.** CMD/CTRL+click the Shape layer in the Layers palette to bring up the shape as a selection.

**7.** Click the Gradient tool, and choose Linear Gradient from the Gradient Options bar. From the Gradient picker, (you can find this by clicking the black arrow to the right of the gradient window) choose the Foreground to Background gradient.

**8.** Draw the gradient through the selection from the upper left to the lower right.

**9.** At the bottom of the Layers palette, click the **Add a layer style** icon (the F symbol). Choose Bevel and Emboss and enter the following settings:

**Bevel and Emboss**

**Structure**

Style: Inner Bevel
Technique: Chisel Hard
Depth: 760 %
Direction: ◉ Up   ○ Down
Size: 5 px
Soften: 0 px

**Shading**

Angle: 120 °
☐ Use Global Light
Altitude: 45 °
Gloss Contour: ☑ Anti-aliased
Highlight Mode: Screen
Opacity: 83 %
Shadow Mode: Multiply
Opacity: 75 %

**10.** You can give the bolt a bit more metal-like tint by applying a Curve. Go to **Image>Adjust>Curves** (CTRL/CMD+M) and create a curve to taste, keeping a close eye on the image so you don't overdo it. Here are the settings used for this image:

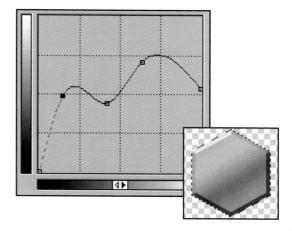

**11.** Our hexagon is becoming more bolt-like, but it lacks realism, so let's add some rust. Again we'll use a layer style, this time Gradient Overlay. Choose the copper gradient from the Gradient picker with the following settings:

**Gradient Overlay**

**Gradient**

Blend Mode: Color Burn
Opacity: 65 %
Gradient: ☐ Reverse
Style: Linear   ☑ Align with Layer
Angle: 90 °
Scale: 143 %

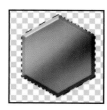

**12.** Then apply another layer style, Inner Glow with the following settings:

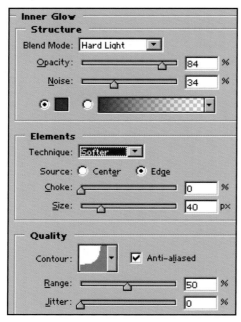

**13.** Create a new layer and make a circular selection within the confines of the bolt's sides.

**14.** Select the Gradient tool. Click the Radial Gradient icon, and fill the bolt, starting at the center and proceeding to the outside edge of the selection.

**15.** Set the Layer Mode to Overlay.

**16.** Apply a Bevel to this layer with the following settings:

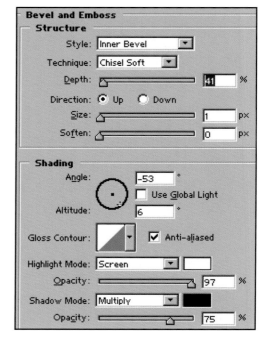

## Adding scratches

You can take this bolt head one stage further by adding it to our sheet metal that we created in the first tutorial; so make sure that this image is open.

1. Reduce your bolt head image to one layer, by going to **Layer>Merge Visible**, (SHIFT+CTRL/ CMD+E). Then to load the image as a selection, CTRL/CMD-click on the single bolt head layer, and drag and drop the selection on to your sheet metal image.

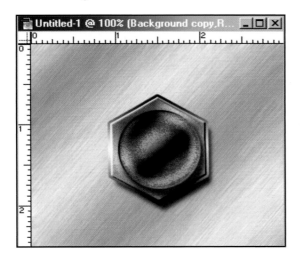

2. Create a new layer beneath the bolt layer and name it 'Scratches'.

3. Change your foreground color to black. Select the **Airbrush** tool, use one of the **Spatter** brushes. Paint some spots around the bolt head. Use a variety of brushes, the shape doesn't matter much, as we'll blur them in a moment.

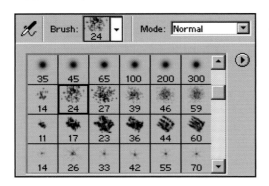

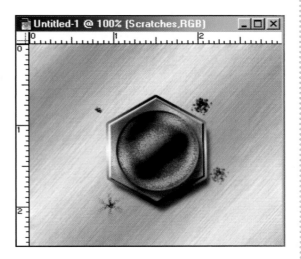

4. Go to **Filter>Blur>Radial Blur**. Set the amount to 40, Blur Method to Spin, and Quality to Best. Click OK.

5. Add a few more paint spots and rerun the filter if you would like more scratching on the metal surface.

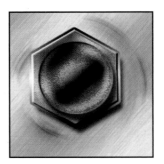

**6.** Access the Layer Styles for the Scratches layer. We'll begin with a Bevel, setting the depth to 1000 and bumping up the Highlight Opacity to 100.

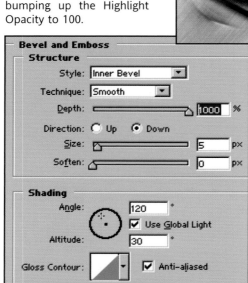

**8.** A Stroke applied with Layer Styles can help give the scratches a hint of color. I'm using a brown set to Color Burn with Size 3 pixels.

**7.** By applying a Texture to the bevel, we can further draw out a worn effect. Any pattern will do, try changing the pattern to see what gives you the better effect.

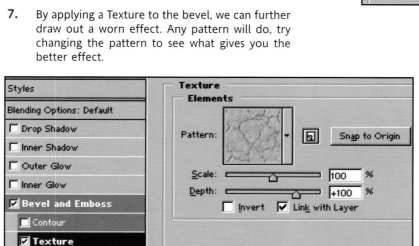

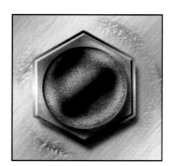

9.  When you are happy with your style, be sure to save it. Along the right-hand side of the styles palette, click New Style. Name your style and click OK. The new style will now appear in the Styles palette for use at a later date. (If you can't see your Styles palette go to **Window>Show Styles.**)

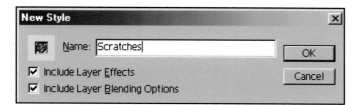

10. To beat up the bolt face, just create a new layer above the bolt, paint some more splotches of color, and apply the style you just saved to it.

# Pattern elements

We will cover creating, altering, and saving patterns in Chapter 6, but as this is a useful technique when working with metal effects we should take a look at the process here. First I'll walk through saving the image as a pattern, and then show you how to apply it to your text.

### 3: Saving a pattern

You'll need a metallic image, photo or background, this can be found on one of the hundreds of websites offering free backgrounds or textures. At first glance these images don't seem to have a whole lot of use, fortunately for us, Photoshop allows us to recycle them for our own creations.

1.  Open your metal background or image. Seamless backgrounds work best for patterns. You may want to open several to define and save as a categorized set. Again, this will be covered in Chapter 6.

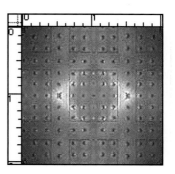

2. You may want to adjust the Hue/Saturation, Brightness, and Contrast. Ultra-dark images aren't very useful as patterns – just something to keep in mind.

3. When you are satisfied with your image, go to **Edit>Define Pattern** and give your pattern a name.

4. The pattern will now appear when you open the Pattern Overlay options in the Layer Styles.

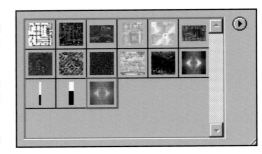

Once the pattern has a home in the pattern group, you can apply it to a layer just like you would a bevel, drop shadow, and so forth.

## Putting the pattern to use

1. Go back to the brushed metal effect we created at the beginning of this chapter. Make a new layer and enter some text.

2. With the text layer active, click the Add a layer style icon at the bottom of the Layers palette. Select Pattern Overlay from the list.

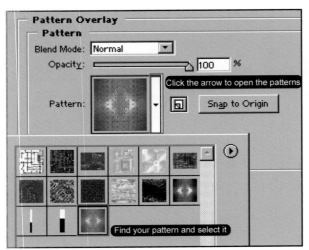

3. Find your pattern and apply it to your text.

4. So now we have a pattern that looks metallic, and a metal-style background but the two don't really mesh as yet. Let's return to the Layer Styles to add more realism.

First, apply a Bevel with the following settings:

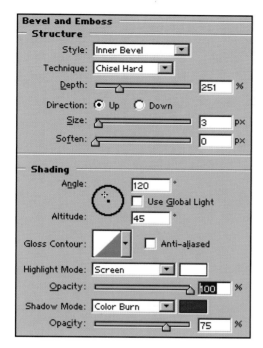

You will note that the background color has been changed to a color bordering between gray and brownish red. The color code used in this example is #190303.

**5.** Apply a Gradient Overlay to your text.

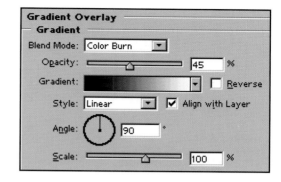

**6.** Finally, let's apply a Drop Shadow.

## 4: Creating extruded text

Once we have the process under our belt, a little experimentation can render some pretty cool variations. Let's say, for instance, you want to use the pattern as your background as well. For this tutorial I'm starting with no style applied to the text.

**1.** Click in the background layer, or layer to which the brushed metal is applied.

**2.** Following the same process as you did applying the pattern to the text above, apply the pattern to the background.

**3.** Apply the same pattern to your text.

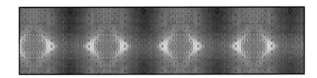

**4.** Naturally, without any other layer style elements applied, the text seems to disappear as the same seamless pattern is applied to both the background and type layers. Re-apply the settings from the previous tutorial to the type layer to reveal the lettering once again.

## 5: Recessing text

**1.** Start with the pattern applied to both the background and text again.

**2.** Let's apply a Bevel once again, this time with the following settings:

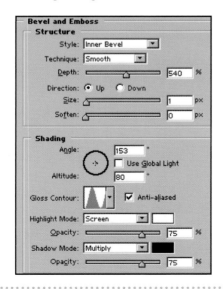

3. Now apply an Inner Glow. Change the color to a light brown or orange, and apply the following settings:

4. Now it's a simple matter of adding an Inner Shadow.

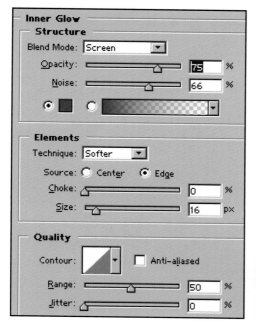

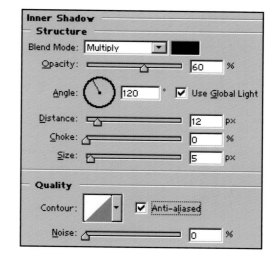

## 6: Heavy metal

Let's go back to the original beveled text on the brushed metal background. We can beef up the depth as well as the metal effect by adding, moving, and combining a few stroked layers, then applying one of the Curves included with the default set already loaded in Photoshop's Layer Styles.

1. Go through the first tutorial dealing with the patterned text until you reach this point:

   Note that the drop shadow was not applied to this version.

2. CTRL/CMD+click the text layer to bring up the type shaped selection.

3. Create a new layer just above the metal background layer by selecting the background in the Layers palette and clicking the **Create a new layer** icon at the bottom of the palette.

4. Select a median gray as your foreground color.

5. Go to **Edit>Stroke**. Apply a Center, 8 pixel stroke to your selection.

6. Apply a Bevel, with the Gloss Contour setting of Ring. This setting is found by opening the Contour picker window, by clicking on the small arrow to the left of the Gloss Contour box.

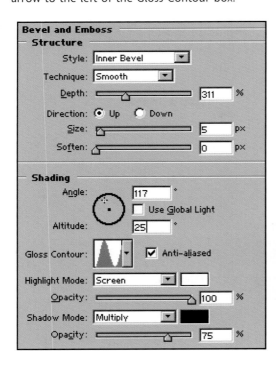

7. Select the background, and create a new layer once again. Select the stroked layer and merge down. Press CTRL/CMD+E or go to **Layer>Merge Down**. This collapses the layer style, leaving the effect.

8. Duplicate the stroked layer, by dragging it to the icon on the bottom of the Layers palette.

9. Select the original stroked layer.

10. Select the **Move** tool from the toolbar, (V). With the arrow keys move the type one pixel up and one pixel left. Repeat this process several times, always moving the bottom-most stroked layer.

*This may seem like a repetitive business, but luckily you can escape the boredom by recording an action to automate the process. For more info on actions check out chapter 6.*

11. When you have a depth you are satisfied with, select the top-most stroked copy layer, and begin merging down until all the stoked layers are combined.

12. Duplicate the layer with the combined strokes. Set the mode to Overlay and reduce the Opacity to 70%.

**13.** Select a white or light color for your foreground.

**14.** Now to add the final touch; go to **Filters>Sketch>Chrome**, and apply this filter to suit your taste. I set my Detail value to 8, and my Smoothness to 4.

## 7: Using channels

Though layer styles have made creating fast metal much easier, channels are still the way to go for richness and depth.

**1.** Open a new image, and create your text/shape selection on a new layer. CTRL/CMD+click to load this as a selection.

**2.** Fill the selection with black. Create a new layer, and fill the selection with 50% gray, **Edit>Fill>50% Gray**.

**3.** With your selection still active, go to the Channels palette and create a new channel.

**4.** Fill (SHIFT+BACKSPACE/DELETE) the selection in the new channel with white.

**5.** Go to **Filters>Blur>Gaussian Blur**, and choose a setting of 6.

**6.** Deselect, and then apply a Gaussian Blur of 1.

**7.** Go back to the Layers palette. CTRL/CMD+click on the topmost layer. This will load the original shape selection.

8. Go to **Filter>Render>Lighting Effects** and apply Lighting Effects with the following settings:

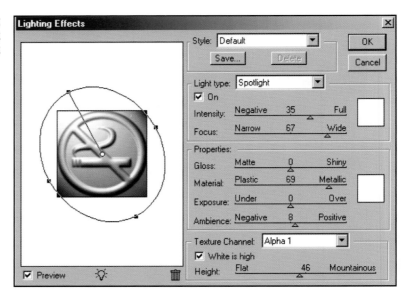

For the remainder of this tutorial, the background will be filled with black so the effect may be clearly seen.

9. We will now apply a Curve that will make the image shine. Go to **Image>Adjust>Curves**, (CTRL/CMD+ M).

10. Enter five additional points on the curve line, as evenly spaced as you can get them. When you are done there should be a total of seven points, including the two defaults. Manually enter the settings for each point, by clicking on the point and typing in the settings for that point in the x/y boxes below the Curve display. For each point, from left to right, the settings are:

Point 1: 0, 0
Point 2: 20, 180
Point 3: 70, 40
Point 4: 140, 110
Point 5: 170, 70
Point 6: 210, 175
Point 7: Leave the final point in its original place.

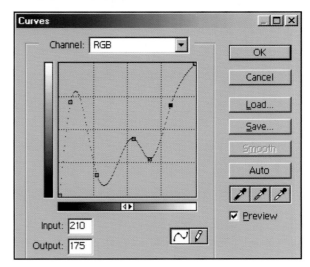

**11.** You may have some jagged edges, but we can take care of that. Ctrl/Cmd+click the metal layer, to load the selection. Go to **Select>Feather**, and feather the image by one pixel (Shift+Ctrl+I/Cmd+D).

**12.** Then select **Inverse** (Shift+Ctrl+I/Cmd+I), and expand your selection by 1 pixel by going to **Select>Modify>Expand.**

**13.** Now hit Delete. Once you have the basic metal, you can dress it up to taste.

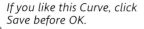
*If you like this Curve, click Save before OK.*

## 8: Quick layer style metal

I'd be remiss if I didn't cover creating a quick layer style for metal, so here we go.

**1.** Create a new image and fill the background with a seamless pattern.

**2.** Place some text or a shape selection in a new layer.

**3.** We'll start with a gradient. With the text/shape layer selected, click the Add a layer style icon on the bottom of the Layers palette. From the menu, select Gradient Overlay.

**4.** Create a gradient similar to the one we did in the sheet metal tutorial, only substitute the gray points for white.

*If you like the look of this gradient, save it now and you can use it again in the future.*

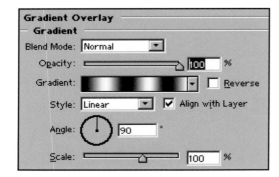

**6.** Apply a Bevel with the following settings. Ensure you change the bevel type to Stroke Emboss.

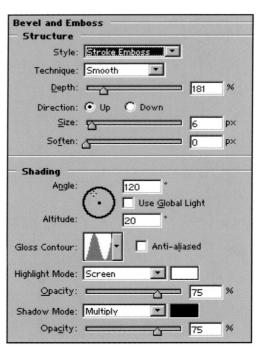

**5.** Select Stroke from the Layer Styles options and apply it to your text with the following settings:

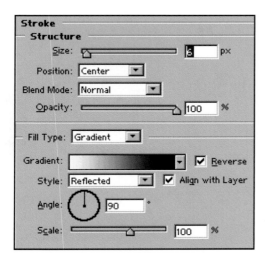

**7.** To add a bit of color without being distracting from the metal effect, we can apply a bit of Satin from the Layer Styles menu.

**8.** Once you are content with the style, be sure to save it for later use!

The nice thing about Layer Styles is that, once you have a technique down and a Layer Style saved, you can alter the effect drastically just by changing or adding a few settings. For instance, using the style we just created, by changing the bevel settings, the result is completely changed, rendering a metal effect that stands in stark contrast to the original.

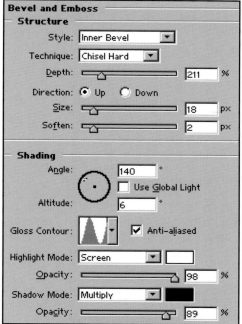

**9.** Using the same premise of tweaking the existing style, we can actually rust our metal with a little Inner Glow.

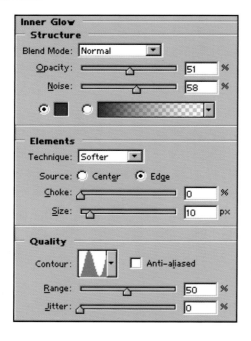

Let me take away the background pattern so you can see the contrast better.

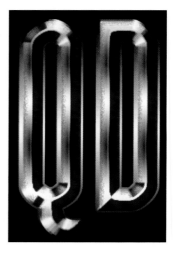

If you saved these styles as you made adjustments to the settings, soon you will have a great set of tools for later use!

## 9:Rust and tarnish

We've had a little look at adding a faint rust effect in an earlier tutorial, now let's take the realism further in just a few steps. This tutorial isn't only exclusive to metal textures; it can be just as easily applied to stone or any other texture. This effect will also give you an insight into bevel options and perhaps even introduce you to filters that you had not previously used.

**1.** Open an image to use as a background, or create your own. For this I'm using a sheet of rusted sheet metal.

**2.** Create a new layer (SHIFT+CTRL/CMD+N) and call it 'Logo'. Import a logo, insert text, or draw your shape in the new layer.

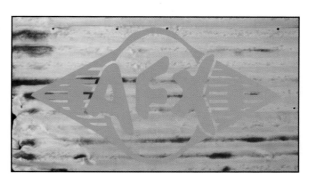

**3.** Click the eye next to the background layer in the Layers palette to render it invisible.

**4.** Select the Logo layer. Select a light gray foreground color and dark gray background. From the Filters menu, choose **Artistic>Sponge** and enter the following settings.

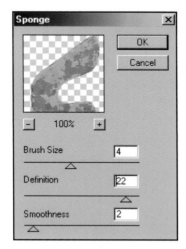

**6.** Choose the background, and go to **New>Layer>Layer via Copy** (CTRL/CMD+J). Move the new layer above the Logo layer.

**7.** Again, make the background layer and the newly created layer invisible. Select the Logo layer and go to **Select>Color Range**. Now we want to invert the selection, so go to **Select>Inverse** (SHIFT+CTRL/CMD+I).

**8.** CTRL/CMD+click the Logo layer to create a logo shaped selection, Go to **Select>Inverse**, (SHIFT+CTRL/CMD+I), click the new layer, and hit DELETE.

**5.** Go to **Select>Color Range**. By default one of the grays will be selected, giving a rough pattern. Click OK.

**9.** Here is where things get interesting. Select the top layer, and go to **Filter>Noise>Add Noise**. Use the following settings:

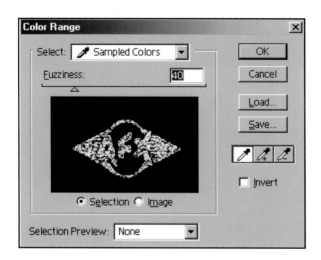

10. Access the Layer Styles for this layer. Apply a Bevel with the following settings:

11. Create a new empty layer (**Layer>New>Layer**) beneath the one we have been working with. Select the recently beveled layer and Merge Down (CTRL/CMD+E).

12. Adjust the Brightness/Contrast for this layer; go to **Image>Adjust>Brightness/Contrast**. Experiment, as this will either make your corrosion stand out or imply subtlety. I'm using the following settings:

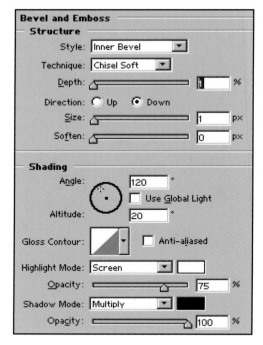

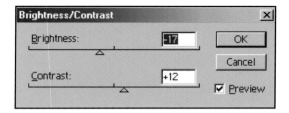

13. If it isn't already, make the Logo layer invisible. Select the other paint-daubed layer we created and change the mode to Color Burn.

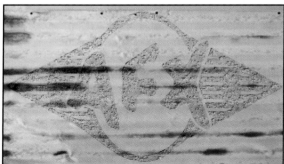

## 10: Final metal effect

So far I've taken a pretty conservative approach in the effects, but I'm going to up the ante a bit now. Thus far we've made bolts, metal that shines, and rusted a background. All of these were done primarily with layer styles and a few filters. Are we restricted to these few effects, or can we squeeze even more realism from the techniques we have learned? The answer is, of course, we can!

1. Find or create a seamless, rusty metal texture and define it as a pattern.

2. Create a new image (CTRL/CMD+N). Fill the background with black (**Edit>Fill>Black**). Apply a pattern overlay to the background. Any pattern will do, but use something that isn't too wild so you can see the effect as we proceed.

**3.** In a new layer, create an image using the Shape and Type tools.

**4.** Access the Layer Styles for this new layer.

**5.** First, click on the Blending Options, and uncheck **Blend Clipped Layers as Group**. Check **Blend Interior Effects as Group**.

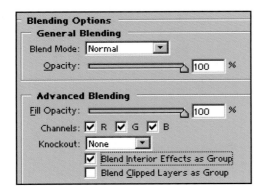

**6.** We are going to set up a style for this layer. First, go to Pattern Overlay and apply the rusty pattern you saved/loaded in step 1.

**7.** Apply a Drop Shadow.

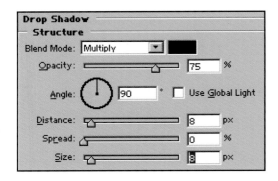

**8.** Now set the bevel options. Go to Bevel and Emboss and enter the following settings:

**9.** We can distinguish areas of contrast on the top and bottom of the logo by applying a gradient overlay set to soft light. Go to Gradient Overlay and try the following gradient and settings:

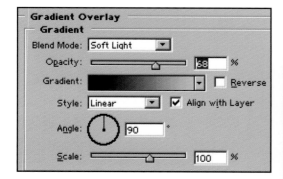

**10.** **Save this layer style now**! You now have an excellent launching point to several effects, but unless you want to repeat this tutorial every time you do a variation, you will want this style in the toolbox. Click the **New Style** button, to the right hand side of the Layer Styles dialog box, then name your style and you'll see it pop up in the Styles palette.

I'm certain that you can think of at least a dozen additional effects for this section. In truth I could most likely fill an entire book just on metal. I have tried to cover the elements that are standard when creating most metal-style effects, and following these tutorials should at least give you a good foundation for creating your own.

# Chapter 3
# Glass and plastic

This chapter is devoted to all things glassy, glossy, and semi-transparent. The authenticity of such objects relies on three main qualities: **Reflections**, **Depth**, and **Transparency**, the interplay between light and shadow. As a result we'll become very familiar with the Layer Styles palette, and we'll see how the settings work together to create realistic surfaces. A little drop shadow here, an extra highlight there makes all the difference. Sometimes it's a question of trial and error, and this chapter will give you the launch pad to your own experimentation. Wouldn't it be nice if your images had that "Reach out and touch it" appeal?

## 1: Glass text

For this tutorial we'll be creating a transparent effect. To allow this to really show up, you need some kind of patterned background. So either find a suitable image, that'll show through nicely, or go through the first few steps, showing you how to set an appropriate background from scratch.

1.  Create a new image (CTRL/CMD+N), 7x 5 inches, 96 dpi, and with a White background.

2.  To generate a background pattern, access the Layer Styles (**Layer>Layer Styles**) for the background layer, choose Pattern Overlay, and apply a pattern to the background layer.

3.  I've found a photo of stones, and have defined it as a pattern, by going to **Edit>Define Pattern**.

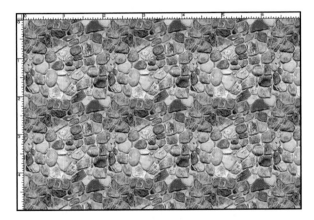

For more information on creating patterns, see Chapter 6.

4.  Create a new layer (SHIFT+CTRL/CMD+N). Enter some text in this new layer. As we are going to create a glass effect, the text needs to be colored white. This effect works best on a fairly wide, thick font, as I've used below. Arial Black should work fine if you do not have any fancy fonts to use, but be sure to set the font size to 140 or so.

5.  Access the Layer Style options for the text/shape layer by clicking the **Add a layer style** icon at the bottom of the Layers palette.

6.  Choose **Blending Options** from the top of the menu.

7.  In the Blending Options, we will set the transparency level for the layer we are working with as below:

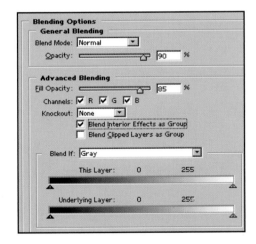

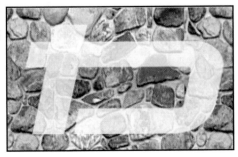

8. Now apply a Gradient Overlay. Select the Copper gradient that is located in the default set. The primary benefit to the copper gradient in this case is that the earthy tones blend well with my stone background.

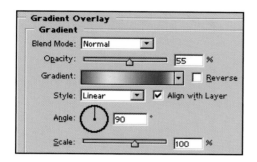

9. Staying with the Layer Style menu for now, go to the Stroke options, and add a single pixel stroke. In the Color field select a complimentary coppery tone. This will play into the definition later, but also helps determine the edges of the area we are working with now.

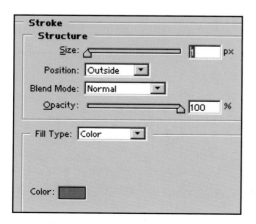

10. Choose Bevel and Emboss and enter the following settings:

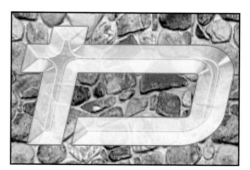

11. Apply an Inner Shadow.

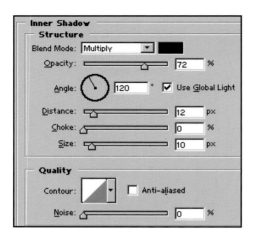

12. By adding a little Satin to the text, we can bump up the white highlights.

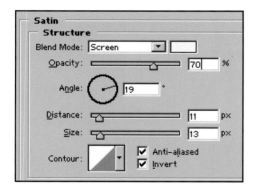

13. Add a Drop Shadow to taste. We can also give this glassy text a little life by applying a Color Overlay.

The effect we've just created was made entirely with Layer Styles. You can save it for use later, by clicking on the **New Style** button. Give your style a name, and you'll be able to access it later from the Styles palette.

For more information on saving layer styles, please see Chapter 6.

## 2: Using displacement maps

By now you can see how useful layer styles can be when creating a glassy effect, but if we use them with other tools we can achieve a heightened sense of realism. We're now going to look at the **Glass** filter from the **Filters** menu, and see how this can be used in conjunction with displacement maps to yield some pretty stunning effects.

1. Create an image, and in a new layer enter your required image. For this example I've created a shape and text, rasterized the layers, and merged them together.

2. We will get back to the pattern later. First we will create a layer style. Select the type/shape layer. Click the **Add a layer style** icon on the bottom of the Layers palette, and go to the Blending Options. Enter the settings seen below. Lowering the Opacity here is a key factor, as it will set the transparency for the effect. In order to be effective glass, we need to be able to see through it somewhat at the end, even though multiple overlays have been applied to it. You will see what I mean shortly. Also, make sure you check **Blend Interior Effects As Group**.

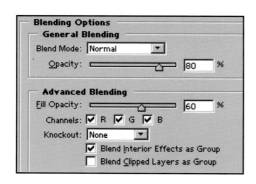

3. Let's start with a Bevel. In this step please note that the Shadow Mode has been changed to Screen, and the color changed from default black to a median gray.

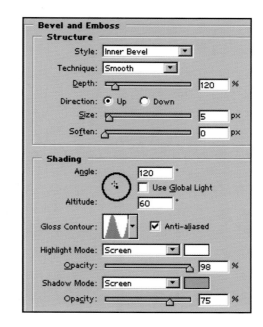

4. We're now going to adjust the Contour settings under the Bevel and Emboss options of the Layer Styles menu. You can access these settings by double-clicking on the Contour heading in the list, which is on the right hand side of the Layer Style palette.

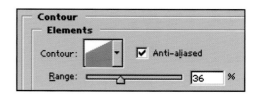

# MOST WANTED: GLASS AND PLASTIC

**5.** Again, from the Layer Styles menu, apply a little Satin and an Inner Glow.

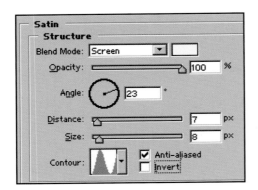

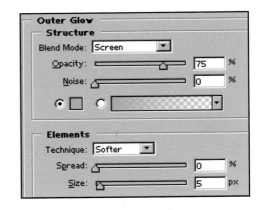

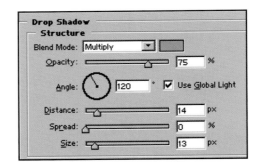

**6.** Apply a gray Outer Glow, and finish off the style with an Inner Shadow and Drop Shadow.

**7.** By duplicating this layer, we can increase the contrast of the image, but, unfortunately, doing so decreases the transparency.

8. Time to get funky! CTRL/CMD+click the shape/type layer to activate the shape as a selection. Go to the Channels palette, and click the **Create new channel** icon on the bottom of the palette. Don't be alarmed if your image goes black, using the **Paint Bucket** tool (SHIFT+G) we are now going to fill the selection with white.

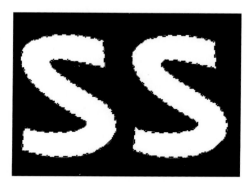

9. Go to **Filters>Blur>Gaussian Blur** and apply this to your selection. Start with a setting of 12, then a setting of 6, and finally a setting of 3. After the filter has been applied three times, deselect the shape layer (CTRL/CMD+D) and apply the blur again, this time with a setting of 1.

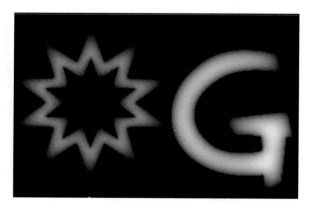

10. Right-click/CONTROL-click on the channel and duplicate it as a new image.

11. Save the new image in a folder on your system. We'll come back to it shortly.

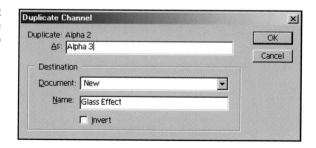

For the next stage of the tutorial we need an image with a lot of blue/white tones, sky and cloud images are ideal. So, you now have a choice; you can either use the cloud image found in the Photoshop 6> Goodies>Stock Art>Images folder, `0005012.jpg`, or you could create your own cloudy sky. I've created my own and I'll cover how to do it over the next couple of steps.

12. Start with a new RGB document, hit the D key to reset the default colors, and then go to **Filter>Render>Difference Clouds**. You'll end up with a black and white cloud pattern.

13. Then go to the Hue/Saturation dialog box (CTRL/CMD+U), check the Colorize box, and adjust the sliders until you have a lovely blue and white cloud pattern.

**14.** Make a copy of this clouds image, and then go back to the original glass image we are creating.

**15.** Create a new layer, and paste the clouds into the new layer. Center it so that it covers the entire shape/text selection. For this example I've saved my seamless image as a pattern. I'm going to create a new layer and fill (SHIFT+BACKSPACE/DELETE) the layer with the pattern.

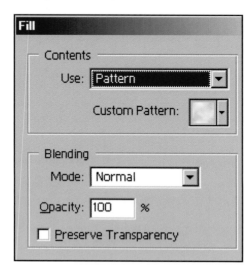

**16.** With the new filled layer selected, go to **Filter>Distort>Glass**. Select **Load Texture** and find the blurred image we just created from our channel.

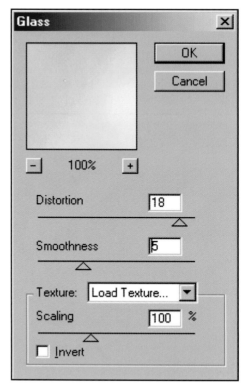

**17.** Run this filter with the exact same settings a second time (CTRL/CMD+F). Your image should look something like this:

**18.** CTRL/CMD+click the original shape/text layer to bring up the selection. Select the filled layer, go to **Select>Inverse**, and hit DELETE.

**19.** Change the Layer Mode to Color Burn.

**20.** We can bump up the highlights to the glass by applying a Bevel to the top layer.

**Bevel and Emboss**

**Structure**

Style: Inner Bevel

Technique: Smooth

Depth: 300 %

Direction: ● Up ○ Down

Size: 13 px

Soften: 0 px

**Shading**

Angle: 120 °

☐ Use Global Light

Altitude: 60 °

Gloss Contour: ☑ Anti-aliased

Highlight Mode: Screen

Opacity: 100 %

Shadow Mode: Screen

Opacity: 35 %

**21.** The above image has both the original layer with styles applied and the duplicate of that layer visible. If we render one of those invisible, our glass takes on greater transparency.

Take a look at the original glass example from the previous tutorial. You should see a marked difference in the quality from the styled glass and the glass we created with the displacement map.

### 3: Glass globe

We'll be looking at globes in greater detail in later sections of the book, but for now let's have a go at making a beautiful glass globe. Yes, we're going to end up with our very own crystal ball!

1. Create a new image (CTRL/CMD+N), and fill (SHIFT+BACKSPACE/DELETE) the background with black.

2. Make a new layer, (CTRL/CMD+SHIFT+N). On this layer use the **Elliptical Marquee** tool (SHIFT+M) to draw a circular selection in the center of the screen. Again fill this circle with black. (If you want to check that this has worked properly, why not switch off the visibility of the background layer so that the newly filled circle is distinct from the background?).

3. With the circular selection still active, create a new layer (CTRL/CMD+SHIFT+N). On this layer we now want to add a white outline to our circle.

*A quick way to bring white up as the foreground color, hit D to reset the default colors, and X to bring white into the foreground.*

4. Go to **Edit>Stroke** and apply an inner stoke of about 8 pixels to the selection. Now deselect (CTRL/CMD+D).

5. Go to **Filter>Blur>Gaussian Blur** and apply a blur of 8 pixels.

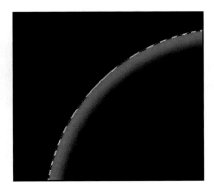

6. Apply a Gradient Overlay to the layer, using the default colors but changing the mode to Hard Light.

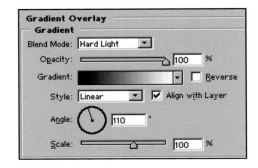

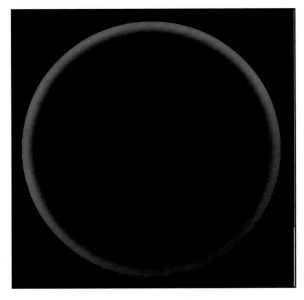

7. CTRL/CMD+click the circle layer to bring up the selection. Create a new layer, and select the **Rectangular Marquee** tool (SHIFT+M).

**8.** In the Marquee Options bar, click the **Subtract from selection** icon. Draw the marquee over the bottom two thirds of your selection. When you are done only the top portion of the circle should have an active selection.

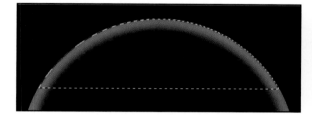

**9.** Go to the Channels palette. Create a new channel and fill the selection with white.

**10.** Go to **Filter>Blur>Gaussian Blur**. Blur the contents of the selection by 35, then by 20, and then by 10. Deselect (CTRL/CMD+D) and blur by 10 again.

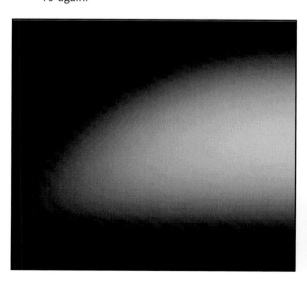

**11.** Hit CTRL/CMD+L to bring up the **Levels** adjustment. Move the sliders together until you have a solid white area with rounded corners.

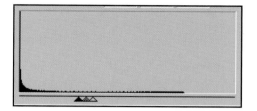

**12.** Use the **Magic Wand** tool (W) and click in the white area. Then go back to the layer you created in step 8. Fill (SHIFT+BACKSPACE/DELETE) the selection with white.

**13.** Apply the Gaussian Blur four times. Start with a setting of 15 pixels, then 10, and then 5. On the last one deselect and use a blur of 3.

**14.** Go to **Edit>Transform>Rotate** and enter 25 in the Set rotation box in the Rotate Options bar. Then select the Move tool (V) and place the reflection in the upper right of the sphere.

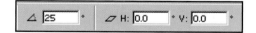

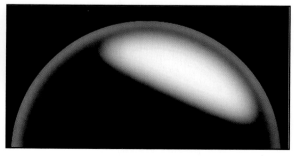

15. Duplicate the highlight layer we just created. Rotate it (CTRL/CMD+T, then right-click/CONTROL-click and choose Rotate) and move it to the bottom portion of the circle.

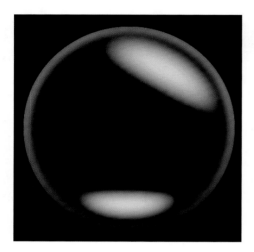

Now we need to distort this highlight to make the globe come to life. You can stretch it; bend it (**Edit>Transform>Distort**); colorize it (**Layer Styles>Color Overlay**). It's your globe; so let your imagination run riot.

16. A great tool for creating reflection distortions is the **Liquify** tool; go to **Image>Liquify** to access it (SHIFT+CTRL/CMD+X). Using this tool we can manually distort the edges of the reflections, curving them inward to match the curve of the bubble.

17. If the reflection is too stark or distorted as in the above example, we can again call on our old friend Gaussian Blur to correct the problem.

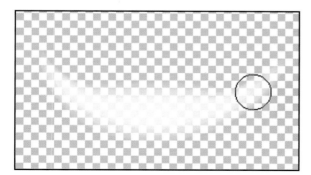

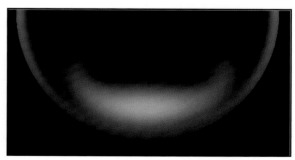

I added some spots of color using the **Airbrush** tool (J), and I applied a Lens Flare (**Filter>Render>Lens Flare**) to the original black circle layer, here is the finished result:

*The reflections should always have a curve or distortion applied that follows the globe's surface. A careful study of real glass object can be a wealth of information when trying to recreate the effect in Photoshop.*

## 4: Plastics

Sticking to our theme of reflections, let's move on to non-transparent glossy objects, like plastics. We can use many of the techniques we've just learned from making glass to create authentic plastic surfaces, and we'll be using the Layer Styles palette extensively again. The best bit is we have more freedom with color this time, so let's see if we can whip up some funky plastic designs.

*A rounded shape or font style really enhances this effect. Check out the font links found later in the book, or do a search online for 'free fonts'. Your search will return many great sites that are dedicated to supplying cool, free fonts to the masses.*

1.  Open a new image, (CTRL/CMD+N) and create a new layer (CTRL/CMD+SHIFT+N). Enter your text or draw your shape on this layer. If you used a selection tool to create it, be sure to fill it (Black is a good color for now) before going to step 3.

    You can download my shape used in this tutorial from the friends of ED web site at www.friendsofed.com/code.

**2.** Head straight for the Layer Styles palette, and start by selecting Bevel and Emboss to apply a bevel with the following settings:

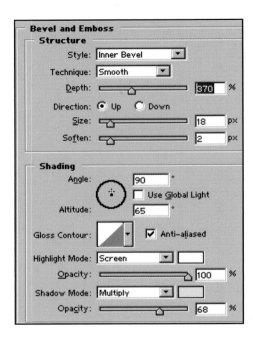

**3.** Add a Gradient Overlay with the following settings, and then a Color Overlay.

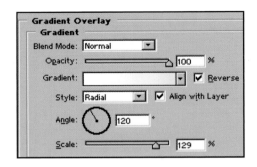

4. Now add an Inner Glow, but use a dark color or gradient with the following settings:

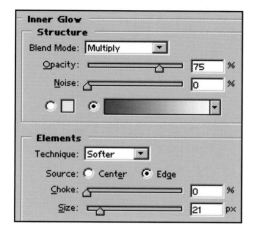

5. That's a pretty fair rendering of plastic, but we can add a few highlights or interior designs and drop shadow to enhance things a bit.

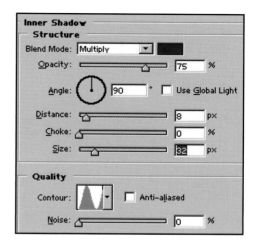

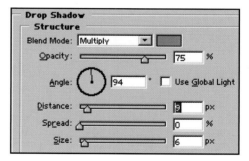

## Variations

Try applying various pattern overlays, colors, and gradients. When you find an effect you like, be sure to save the style! Here are a few examples of variations of the above effect

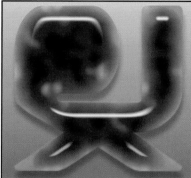

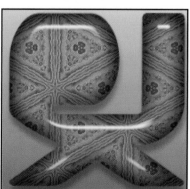

As, we've seen, glass and plastic are basically exercises in reflections and transparency. Once you have a few of these techniques under your belt, you'll be creating fuller glossy effects in no time! Keep in mind what was discussed earlier. In order to duplicate glass or plastic, a careful visual study of how light plays on a real object can definitely help to understand what elements, reflections, and so forth need be applied to a digital version to increase or enhance the realism of the effect.

# Chapter 4
# Surfaces and textures

Textures are the building blocks for reality; all things natural and man-made are made up of textures. We are going to examine a variety of different textures and surfaces in this chapter.  And we'll be taking things a step further by looking at techniques such as using displacement maps, and alpha channels to create realistic effects. Again, my advice is not to limit yourself to the examples you see on these pages: use your creativity and apply them in all kinds of places and produce something different. These textures will come in handy for backgrounds, photo retouching, text effects, special effects, and when all that is done, just for fun! If you don't have a little fun while creating, your designs will show it, they will be dry and stagnant. Don't be afraid to take a few risks. These effects will help expand your horizons and give you new avenues to explore.

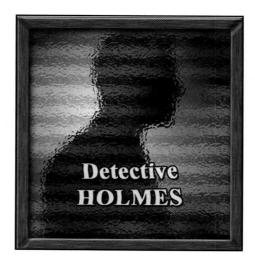

## 1: Glass window

In this section we are going to combine a few effects to create a 50s style silhouette in a window. We are going to create the glass texture, apply it to the picture, wrap some text to the texture, then tweak the lighting, and lastly make a wooden frame from scratch.

1. Begin with a silhouette of a person. A good source for this is clip art, or you could modify a photo or even draw one yourself. This example is 550X600 at 72dpi and RGB mode. Press D to reset the foreground and background colors.

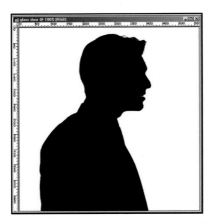

2. Create a new layer, (CTRL/CMD+N) and name it, 'glass'.

3. Let's build up the texture for the glass, go to **Filter>Render>Clouds.**

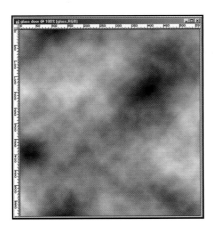

4. Now apply a motion blur to the clouds. **Filter>Blur>Motion Blur**, I used a setting of 92 pixels.

5. What we want to do now is add a louvered texture to simulate the texture on some of the old windows. So choose **Filter>Sketch>Halftone Pattern**.

6. Change the Pattern Type to Line, Size to 12, and Contrast to 5. The size needs to be as large as it will go. So, here is the completed window texture. This is a pretty useful texture that you could use to overlay a collage.

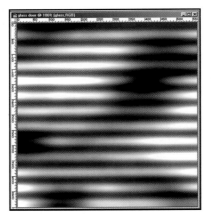

7. Now we want to frost the glass. This is very simple and produces good results. Go to **Filter>Distort>Glass**. Set the Distortion to 7, the Smoothness to 3, and, of course, choose Frosted as your Texture.

8. We now have our textured glass, let's apply the frosted texture to our silhouette.

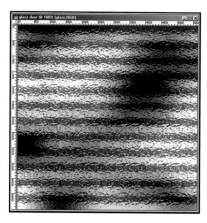

9. Hide the glass layer, by clicking on the eye icon, and select the Background layer, which should hold your silhouette.

10. Press CTRL/CMD+F to apply the previous filter with the same settings. You will now see the image as if looking through a shower door.

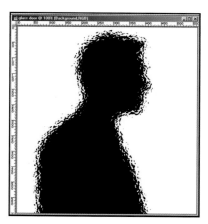

11. Now we'll combine the two steps. Show the glass layer and lower the Opacity to 40%

12. Here we have our basic effect, very Philip Marlowe. You could stop here or continue to add some extra realism and atmosphere.

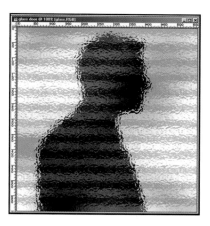

## Lighting trick

We are going to create a little lighting effect to make the image seem as if there is a single light source coming from behind, perhaps a window, or maybe one of those sultry lamps you always see in detective movies.

1.  Create a new layer, name it, 'lighting' and position it between the Background and the glass layer.

2.  We are going to apply a Black to White, Radial gradient. The effect we want is light around the middle and blending to dark on the edges. This will also pull the eyes into the center of the image more, and strengthen the image.

3.  Hide the glass layer so you can see what you are working on. Apply the gradient by drawing a line from top to bottom across the center of the image, the bigger the line, the larger the radius of the gradient. You may need several attempts before you get a result you like. Here is an ideal gradient. It's nice, smooth and even.

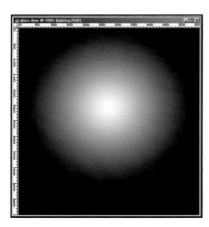

4.  Switch the layer blending mode to Darken. This will allow our silhouette to show through. You can adjust the Opacity if necessary, to get a good balance between the silhouette and the gradient.

5.  Here is the result, I like the feel of it, so we'll continue.

6.  The following image shows the three layers combined. See how much stronger the image looks now. Definitely some kind of cagey business going on behind that frosted glass.

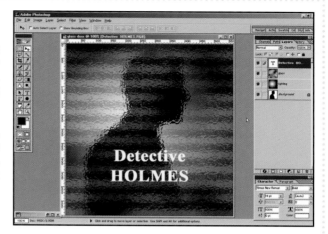

## Wrapping text to the surface.

1. Next, let's create a displacement map so we can wrap the text to the glass. Choose the glass layer and right-click/CTRL click; select Duplicate Layer. In the Document field, select New, and call the document, 'map'.

2. You will now have the layer as a new document. The new document kept all the properties of the glass layer. Just scoot the Opacity up to 100%. Here is the image we are going to use for a map:

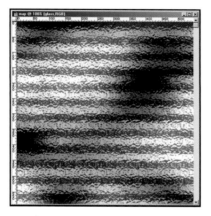

3. Apply a pretty heavy Gaussian Blur to the image because frosted glass is relatively smooth on one side. Of course the text would be painted on the smooth side. Go to **Filter>Blur>Gaussian Blur**, I used a 9.9 pixel blur here.

4. Save your displacement map to your hard disk. Save it as `map.psd`. It must be a psd file to work.

5. Apply some type to your image and move to the top layer.

6. Now add a 3 pixel, black stroke outside the text, we'll do this by selecting the Stroke option from the Layer Styles menu. For extra emphasis you can also add a hard Drop Shadow by turning up the Spread option in the Drop Shadow layer style.

7. Before you can run most filters on a type layer you must first rasterize it, which basically converts it to a regular, editable layer. Right-click/CTRL click the type layer in the Layers palette and chose Rasterize Layer from the menu.

8. Let's get warped, go to **Filter>Distort>Displace.** Change the Scale to 5% because we only want a subtle effect.

9. Photoshop will now ask you for a displacement map. Navigate to your `map.psd` you saved earlier. Load the map and your text will twist and turn to follow the contour of the pattern on the glass.

### Final touches

I think it's time to add a little bit of color to the glass to make it pop. This is the same method found in the Creative Colorizing chapter.

1.  Select the glass layer.

2.  Click CTRL/CMD+U to open the Hue/Saturation box. Click Colorize and adjust the setting to suit your tastes, I would suggest a blue hue, to lend some realism to our image. I used the following settings: a Hue of 209; Saturation at 64; and Lightness at 0.

3.  Isn't it amazing what a bit of color can do to an image? This demonstrates the power of subtlety. Our image is basically finished. How about adding a final touch, with a wooden frame?

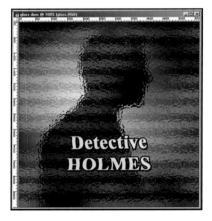

4.  Create a new layer and name it, 'wood frame'. Make sure that this layer is at the top of the Layers palette.

5.  Use the **Polygonal Lasso** tool (L) to draw the shape of the left-hand side of the doorframe. Hold down the SHIFT key to constrain the lines to angles of 45 degrees.

6.  Fill (SHIFT+BACKSPACE/DELETE) this selection with black, and then go to **Filter>Noise>Add Noise**. Use the following settings to add Gaussian Noise, at a percentage of roughly 84%. Ensure that the Monochromatic box is checked.

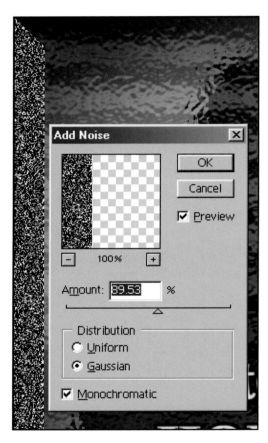

7.  Blurring the noise creates a nice wooden texture, **Filter>Blur>Motion Blur**, I think you get the idea. I used a 90-degree angle, with a distance of 32 pixels.

8. Now we need to colorize the wood. Once again Hue/Saturation comes to the rescue. Click Colorize and play around with the settings until you get a deep brown/red color.

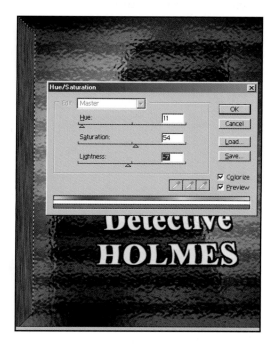

9. Duplicate the frame layer, and flip it horizontally, **Edit>Transform>Flip Horizontal**. Slide it into position on the right-hand side.

10. Duplicate again and rotate 45 degrees for the bottom. Duplicate once again and flip vertically for the top. You can use the free transform command (CTRL/CMD+T) to tweak the frame to fit.

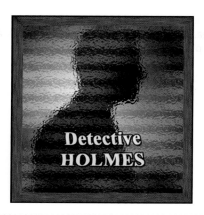

11. Now we now have four frame layers. Let's make them one entity. Link them in the Layers palette by clicking to the left of the thumbnail. You will see the little chain-link icons.

12. Choose Merge Linked from the Layers menu, and we now have one layer for the frame, this is a lot easier to apply extra effects to.

13. Add the Bevel layer style as shown here. Also add a default Drop Shadow while you have the dialog box open.

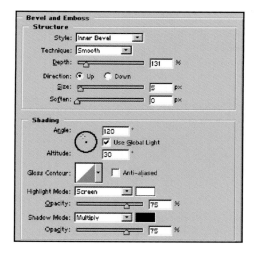

And here we a have our finished image that sports quite a lot of realism. Congratulations, you learned a few tricks along the way too.

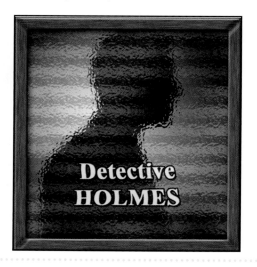

## 2: Making aged metal

Fasten your seatbelts; you are about to go on a journey of metal, rust, and time. We are going to create a highly detailed piece of metal. The metal will be beveled, shiny, and pitted. We are going to make the corners worn and smooth, but with a touch of discolor from the weather. Then we will add rusty rivets and discoloring where water has dripped from the rivets for a few years. This is about as realistic as it gets. Imagine what you will be able to do with these techniques. You can use them in sequence, or stand-alone. You can use them on interfaces, backgrounds, text, whatever you please. So without further delay, let's go...

### Creating the beveled metal

1.  Begin with a new document of 600X600 at 72ppi and RGB mode.

2.  Create a new layer and call it, 'shape'. Using the Polygon Lasso tool, draw the outline of your shape.

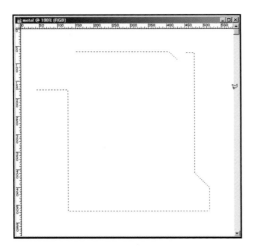

3.  Press D to reset the default colours and then fill with a Foreground to Background Linear gradient.

4.  Take the Polygon Lasso tool again and draw a shape that will be carved out of the center.

5.  Press DELETE to cut out the shape. Press CTRL/CMD+click on the layer thumbnail to load the entire shape again as a selection. You should see the "marching ants" around the entire shape.

6.  Open the Channels palette and add a new alpha channel by clicking on the **Create new channel** icon.

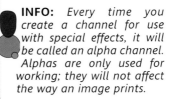

**INFO:** *Every time you create a channel for use with special effects, it will be called an alpha channel. Alphas are only used for working; they will not affect the way an image prints.*

7. Click on Alpha 1 to make it the active channel. Choose a mid gray color for your foreground color.

8. We are now creating a **bump map**. This will give the image depth when we apply the lighting effects filter. Apply a Foreground to Background gradient from the right to the center; this is a very subtle effect. What will happen in 3D is this: the white parts of the channel will be higher, the black parts will be lower, and the gray will be angled.

9. Apply an 8.4 pixel Gaussian Blur (**Filter>Blur>Gaussian Blur**). By keeping the selection active, we can ensure that only some darkening of the edges occurs.

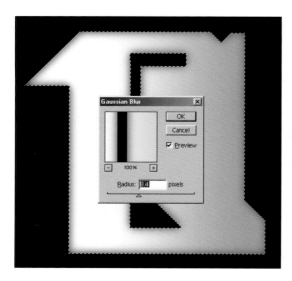

10. Deselect and run the Gaussian blur again, at 5.6 pixels. This two step process creates sharper beveled edges.

11. Click on the RGB channel to display all the channels again.

12. Go back to the Layers palette and choose the 'shape' layer.

13. Now, rather than using a Layers palette bevel, let's apply lighting effects to make our shape 3D, **Filter>Render>Lighting Effects.**

14. Here is the Lighting Effects dialog box. Choose a light blue Spotlight. In the Texture Channel, choose Alpha 1. This will load the channel we worked on earlier.

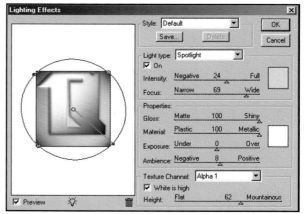

15. Here is the shape with the Lighting Effects bevel. In my opinion, using the Lighting Effects option is one of the best ways to produce a realistic bevel.

## Making the metal shiny

Here is a simple technique to give any surface a highly reflective surface.

1. Go to **Image>Adjust>Curves** to create a curve that looks similar to the example here.

*The curve gives a visual representation of the tonal properties of an image.*

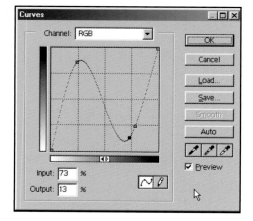

2. Press CTRL/CMD+ALT/OPT+M to open the Curves box again with exactly the same settings. Press OK to apply to the image. We now have a very shiny titanium look.

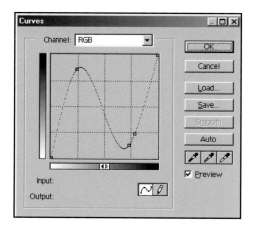

3. To lose the titanium coloring, but keep the shiny effect, go to **Image>Adjust>Hue/Saturation**. Click on Colorize and shift the Hue to a blue/gray color.

Here is our shiny, chrome metal.

## Adding texture to the metal

I believe the difference between a good image and a great image is the little details. This step will add a lot of realism to the metal and take it beyond just another chrome clone image. We are going to add a texture to the metal, but at the same time keep it smooth on the edges as it would look after it had been polished frequently.

1. Duplicate the 'shape' layer.

2. Select the copied layer and apply some noise, **Filter>Noise>Add Noise**. Add roughly 20% noise with Gaussian distribution, check the Monochromatic box.

3. Invert the selection, (SHIFT+CTRL/CMD+I).

4. **Select>Feather** and choose a large radius, say 25 pixels.

5. Here is the image with the soft selection. Press DELETE 5 times or until you are happy with the blend of texture to smooth.

6. Change the blending mode to Multiply and change the Opacity to 48%. Here is the metal with the texture:

## Drilling holes

Now we are going to drill some holes in the metal.

1. Merge the 'shape' and 'shape copy' layers. Using the Elliptical Marquee tool, make a circular selection around the metal.

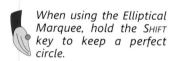
*When using the Elliptical Marquee, hold the SHIFT key to keep a perfect circle.*

2. Press DELETE to cut out the hole, don't deselect yet.

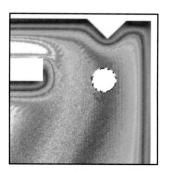

3. Using the arrow keys on the keyboard and holding the SHIFT key, move the selection and hit DELETE to make your second drill hole, move it again and hit DELETE again until you have four holes in the metal. (Using the arrow keys helps you to keep the holes evenly spaced).

4. Now we'll apply a Bevel and Drop Shadow layer style to the image. Use the following settings:

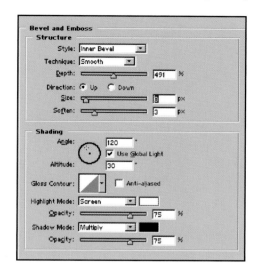

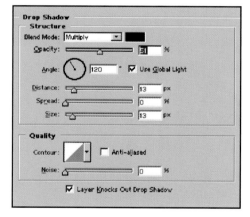

Here is the finished metal with the beveled holes in it:

## Aging the edges

This effect is a lot of fun. We are going to add coloring to the edges to make it appear that the object has been out in the weather for a while.

1. CTRL/CMD+click on the layer thumbnail to load the 'shape' layer as a selection and create a new layer.

2. Invert the selection (CTRL/CMD+I). This will select everything but our metal.

3. **Select>Feather** with a setting of 20. This will cause a soft selection over the edges of our shape. Then choose a nice rusty orange color and set it as the foreground color.

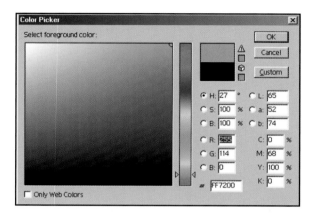

4. Fill (**Edit>Fill**) with the foreground color. Repeat four times until you build up a nice orange edge.

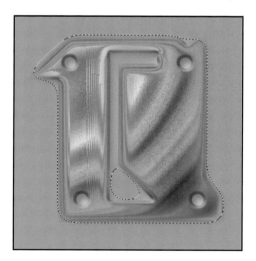

5. With the orange layer still active, load the selection from the edge layer again and invert. Press DELETE and you will have your image with soft orange edges.

6. Deselect (CTRL/CMD+D) and change the layer mode to Color Burn. For future clarity, name your 'edges' layer as such. Here is the finished effect. Notice how the color adds so much to the realism of the image.

## Making rivets

Now we come to the point where we want to create some rivets to add to the industrial feel of the metal.

1. Ensure that the 'shape' layer is active by clicking on it in the Layers palette, then using the **Magic Wand** (W), select one of the holes.

2. You will now have a circular selection the same size as the hole. (If you are doing the rivets as a stand-alone effect, just draw a circular selection using the Elliptical Marquee tool).

3. Create a new layer, called, 'rivets'. Click on this layer to activate it.

4. Choose a dirty brown color for the foreground and white for the background. Then select a Radial, Foreground to Background gradient. Apply the gradient to the selection; you should have a dome look.

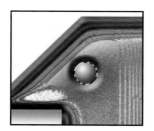

5. Let's age the rivet a bit, go to **Filter>Noise>Add Noise**. I used a setting of 8.79%.

6. Add a standard Drop Shadow layer style to the rivet.

7. Duplicate the rivet layer three times and position them over each hole.

*To make a duplicate of a layer, hold down the ALT/OPTION key and drag the object, you will notice a double arrow; this indicates you are dragging a copy.*

## Adding the drip-stains

1. Merge the rivets layers together until they are all on one layer. We want to do this so that we can create the effect for all four rivets in one go and save time. Link the layers together, and then select Merge Linked from the Layers menu.

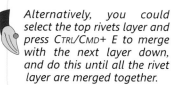

*Alternatively, you could select the top rivets layer and press CTRL/CMD+ E to merge with the next layer down, and do this until all the rivet layer are merged together.*

2. Let's do the effect now: Duplicate the rivets layer. Apply a motion blur, **Filter>Blur>Motion Blur,** use a setting of 90 degrees and distance of 49 pixels.

3. Reposition the blurred rivets so they are under the original rivets.

4. Duplicate three times to thicken them up, then merge the three blurred rivet layers and rename the layer, 'drip'. Your image should now look something like this:

5. Apply a Gaussian Blur (**Filter>Blur>Gaussian Blur**), use a setting of 4.7, then move the 'drip' layer beneath the 'rivets' layer.

6. Use the Hue/Saturation (CTRL/CMD+U) filter to change the color of the drip to orange. (For more info on Hue/Saturation see the Creative Colorizing chapter).

7. Now change the layer blend mode to Overlay to make the drips blend in better. We're almost there; just need to do some clean-up work, as the drips extend off the bottom of the metal.

8. With the 'drip' layer still active (highlighted blue in the Layers palette). Load the selection for the 'shape' layer. Remember we CTRL/CMD+click on the layer thumbnail to load a selection.

9. Invert the selection, (SHIFT+CTRL/CMD+I), and press DELETE. The edges will be cleaned up and the overlap is now gone.

One way you could use this effect is for an interface for a website or CD-ROM.

### 3: Gems

Throughout the book, we have looked at various ways to make glass, stone, metal, backgrounds, and so forth, using a lot of filters in the process and variations of Layer Styles. There is one filter that is rarely seen in design, primarily because its application is a dead give away that a filter was used. I'm talking about the Stained Glass filter. The name implies that one should be able to create some visually stunning effects, but people steer away from it nonetheless.

I'm not one to leave well enough alone, so I'm going to show you a use for this neglected filter.

1. Create a new image (CTRL/CMD+N). For this example, the image size is 9 by 6 inches, 100 ppi, RGB, with a White background.

2. Create a new layer (SHIFT+CTRL/CMD+N) and call it 'gems'.

3. Select the **Type Mask** tool, and set your font size fairly large. Enter your text selection on the new layer.

4. Select the **Gradient** tool, changing the foreground and background colors to something bright. I'm using a red/purple combination.

5. Change the Gradient Blend Mode to Difference. Fill the selection three times with the Foreground to Background Gradient, drawing from a different direction each time.

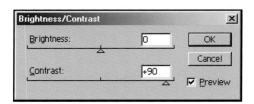

6. Now go to **Filter>Render>Difference Clouds** and run the filter twice (press CTRL/CMD+F to run the filter again). Go to **Image>Adjust>Brightness/Contrast**, and increase the contrast considerably so the separation between the two primary colors becomes sharp.

7. Make a copy of the type layer (**Layer> Duplicate Layer**) and hit 'D' to reset the default colors.

8. To apply the Stained Glass filter go to **Filter>Texture>Stained Glass**. Set your Cell Size to 15, Border Thickness to 4, and Light Intensity to 3. Click OK.

9. Go to **Select>Color Range** to delete the black lines separating the colors. With the eyedropper, click on a black line directly on the image. Click OK, and hit DELETE. Deselect.

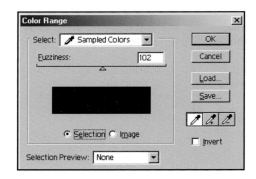

10. Go to the Channels palette and duplicate the Blue channel.

11. In the original Blue channel, click the area outside of the text cells using the Magic Wand tool (W).

12. Select the duplicate Blue channel and fill the selection with Black. Go to **Select>Inverse**, and fill the cells with White. When you are finished you should have a duplicate of the Blue channel with white cells in the shape of your type on a black background. This is important, as in the following steps we will be rounding the corners on the cells. In order to do this effectively, we need white cells blurred on a black background so the coming levels adjustment can round the cells for us.

13. We need to round out the edges. First, go to **Select>Deselect** (CTRL/CMD+D).

14. Let's apply a blur for the rounding process. Go to **Filter>Blur>Gaussian Blur** and apply a setting of

3 to 4. Keep an eye on the viewer window to make sure you can still see the black lines, even though they are blurred somewhat.

**15.** Hit CTRL/CMD+L to bring up the Levels control to adjust the levels in the duplicate Blue channel. Move the sliders closer together until you have distinct, rounded cells in the viewer.

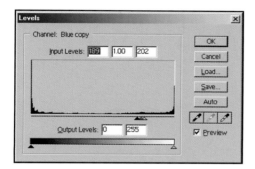

**16.** CTRL/CMD+click the rounded 'gems' channel to bring up the selection. Go back to the Layers palette and select the bottom type layer. Click the eye to render this layer invisible, we will need it for the next part of the tutorial.

**17.** Select the topmost type layer. Go to **Select/Inverse** and hit DELETE.

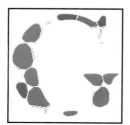

**18.** Time to make the gems shiny! Access the Advanced Blending Options in the Layer Styles. Drop your Opacity settings to 85% each.

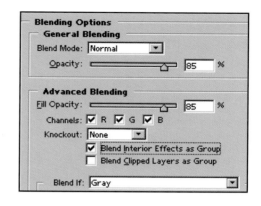

**19.** Apply a Bevel/Emboss with the following settings:

**20.** Now an Inner Shadow:

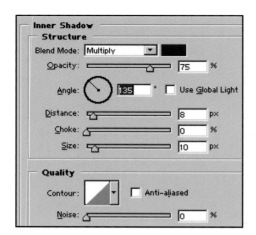

**21.** Now a Drop Shadow to seal the deal and deselect (CTRL/CMD+D).

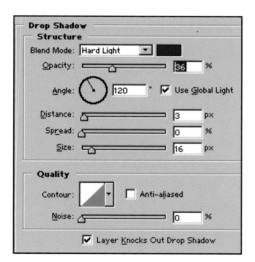

Of course, you can stop the effect right there. However, since we saved the original gradient filled layer, we can embed the gems in just a few more steps.

**22.** Click the lower type layer, making it visible again. CTRL/CMD+click it to bring up the original type selection.

**23.** Select a light gray foreground color and dark gray background. Click on the Gradient Tool. In the Gradient Options bar, select the Foreground to Background Gradient, Reflected, in Normal Blending Mode.

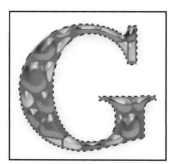

**24.** Starting in the middle of the selection, draw the gradient straight down to the edge of the text.

**25.** Access the Layer Styles for this Layer. Select Stroke first, as we will be applying a Stroke Bevel shortly.

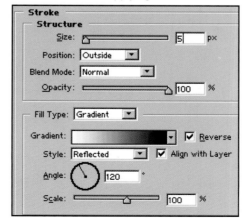

26. Now apply the Bevel. Be sure to change the Bevel style to Stroke Emboss. Also note the curve change from the default in the example.

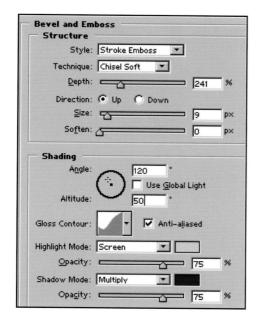

28. We are almost there, but we should really try to make the gems actually look embedded. Duplicate the gems layer.

29. Select the 'gems' layer (not the duplicate) and access the Layer Styles. Open up the Bevel/Emboss options again. Change the Bevel Style to Pillow Emboss, and adjust the settings to match those in the image below.

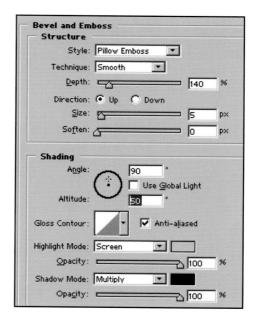

27. Apply a dark Inner Glow, changing the blending mode to Color Burn and bumping up the noise.

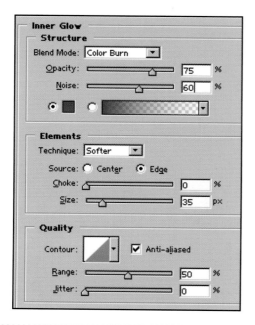

30. Go back to the Blending Options. Change the Blending Mode to Color Dodge, increase the Opacity to 100%, and lower the Fill Opacity to 60%.

And here's our final result:

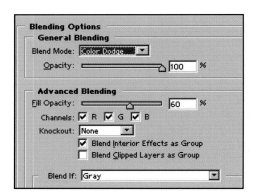

This completes our look at textures and surfaces. Over the past three chapters we have covered wood, stone, metals, glass and plastic. You have just taken your skills to a whole new level and you should be experimenting with some new textures by now. We're now going to move things up a gear and take on the world of electronics and science fiction. You'll be using some of the techniques that we have already covered; you should be feeling more confident in your skills with every new effect.

# Chapter 5
# Circuits and electronics

In this chapter we will be creating objects from the world of electronics. Math was never this much fun at school. When we discussed nature in Chapter 1, I put forward the idea that despite nature's random appearance, its roots are in complex math. By running formulae on a computer, we can generate the appearance of a tree, but never capture the complexity of a living plant. We don't have the formula. Recreating man-made objects is actually easier, as the math involved is much simpler. Photoshop understands the formulae, and so in a few steps we can have visual representations of items we would expect to see in the man-altered world.

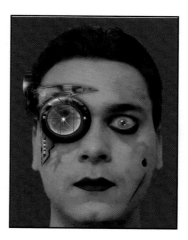

## 1: Circuits

There is a cool little trick built right into Photoshop for creating designs that give the appearance of circuitry.

1. We'll start with a new image (CTRL/CMD+N), 3X3 inches, 100 dpi, RGB color mode, and Transparent.

2. Fill (SHIFT+BACKSPACE/DELETE) the background layer with a dark green, the settings for the color I used are shown below:

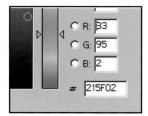

3. Press CTRL/CMD+SHIFT+N to create a new layer.

4. Select the **Gradient** tool (G), and choose a Copper, Reflected Gradient, with the blending mode set to Difference.

5. Fill the new layer from the center to the bottom with the gradient.

6. Starting a little off center, apply the gradient again, this time horizontally, from left to right.

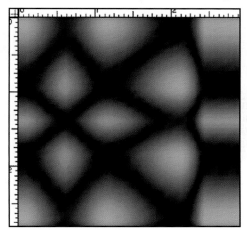

7. Go to **Filter>Pixelate>Mosaic**, and enter a cell size of 10.

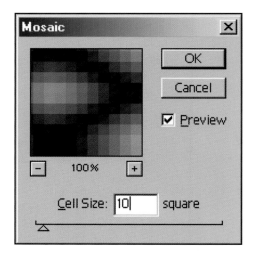

8. Go to **Filter>Stylize>Find Edges**.

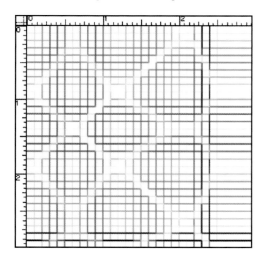

9. Now go to **Filter>Stylize>Glowing Edges**. The setting you apply here is going to dictate the circuitry pattern. Set the **Edge Width** to 1, **Edge Brightness** to 8, and then try experimenting with various **Smoothness** levels. I suggest you use a value of 2, but anywhere between 1 and 6 is good.

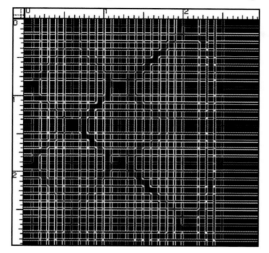

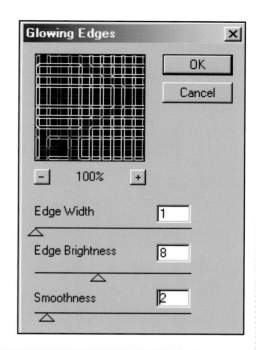

10. Set the layer mode for the circuit layer to Overlay, and voila, we have a nice little electronic circuit.

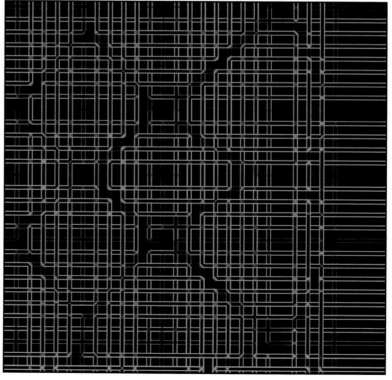

## 2: Lightning

Let's heat things up a bit now and look at creating lightning bolts. This is a great effect for lightning and electric shock effects. We will be using difference clouds and levels to create this effect.

1. Start with a 600x600 document in RGB mode.

2. Create a new layer (SHIFT+CTRL/CMD+N) and name this new layer 'effect'.

3. Now diagonally apply a Black to White Linear gradient, this effect is going to be created around the area that is 50% gray.

4. Go to **Filter>Render>Difference Clouds.** Your image should now look something like this. It won't be exactly the same, as this is a random effect. Notice the dark line in the middle. This is the base of our lightning.

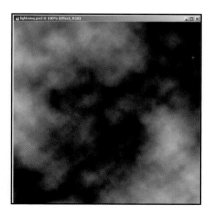

5. We want to invert the tones, similar to changing the image to a negative, so select **Image>Adjust>Invert** (CTRL/CMD I).

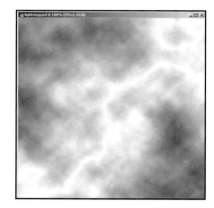

6. Now adjust the levels to clean up the lightning bolt and accentuate it using **Image>Adjust>Levels** (CTRL/CMD+L). Move the middle slider most of the way to the left and then move the left slider to the right until you get a satisfactory result. For reference my settings ended up at 157, 0.10, 255. Click OK.

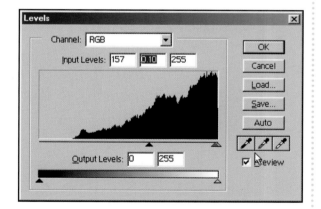

This is roughly what your image should look like after the Levels adjustment.

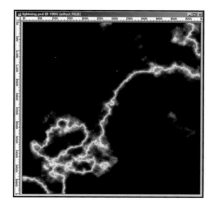

7. There are still a few stray areas to clean up. Use a 100px soft brush, set it to black, and paint over the areas we don't want.

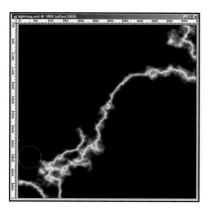

8. All we need to do now is adjust the color using **Image>Adjust>Hue/Saturation** (CTRL/CMD+U). Check the Colorize box and play with the sliders until you get a suitable color. To get an electric purple-blue color I set the **Hue** to 257, the **Saturation** level to 25, and the **Lightness** value to 0.

Here is the finished lightning bolt. The great thing about this technique is that you will never get two bolts exactly the same, just like real lightning in nature.

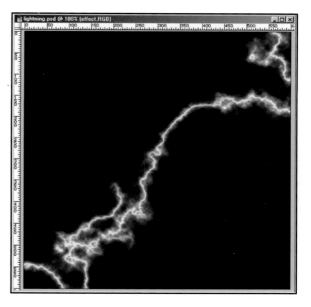

## 3: Lightning strikes

Okay, so now we've got our authentic looking lightning; let's apply it to some images. For the next few steps, we'll be making full use of the layer blending modes again.

1. Open (CTRL/CMD+O) the image you want to apply the lightning to.

2. Drag the lightning from the 'effect' layer into the new image. It really is as simple as that, just select the layer from the Layers palette, and drag it over to the new image.

*Hold down the SHIFT key as you drop it into the new document to ensure it will be centered.*

5. There we have the two images perfectly blended together. Congratulations, you have just learned how to electrify your images.

*You can get some cool effects by duplicating the lightning layers and then transforming them – rotating, scaling, skewing, whatever. Play around with those layers and make sparks fly!*

3. We have the document with a new layer on top with our lightning. By changing the layer mode, we can remove all the black and reveal the image below.

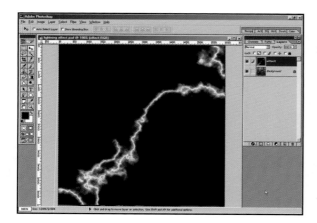

4. Change the effect layer blending mode to **Screen** and watch what happens.

## 4: Cybernetics

I'm a science fiction fan, and I would love to be able to draw the images I see in my head when my imagination is going wild, but sadly I'm not much of an artist. I do know a thing or two about Photoshop though, and fortunately, with this powerful tool, I can apply fantastic science to everyday images. So, it's time for a bit of futuristic Photoshop experimentation.

## Cyborg eyepiece

My good friend, Andrew, has volunteered to help me further the cause of warped science, by offering his services as my first guinea pig. He's fully conscious and firmly tied down, let's see what horrific transformations we can achieve.

1. Find an image of someone's face. Choose a picture with a fair amount of contrast between the background and the skin tones, so that the two are easy to separate.

2. Double-click on the background layer to turn it into a regular, editable layer.

3. Select the background area around the face with the **Magic Wand** tool (W).

4. Once the background is selected, go to **Select>Inverse** (SHIFT+CTRL/CMD+I). Go to **Layer>New>Layer Via Copy** (CTRL/CMD+J) to paste a copy of the face area into a new layer. Call your new layer 'face'.

5. If the edges appear too jagged around the head, you can blend the edges a bit by selecting the area around the head with the Magic Wand. Go to **Select>Feather**, and set it to 2-3 pixels, and then hit DELETE. Deleting the feathered selection will erase and blend the edge around the head, but don't overdo it.

6. Choose a dark gray foreground color. Create a new layer (SHIFT+CTRL/CMD+N) beneath the face layer and fill it with the foreground color (ALT/OPT+BACKSPACE/DELETE).

7. Create a new layer (SHIFT+CTRL/CMD+N) above the face layer and call it 'eyepiece'. With the **Elliptical Marquee** tool (M or SHIFT+M), make a selection around an eye, from about the brow to the lower portion of the nose.

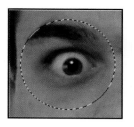

*When drawing your circle, remember that to ensure that your selection is perfectly circular, hold down the SHIFT key as you drag out the shape.*

8. Fill (SHIFT+BACKSPACE/DELETE) the selection over the eye with gray. This would be a good time to move the circle if you are not happy with its position, do this using the **Move** tool (V). Then deselect, CTRL/CMD+D.

9. Make another circular selection within the gray circle, about a third of the size of the original. You may want to draw out guides to help you place the circle, or you can hold down the SHIFT key 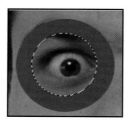 while creating the selection, which will maintain the aspect ratio of the circle. Position it manually with the arrow keys. Press DELETE to clear the selection.

10. For the next few steps we are going to work on a layer style to give the eyepiece some character. Click on the **Add a layer style** icon at the bottom of the Layers palette, and choose the **Bevel and Emboss** option.

11. Use the settings shown in the screenshot below. Notice that we have created a customized **Gloss Contour**. To do this, you need to click directly in the Gloss Contour window. The **Contour Editor** will then pop up, and you may adjust the points by moving them with the mouse. You can add additional points by clicking on the contour line, and move it as you see fit. Try applying a contour similar to the one seen below. You can also save the contour for later use.

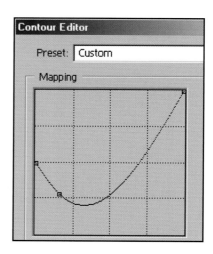

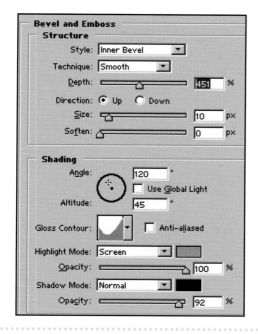

12. Next, let's apply an Outer Glow. We are actually using the glow to apply a shadow by changing the blend mode to Multiply and choosing a dark gray color.

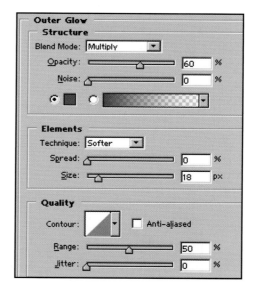

13. Go to Color Overlay. Choose a light color and change the blend mode to Color Burn.

**14.** Next, apply a Gradient Overlay.

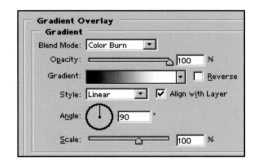

**15.** Let's give the eyepiece some variation by applying a Pattern Overlay. For this example a pattern from the default set will suffice. Change the Blend Mode to Soft Light.

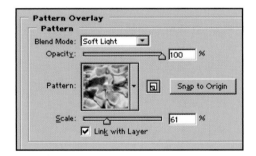

**16.** If you don't still have your inner circle selected, then use the Magic Wand tool (W), and click in the empty space within the circle.

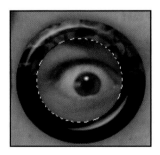

**17.** Create a new layer (SHIFT+CTRL/CMD+N) and call it 'edge'. Go to **Edit>Stroke** and stroke the selection by 3 pixels, centered, and with the Opacity set to 75%.

**18.** Apply a bevel to the strokes layer with the following settings. Note that we are applying a **Pillow Emboss** to give the illusion that this portion of the eyepiece is raised. Control this by altering the **Depth** and **Size** settings.

**19.** Again, select the Magic Wand tool and click in the empty area in the middle of the circle. Create a new layer, called 'lens', and fill it with gray.

**20.** Again we'll apply a nice bevel. Change the **Shadow Mode** color from black, which is the default color, to a dark green.

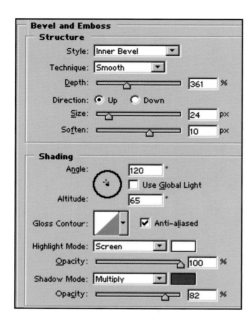

**21.** Apply a light green Inner Glow, set the Blend Mode to Screen, and the Elements Technique to Softer.

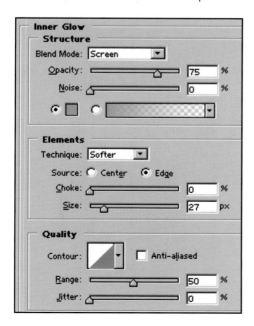

**22.** Now for an Inner Shadow:

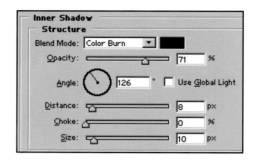

**23.** Apply a dark green Color Overlay. Reduce the Opacity to about 40%.

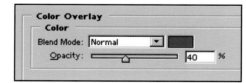

**24.** The lens is coming along nicely now, but it needs more character to really make it shine. Deselect the circular selection, and create a new layer, called 'lines'. Select the **Single Row Marquee** tool.

**25.** In the Marquee Options bar, click the **Add to selection** button. This enables you to add more than one line.

26. Make a couple of selections crossing the lens. Then use the **Single Column Marquee tool** for a little vertical line action. Once you have three or four lines crossing the lens area, go to **Edit>Fill** to fill the selection with black.

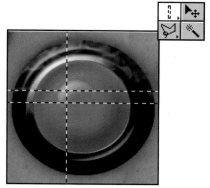

27. If your 'lines' layer isn't at the top of the list in the Layers palette, move it there now.

28. Go to the 'lens' layer and select the Magic Wand tool. Click within the circle, and yet again you have the circular section active.

29. Go back to the 'lines' layer and **Select>Inverse** (SHIFT+CTRL/CMD+I). Now you can delete the excess lines outside of the lens area, simply by hitting the DELETE key. **Select>Inverse** again, before moving to the next step.

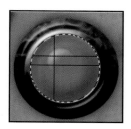

30. Create a new layer at the top of the Layers palette. I'm calling this one, 'lens highlights', we'll be applying still more glow to the lens to give it a bit more life.

31. Select white as your foreground color and click on the **Airbrush** tool (J). In the Airbrush Options, change the pressure to 11% and choose a soft, round brush. I'm using the 35 pt brush from the default set, but this will depend on the size of your image.

To access the default Brush options, click on the arrow to the left of the Brush window.

32. Run the Airbrush along the bottom portion of the lens, covering roughly half the circumference, with a heavier application of color on the nose side.

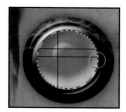

33. Select the **Smudge** tool (R), and in the Options bar, choose a small, precise brush. I'm using one that is 9 pts in size. On the outward edges of the painted highlights, smudge the highlights outward and up in a slight circular pattern. You may need to zoom in close to do this most effectively.

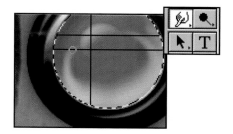

34. Change the layer blending mode of the 'lens highlights' layer to Overlay.

35. Create a new layer, called 'lens shadow'. Click D *to reset* black as the foreground color, and with a small, soft Airbrush, paint a small dab in the center of the lens. If it seems too harsh along the edges, simply apply a Gaussian blur for blending.

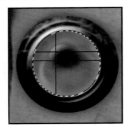

36. Change your foreground color to white by pressing X. Create a new layer above the eyepiece called 'top highlights'. Use the Airbrush tool to paint some highlights and reflections in the center of the eyepiece.

37. Create a new layer, 'circuits'. Select a gray foreground color and add a Foreground to Transparent, Linear gradient. Fill the top portion of the lens with the gradient starting at the top and drawing down to the center.

38. On this layer, go through the tutorial on creating circuits found earlier in this chapter. Once that is done, change the layer blending mode to Overlay.

39. Repeat step 36, but this time, draw the gradient from the bottom to center. Apply a **Pattern Overlay** to this layer.

40. Create a new layer beneath the 'circuits' layer; and then immediately re-select the 'circuits' layer and Merge Down (CTRL/CMD+E).

41. Change the blending mode to Color Burn, and drop the Opacity of the layer to around 60%.

## Metal plating

We've spent a lot of time drawing character out of the eyepiece, but there are other elements we can apply to our subject to further the marriage of flesh and electronics. This effect deals with applying metal structures to the face piece.

1. Create a new layer (SHIFT+CTRL/CMD+N). Place this layer just beneath the original eyepiece circle layer. Name the layer so you can keep track of it in the Layers palette.

2. Select the **Polygon Lasso** tool (L or SHIFT+L). Make a selection with sharp, jagged edges on the new layer. Make your selection so that one edge goes beneath the eyepiece.

3. Hit D to reset the default colors. Choose a Foreground to Background, Linear Gradient. Change the Gradient Mode to Difference.

4. Fill the selection several times with the Gradient tool (G). Direction doesn't matter so much as a stark variation in the pattern when you are done. If areas come out too bright or dark you can always adjust them with Brightness/Contrast.

5. Contract (**Select>Modify>Contract**) the selection by 6 pixels or so. Go to **Layer>New>Layer Via Copy** (CTRL/CMD+J).

6. Go to **Image>Adjust>Invert** (CTRL/CMD+I). Reduce the Brightness of this new layer.

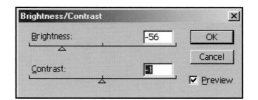

7. Let's give this layer a bit of texture. Go to **Filter>Distort>Diffuse Glow**. Set your **Graininess** to 9, **Glow** to 1, and **Clear Amount** to 17.

## LED Lights

For the final portion of this lengthy tutorial, we are going to create small LED style lights to add to the apparatus.

1.  Create a new layer above the metal plate. Using the Rectangular Marquee tool (M or SHIFT+M), make a small rectangular selection above the edge of the eyepiece. **Edit>Fill** to fill the selection with black, and apply a Bevel.

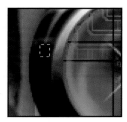

2.  Contract (**Select>Modify>Contract**) the selection by 2 pixels. Create a new layer and fill it with black. Apply a Color Overlay (red works well) and apply a slight Inner Bevel with a Depth of 10 and Size of 2-4. When you are satisfied with the look, merge this with the previous layer so that both light elements are on the same layer.

3.  Now you can duplicate the light several times. Select the Move tool (V), ALT/OPT-click on the light and drag it to a new area of the faceplate. Each time you drag a new light to a different portion of the image, a new layer is created, making it easy to change the hues of the individual lights. To line the lights up vertically, simply pull a guide in from the left and position the lights with the Move tool.

4.  Be sure to go back and apply the appropriate drop shadows to the layers.

    So, how does our victim...I mean 'volunteer' look thus far?

We are well on our way to creating one very handsome Cyborg! Relatively speaking, of course.

Try creating more plates following the process above, placing them on other areas of the face. Use your imagination! Cables are great objects to insert into a cyborg, and by manipulating the textures and hues of the fleshy areas we can have a rather striking looking man in a very short time. To close this chapter, allow me to introduce my newest creation:

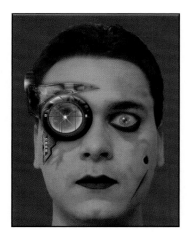

Introducing the new, improved Andrew, the Photoshop Most Wanted Borg! He's already taken, ladies, sorry!

# Chapter 6
# Building your own toolbox

In this chapter we'll look at all kinds of ways to fully exploit the Layer Style palette. We'll cover how to create actions in order to optimize your workflow, and we'll consider all the other things we can customize in Photoshop, from curves to brushes, and color swatches.

Why is all this stuff so important? Well, in my working life I create so many effects, and alter so many settings, that it would be a shame to lose all the things I'm really proud of. So I like to save those settings, and record those effects. To me, this is one the most useful features in Photoshop - the ability to create plug-ins from your settings for application later.

The great thing about **Actions** is the fact that you can not only record your own actions to create type treatments, but also actually load and use an action file created by other designers from around the world. If a person in Hong Kong creates an action that transformed mild-mannered type into melting fire, someone in Montana can download it from the web, load it into the Actions palette, and melt his own text in minutes with the exact settings recorded half a world away. This shows Photoshop harnessing the power of the Web.

## Actions

Actions enable us to record a series of steps in Photoshop, so that they can be used again and again. Their function is similar to that of macros in Word. They are pre-recorded commands that can be played back through the Actions palette to reproduce the effect or shortcut recorded into them. Throughout this book we have encountered some great effects, if we recorded them all as actions then we could run these effects on any shape or text that we choose, thus saving an awful lot of repetition.

The Actions palette (**View>Show Actions**) can be seen in one of two modes; **Button Mode** or **Edit Mode**.

- Button Mode displays the actions as a button, which you press to play the action. You may not edit or record when in Button Mode.

- Edit Mode displays the action as a list of commands. In this mode you can record, edit, re-arrange commands, and so forth. You may also play the action by clicking the play icon located at the bottom of the palette.

You can switch between the two modes by checking or unchecking the Button Mode option in the Actions palette menu. I'll demonstrate how to record an action later, when we'll make a handy action for creating pattern sets in the next section.

## 1: Layer styles and their elements

Many of the features we can record in Photoshop are found tucked into the **Layer Styles** palette. Not only can we create and save layer styles themselves, but we can also use the Layer Styles dialog box to load and create gradients and contours. We can create pattern sets for use in styles, and when we save a style set (group of styles) those patterns will be available to any user of the style set.

## Generating pattern sets

To begin with, you will need a few seamless patterns. There are literally hundreds of websites that provide custom-made background images, free for the taking.

For this section, I've downloaded patterns from a favorite website of mine – www.infinitefish.com, many thanks to designer Scott Balay for allowing us to use his creations. Check out his site for yourself to find some great textures and other Photoshop goodies. Another excellent site for patterns, textures and backgrounds is Eyeball Design (www.eyeball-design.com/fxzone/).

It's helpful to create an example image on which to test the patterns once we have a set put together. Let's create one now and leave it open in the background for use a little further on. Start by downloading some patterns, and then save them to a folder of their own on your hard drive.

1.  Create a new image (CTRL/CMD+N), 8x5 inches, 100 dpi, RGB, with a black background.

2.  Create a new layer (SHIFT+CTRL/CMD+N). Select the **Type** tool. Hit 'D' to reset your foreground/background colors, then hit 'X' to swap them, placing white in the foreground.

3.  Enter some text; make it fairly large, as it will be easier to see the pattern effect when we get to the Overlay step.

4.  Highlight the type layer in the Layers palette. Click the **Add a layer style** icon on the bottom of the Layers palette and select **Pattern Overlay**.

5.  Click the small arrow to the right of the pattern icon to open the default Pattern set, this is the set that loads with Photoshop.

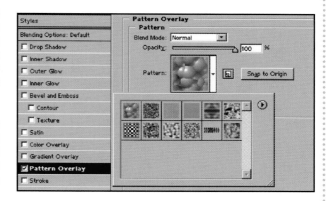

6.  As we will be making an entirely new pattern set, we need to get rid of those in this set. Right click/CTRL-click each example icon and select **Delete Pattern** until the set is empty.

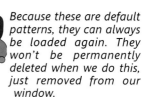

*Because these are default patterns, they can always be loaded again. They won't be permanently deleted when we do this, just removed from our window.*

7.  Ok, it's time to create a custom pattern set. Minimize the current image. Go to **Image>Open**, and open several of the seamless backgrounds you downloaded previously (or some you may have already on your computer or an image CD).

Here I have opened a series of patterns including one of a dilapidated wall, which is rather charmingly entitled, "Stinking Plaster"!

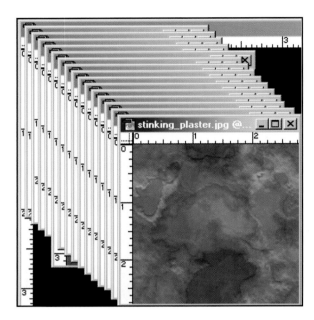

This next section is actually a tutorial within a tutorial. I'll demonstrate the use of actions by making one which will help us to create pattern sets. This allows us to automate the process so that we can create literally dozens of entire pattern sets in a matter of minutes, provided we have the images to fill dozens of sets tucked away in a folder on the computer.

*Pattern sets, while incredibly useful, can have some rather large file sizes when saved. For this reason I try to restrict a new set to 12-15 patterns. This is of particular importance if you'd like to distribute your patterns for others to use. A smaller pattern set will save on bandwidth.*

1. Open the Actions palette. In the Actions menu, select **Clear Actions**. You should now have an empty Actions palette.

2. Click the **Create new set** icon on the bottom of the Actions palette. When the Action set dialog box pops up, name the set, 'Pattern Set Creator', or something similar.

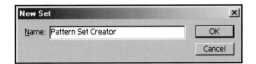

3. Click the **Create new action** icon on the bottom of the palette. Name the action 'Define Pattern-Add to set'.

4. In this dialog box, you are also given the opportunity to assign a shortcut key combination, and a color code to the action, both of which will aid efficiency when using actions, so go ahead and assign them now.

*Color-coding may not seem very useful at first glance, but it can help categorize actions according to their function. For example, you could create several actions for image adjustments, and use red buttons for all of these. If you made some actions of various type effects these could be indicated with green, and so forth.*

5. Once you click OK, the action will begin recording. It will record every step you take in Photoshop, until you click Stop, rather like a macro.

6. Click on one of the open backgrounds to make it active.

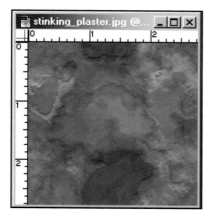

7. Go to **Edit>Define Pattern.**

8. Name the pattern and close the image.

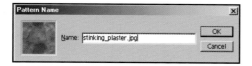

9. Press the **Stop** button on the bottom of the Actions palette to quit recording. If you have the Actions palette set to edit mode (toggle edit/button modes from the Actions menu), your action, when expanded in the palette, should look something like this.

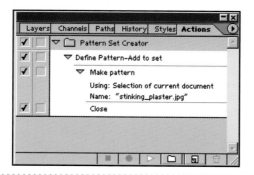

Now would be a great time to save the action.

10. Select the action set name at the top of the list. All actions must be saved in sets, even if there is only one action in the set. Click the small arrow in the upper right corner of the Actions palette to access the Actions menu.

11. Click **Save Action** and save it to a folder on your system. You may want to create a specific actions folder to house your custom made actions, and place it somewhere you can find it again easily.

12. In the Actions palette, switch to **Button Mode** to see the keyboard shortcut, and color-coding, that you assigned to this action. You can now use this shortcut to run the same action on another image.

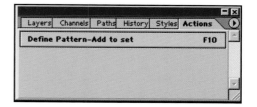

When you run this action it will define the background on which you run it as a pattern. We have included a close command in this action, so ensure that you have a new background active, but not the example image. If we run the action on our example it will close automatically, and we'll lose our test image.

13. Repeat the action on each background you opened.

14. Once you have several patterns defined, go back to the example image and select the type layer.

15. Click on the Add a layer style icon on the bottom of the Layers palette. Select **Pattern Overlay** from the menu.

16. Once the Layer Styles dialog box is open with the pattern options visible, click on the small arrow to the right of the Pattern thumbnail. All the patterns you just defined should be visible in the pattern set.

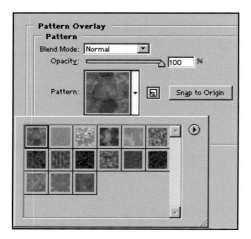

17. Click on the first pattern you defined. Take a look at your example image to see the effect this pattern has had.

*You can drag the pattern around over the type layer just by click-dragging the cursor on the main image when the layer styles box is open.*

18. Click on each pattern to see the effect on your text.

19. With the pattern set open in the Layer Styles dialog box, click on the small arrow to the upper right of the set. Select the **Save Patterns** option from the menu. As with the action saved earlier, you may want to create a folder in which to place your custom pattern sets. Once saved, the pattern set will be available to load whenever you so desire.

*In addition to the Layer Styles option, you can also access your custom pattern by going to **Edit>Fill** and choosing **Pattern** from the **Fill** dialog box.*

## Creating, using, and saving custom gradients

You can create gradients via the Gradient Options bar. However we are going to look at a different technique that will allow you to see the gradient in progress. Also, you can tweak it where necessary, depending on what it does to the example image, add the gradient to the loaded set, and save the set for use later.
Go back to the original type example image or create a new one before you proceed.

1. Access the Layer Styles for the type layer again; this time select **Gradient Overlay**.

2. Once you select the Gradient Overlay from the list, your type will automatically be covered with the default gradient. As the gradient also defaults to Normal blending mode and 100% Opacity, you will not be able to see the pattern applied before.

3. Click directly on the Gradient in the center of the Layer Styles pop-up. Doing so brings up the **Gradient Editor**.

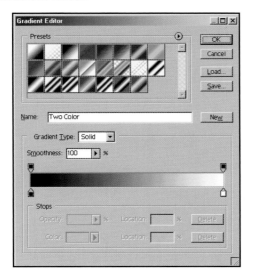

4. The top portion of the editor, **Presets**, shows all of the loaded gradients. In the example above, you will notice the first few are default gradients. The last eight icons represent those I've created and added over the course of this book. I've not yet saved them as a set, however. We shall go through this shortly.

5. The bottom section of the Gradient Editor is where we actually set the characteristics for a new gradient.

6. There are two pointers above and below the gradient. These are called **stops**. By default, there are two stops above, which control the opacity of the gradient at that point on the scale, and two below, which control the color of the gradient at that point. These can be moved by sliding them left or right, and also by clicking on a stop and entering percentage values in the **Stops** area below the gradient editor section.

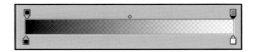

7. You can add points of color or transparency to the gradient by changing the values for each point in the **Stops Editor**.

8. Notice that the stops change when you alter the opacity or color of a stop. To change a color, select a stop, click in the color box, or open the color window by clicking the arrow, and the color picker will become available.

*Although you can save the Gradient Set as it is, it is good policy to delete the default gradients first and save your set of custom gradients as a stand-alone group. Right-click/CTRL-click each default gradient and delete any gradients you do not want included in the set.*

9. Once you are satisfied with a gradient, click New to save it in the current gradient set. Once saved it will be added to the group of icons above.

10. Click Save, and find or create a folder in which to keep your custom gradient set. Name the set and click Save again.

11. Apply the gradient (if you haven't already) to the type layer.

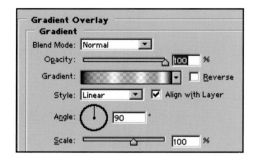

## Gradient stroke

Since we are playing with Gradients and creating a Layer Style at the same time, there is another cool way you can use your gradients. With the Layer Style Stroke option, you can apply a gradient stroke to the outline of the type layer.

1. Access the Layer Styles again, this time selecting **Stroke** from the menu.

2. In the **Stroke Options**, change the Fill Type to Gradient. Select a gradient from the set you have loaded, or click on the gradient to access the Gradient Editor, create and save a new gradient as above, save it and apply it to the Stroke.

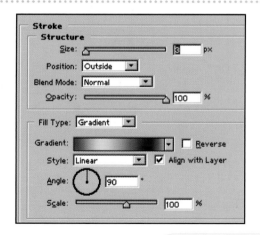

*You can also change the hues of the overall style by applying a Color Overlay set to Difference Blend Mode. Try a few colors, keeping an eye on the example to see which one works best*

## Creating, applying, and saving custom contours

As we move on with the process of generating elements of, and ultimately a complete layer style, I bet you probably guess we'd get to a bevel eventually. Well, we made it to that point, and our bevel is also going to allow us to create a custom contour to save for later use.

1. Access the Bevel and Emboss area of the Layer Styles palette.

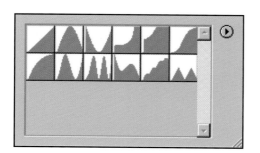

2. In the **Shading Area**, you will see **Gloss Contour**. The icon represents the default contour currently applied to the bevel of the image, affecting how the shading and reflections play on the surface of the image. Click the small arrow to the right of the example to see the loaded default contours.

3. Click directly on the contour example to open the **Contour Editor**.

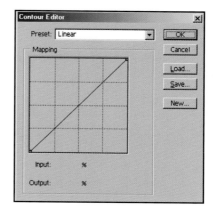

4. By clicking on the contour line, you can add points that you can drag to create a curve in the line, thereby affecting the reflections and shading on the bevel. You can see what the curve is doing to the bevel by watching the preview icon to the right of the Layer Styles dialog box.

This example shows the style with the default Contour applied along with the bevel settings and other style settings (gradient, stroke, color overlay) that we added before.

5. By moving a point on the contour line, we affect the reflections on the surface of the bevel.

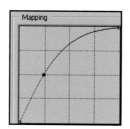

**6.** We can manipulate the contour by adding more points to the line and moving them with the mouse.

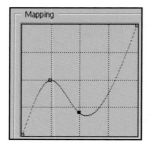 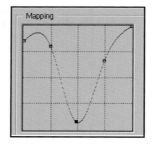

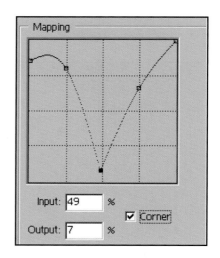

**7.** To generate a sharper contour and effect, we can change the smooth corner through a point into a sharp alteration in direction by clicking on a point and checking the **Corner** box.

Again, keep an eye on the example. Once you are satisfied with the contour, you will want to save it for later use.

## Completing and saving the layer style set

The last few pages have been devoted to creating elements of a layer style while creating an entire Style for later use. In the process we have also created a custom gradient, pattern set, action for making pattern sets, and custom contours. Now we have a style; what's next?

Let's save our new style to a set.

**1.** With the Layer Styles dialog box open, click the **New Style** button on the right hand side.

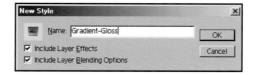

2. By accessing the Styles palette, the new style can be found as the last icon.

3. You can delete styles from the loaded set by right-clicking/CTRL-clicking the icon representing the style, and selecting Delete Style from the menu.

4. Once you have created several styles and would like to save the entire set, click the Save button on the right-hand side of the Layer Styles dialog box. Save the new set to a folder on your system, preferably one you have created for holding your custom styles.

Once you get the hang of the Style creation process by changing patterns, bevels, overlay modes, and so forth, you will soon have several Layer Style sets to apply to text, shapes, and frames.

*But remember; alway save your settings!*

## 2: Filling the toolbox

We've taken a look at creating patterns, actions, layer styles, gradients and contours. Are there any other items we can create and save for use in Photoshop with the tools at hand?

There most certainly are, and we'll cover a few of these here.

## Curves

Curves are a method for re-mapping pixel tonal values. They are far more powerful than levels, as curves give us the ability to change the value of a single pixel rather than an entire range of pixels over the whole image.

Curves are essential when working on some types of metal effects. If we create a curve that we like, we can save that curve as a preset for later use.

1. For this example, I've simply created a two-layer image: a gradient background layer and a spherical selection filled with a white to black radial gradient.

117

2. Now if we apply a standard metal curve, our ball goes from a rather dull white-to-black to a rather cool looking steel ball. Go to **Image>Adjust>Curves** (CTRL/CMD+ M) and create a curve similar to below:

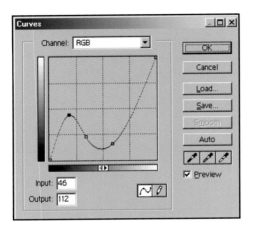

3. Keep your eye on the ball, and when you are satisfied with the modifications the curve makes to your gradient, click Save. Name the curve, and save it to your system for later use.

Now you have a great curve that can be applied over and over again. When you want to reapply a curve that you had earlier saved, you simply click the **Load** button in the Curves window, and then navigate to the folder in which your curves are saved.

## Custom shapes

Shapes are another goodie that can be created and saved. The primary thing to remember here is that shape creation works best if you have a black shape on a white background.

1. Let's use the sphere image created above. I've filled the background layer with white, and then merged all the spheres into one layer separate from the background. CTRL/CMD+*click* the spheres layer in the Layers palette to load the sphere as a selection.

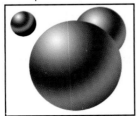

2. For the next step, go to **Edit>Fill** to fill the selection with black.

3. Before we can define the shape, we need to turn the selection into a path. This is done by going to the Paths palette and clicking the **Make work path from selection** icon on the bottom of the Paths palette.

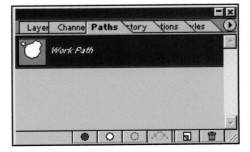

**6.** Once the selection is converted to a work path, go to **Edit>Define Custom Shape**. Name the shape and click OK.

You can now find the shape in the **Custom Shape picker** in the Shapes option bar.

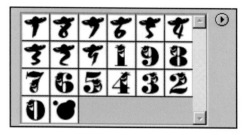

**7.** Let's say you have defined several custom shapes, and now want to save the set for later use. With the **Custom Shape picker** open, click the small arrow to the upper right. Choose **Save Shapes** from the menu, find a folder in which to store them, name them, and click OK.

## Custom brushes

This process is nearly identical to that of creating custom shapes, but this time we need not convert a selection to a path. What I love about custom brushes is we can use nearly any picture as a brush! Our only restriction is that the image has to be under 999 x 999 pixels. You can even define and paint with a human face if you like.

**1.** Again, go back to the shape we converted into a custom shape.

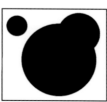

**2.** Most brushes seem to work better slightly blurred, so apply a Gaussian Blur to this image.

**3.** Now turn this into a brush by going to **Edit>Define Brush**.

**4.** Once defined, the brush is given a name and saved to the **Brush picker**.

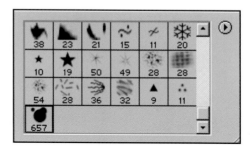

Maybe you have noticed a problem with this brush. Take a look at the size of the brush. This thing is huge! Imagine trying to paint with it... the picture may not be too pretty.

In just two swipes of the brush I completely obliterated the image it was created from. So in order for this to be an effective brush, we need to reduce the image size, and define it again, perhaps even a couple times to give us some size variation with the same shape.

5. Go to **Image>Image Size** to open the following dialog box and adjust the size of your image to make a smaller brush. You may have to try a few different sizes until you come up with one you are happy with.

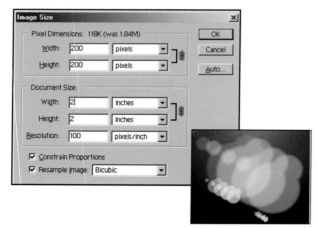

Take a look at the image below. Every picture element in this image is actually a brush, including the keyboard, the photo, and the image of the Actions palette!!!

Photos can also be defined as brushes. Take a look at how to take fire from a picture to create a custom brush.

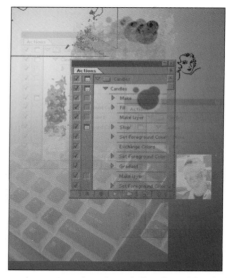

6. This image will be easy to convert, as the black is nicely contrasted with the fire. With the Magic Wand we can select the black areas and fill them with white. Then reduce the image size, and define the brush as before.

Once you have your brushes defined and loaded into the Brush picker, you can save them by clicking the small arrow on the upper right of the Color Picker. Select **Save Brushes** from the **Brushes Menu**, name the brushes, and save the set to your computer.

In this chapter we've covered many of the features that can be customized in Photoshop, this will really help to increase your productivity, and optimize your workflow. Photoshop is a powerful tool, and like any tool, you'll get the most from it the more you learn, and the more you modify it for your own purposes.

# Chapter 7

# Text effects

Hopefully by now you have found a few new ways to manipulate your images in Photoshop without resorting to a lot of hair pulling. In this chapter we'll look at effects that can be best applied to text to create really stunning typefaces. We'll see that given the right amount of creativity, we can create text which is an art form in itself.

## 1: Designing for the background

Before we get into the die-hard text effects, I wanted to approach things from a different angle. As an unspoken rule, most designers generate a background with the primary image in mind. But what if you have a great background that you don't want to go to waste? In this tutorial we're going to elevate the background's role, and design the type effect in order to best compliment the background.

1.  Open your background image (CTRL/CMD+O).

2.  Create a new layer (SHIFT+CTRL/CMD+N).

3.  Select the **Type** tool (T). In the Type Options bar, select the Type Mask tool, a cool font, and set the size to around 140 pt.

4.  Fill (**Edit>Fill**) the type selection with Black.

5.  Access the Layer Styles for the filled type selection layer, and go into the Advanced Blending Options. Change both Opacity settings to 80%, uncheck **Blend Clipped Layers as Group** and check **Blend Interior Effects as Group**.

6.  Let's apply a quick style to the new text. Start with a Bevel:

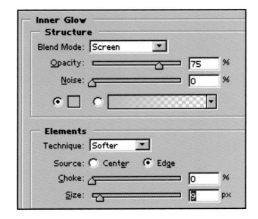

7.  We need to define our type against the background a bit better, so let's add an Inner Glow with the settings shown below. Deselect (CTRL/CMD+D).

For a subtle text effect, we could stop right here, but let's forsake subtlety and see how far we can take this text and this background.

8. Duplicate the type layer by right-clicking/control-clicking on the layer in the Layers palette and selecting Duplicate Layer. Go to **Edit>Transform>Flip Vertical**. Move the two type layers so that they just touch at their closest point.

9. Let's have some fun with the background. Select the background layer. Pick the **Rectangular Marquee** tool (M), and select the lower portion of the background image. Once selected, go to **Layer>New>Layer Via Copy** (CTRL/CMD+J).

10. Select the new copy layer. Go to **Edit>Transform>Perspective**. Move the side point in until you have a trapezoid roughly the width of the type. Press ENTER/RETURN.

11. Select the background layer and make a copy (CTRL/CMD+J). Apply the **Edit>Transform>Perspective** command again, this time moving the bottom corners closer together.

12. Select the background layer and fill it with black (SHIFT+BACKSPACE/DELETE).

13. Repeat the Perspective Transform for both of the type layers. You will not need to make the transform as harsh as the pattern layers.

14. Select the original type layer (not the reflection layer). Bump the Opacity up to 100%.

**15.** Apply an Outer Glow to taste to the topmost type layer.

**16.** Select the bottom type layer, and go to **Image>Adjust>Brightness/Contrast**. Decrease both settings for this layer.

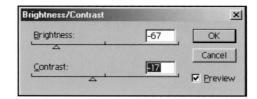

## 2: Cells

Now we'll to delve into the area of type treatments in greater detail.

**1.** Create a new image that is 7 inches by 5 inches, with a resolution of 150, is RGB, and has a transparent background. Any resolution will work, but as stated in Chapter 1, I like to alter the resolutions on occasion and see how the effects play on the image.

**2.** Go to **Edit>Fill** (SHIFT+BACKSPACE/DELETE). From the Fill dialog box, choose Pattern and select the Molecular Pattern that is loaded into the default set. Click OK to fill the layer.

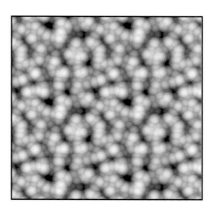

**3.** Create a new layer (SHIFT+CTRL/CMD+N).

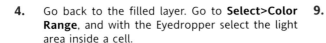

**4.** Go back to the filled layer. Go to **Select>Color Range**, and with the Eyedropper select the light area inside a cell.

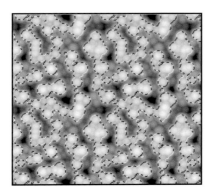

**5.** Copy the selection (CTRL/CMD+C) and paste it into a new layer (CTRL/CMD+J). You may want to name the layer, as the layer contents are difficult to see in the Layers palette icon for the pasted layer. I've named mine 'cells'.

**6.** Uncheck, or make invisible, all layers except the cells layer.

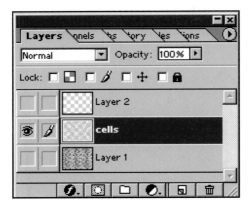

**7.** To create a displacement map, go to the Channels palette, and select one of the existing channels (in this case I've chosen the Blue channel). Drag it to the **Create new channel** icon to create a duplicate.

**8.** Select the newly created duplicate and go to **Image>Adjust>Invert** (CTRL/CMD+I).

**9.** Adjust the Brightness/Contrast to bring out the whites and blacks.

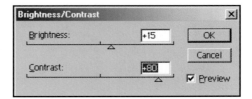

**10.** Right-click, control-click on a Mac, on the new channel. Hit Duplicate Channel, and save the duplicate image as a new file. Save the new .psd file somewhere on your computer to use as a displacement map.

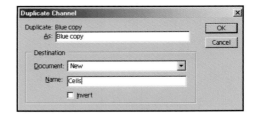

**11.** Go back to the Layers palette in the original document and select the new layer we created at the start of this tutorial.

**12.** Select the **Type** tool (T), and in the Type Options bar select the type characteristics. In this case I'm using a font called 'Vectroid' set to 150 pt, as the style is a bit futuristic and so is the effect I have in mind. You can use any font you like for this step, but try to use a thick font for the best effect. Once you have made your selection, hit D to reset the default colors and type your text in the layer.

**125**

**13.** In the Layers palette, CTRL/CMD+click the type layer to bring up a type selection.

**14.** With the selection active, click the **Add a mask** icon.

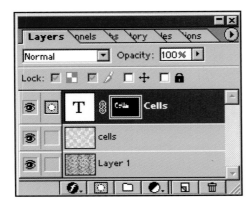

**15.** Go to **Filter>Distort>Displace**. Change the Horizontal and Vertical settings to 5%. When you click OK, a new dialog box will open enabling you to select your displacement map.

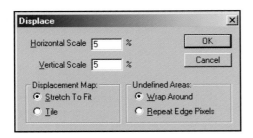

**16.** Find the displacement map we created earlier and apply it to your mask.

From this point on, I'll be creating and applying a layer style for the Cells text. Try experimenting with different settings in the styles. The whole point to the first part of this tutorial was to generate the clipped edges to the type. Now that we have chipped away some of the edges, our styles will complete the effect nicely.

**17.** Access the Layer Styles for this layer and select Pattern Overlay. Choose the same Molecular pattern we used on the background.

**18.** CTRL/CMD+click the type layer to bring up the selection. This is primarily to keep track of the location of the text it isn't really needed. Since we applied the same texture as the filled background layer, the type will become 'invisible' until we apply more styles.

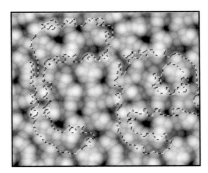

**19.** On to more Style settings. Let's start with an Inner Shadow with the following settings:

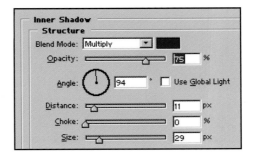

**20.** Next comes a Drop Shadow:

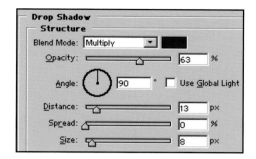

**21.** Now the Bevel:

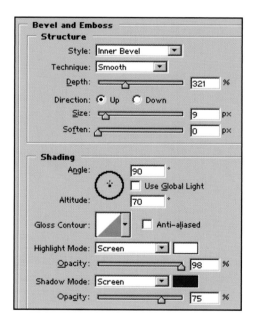

**22.** Just for fun, let's also tack on a Gradient Overlay:

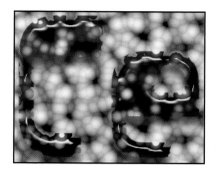

**23.** This particular effect might work better on a dark background, so let's apply an Outer Glow. Since I've already applied a reddish tint with the gradient, I'll do the same with the glow.

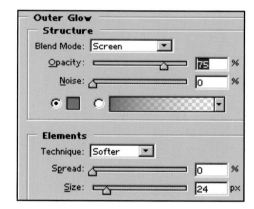

**24.** Now an Inner Glow:

**25.** Let's finish off the effect with a Stroke to further define the edges against the background. I generally prefer a gradient set to Shape Burst to pull this off.

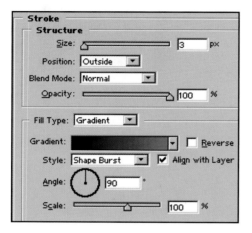

**26.** **Save the Layer Style now!!!** Click the **New Style** button to the right of the Styles dialog box. This will save the style in the set loaded into the Styles palette. You may want to name it 'Cells' or something along those lines for future reference. For more on saving and loading Layer Styles, please see Chapter 6.

**27.** Finally, press D to reset the default colors and fill the background layer with black (ALT/OPT+BACKSPACE/DELETE) to really bring out this effect.

## 3: Transparent text

For this next tutorial, we'll create a logo with a see-through appearance. As we go through it look at the ways that a simple effect can be altered to something totally different simply by changing a blending mode, a pattern, a bevel, and so on.

**1.** Create a new image (CTRL/CMD+N). For this example, the image characteristics are: 900 px wide, 600 px high, resolution 100 PPI, RGB, with a transparent background.

**2.** We are going to have some fun with a stock photo that came with the Photoshop package. Go to **File>Open**, and in the Photoshop 6 directory find the **Goodies>Stock Art>Images** folder. All of these images are named with a numeric value. Open the image named 0004654.

**3.** With the stock image active, hit CTRL/CMD+A to select the photo, and CTRL/CMD+C to copy it. Go back to the new image you created, and hit CTRL/CMD+V to paste the photo into the new image. Once pasted into the new image, make a copy of Layer 1 (CTRL/CMD+J).

**4.** Blur the copied layer by with a Gaussian Blur, **Filter>Blur>Gaussian Blur**, of 30 pixels.

**8.** You may want to bump up the Brightness/Contrast to make your color variations more dynamic. Do so now.

**5.** We can render the background image totally unlike the original, even more so than the blur allows. In fact, in this step I'll show you the power of using a Gradient in Difference mode to achieve some really crazy designs. Select the Gradient tool (G), and choose a light tan foreground color and a darker brown for the background color. Try using the **Eyedropper** tool (I) to select a light or dark brown from the image itself.

**9.** Select the Type tool (T). In the Type Options bar, choose the **Type Mask** tool. Pick an interesting font, set the size to something fairly large (I used 130 pts) and type your selection onto the layer.

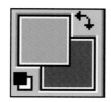

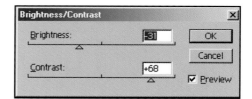

**10.** Go to **Layer>New>Layer via Copy** (CTRL/CMD+J).

**11.** Select Layer 1, copy (CTRL/CMD+C), and click the Create new layer icon.

**6.** In the Gradient Options bar, select the Foreground to Background gradient, click the Radial Gradient button, set the Blending Mode to Difference, and the Gradient Opacity to 85%.

**12.** Your selection should still be active. If not, CTRL/CMD+click the layer with the type pasted into it. Make the new layer active. Select a dark gray foreground color.

**7.** Fill the image with the gradient several times until you have a pattern you like.

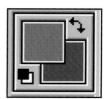

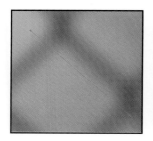 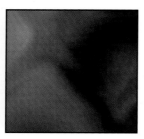

**13.** We will be applying a Stroke to this selection, but without using the layer style Stroke. Why? Because if we have a stroke on its own layer, we can create a layer style that only applies to the stroke. Go to **Edit>Stroke**. Apply a 16 pixel centered stroke to the selection.

**14.** Access the Layer Styles for this layer and apply a Bevel.

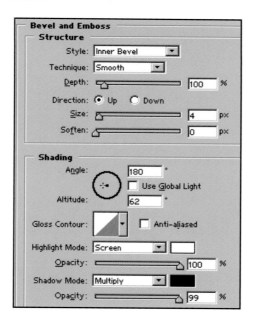

**15.** Reselect the top layer, the one with the text on it.

**16.** Now we'll apply our style to the top layer. Start with a Bevel and Emboss:

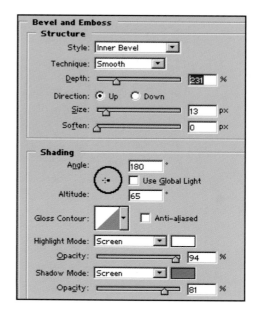

**17.** Under the Bevel and Emboss menu, apply a Texture. I'm using a texture of circuits I have on my system similar to that created in Chapter 5, but any texture will do. For information on creating and loading patterns to use as textures, please see Chapter 6.

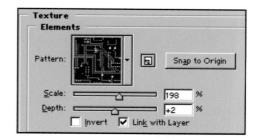

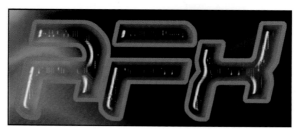

18. Now apply a few other settings to define this particular style. Inner Shadow will help with the transparency effect.

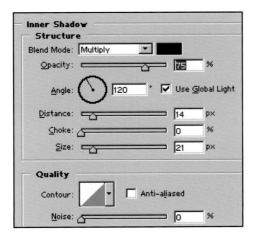

19. Satin gives it a bit of a reflection. Take special note of the Contour in the example. This particular Contour centers the reflection, reducing it toward the edges of the bevel.

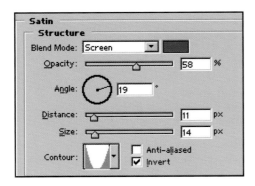

20. Now apply a Gradient Overlay set to Soft Light:

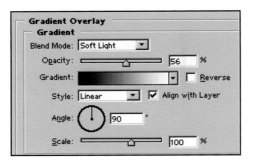

21. Apply a Pattern Overlay set to Color Burn:

22. Go back to the Stroked Layer, Layer 3. Open the Styles. We have already applied a Bevel to this layer, so let's apply a Pattern Overlay and an Outer Glow.

131

To give the following result:

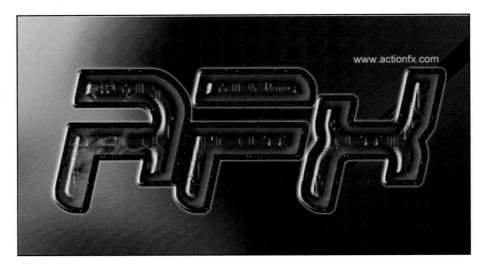

### 4: Explosions

The last effect we will look at in this chapter is an explosion type effect with added sparks. This is a dynamic effect and should be used sparingly. It can be used with shapes, text, or just for effect.

1. Create a new document (CTRL/CMD+N) and name it 'explosions'. Make it 600x300 in RGB mode.

2. Create some text that you'll want to explode (perhaps your boss's name...?). We'll need to rasterize the text in order to manipulate it. So, right-click/control-click on the thumbnail name in the Layers palette and choose **Rasterize Layer**.

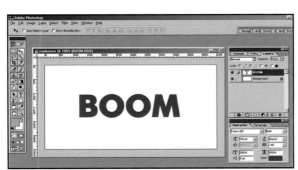

3. Now to break apart the text, get ready to get your hands dirty, select the **Lasso tool** (L), and make a selection around a portion of the text

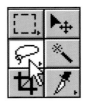

4. Now choose the **Move tool** (V) and drag it away slightly. Deselect (CTRL/CMD+D).

**5.** Make another selection.

**6.** Drag it away again.

**7.** Continue doing this until you have your object all broken up. This will form our main image.

*It's best to start at the edges and work your way to the middle. This will produce more movement at the edges, which is what you are looking for. The smaller pieces should be dragged further than the large pieces, since in the real world they would fly out further because they are lighter.*

**8.** Now for the explosion effect. Duplicate the text layer, and CTRL/CMD+click, to load the text as a selection. Use the **Paint Bucket** tool (SHIFT+G) to fill with a brighter color. Here, I choose a golden yellow.

**9.** Drag the duplicated layer under the original layer. The copied layer will become our effect layer.

**10.** With the duplicated layer selected, go to **Filter>Blur>Radial Blur**. Choose Zoom as the Blur Method, and set the amount to 100. Here's where we begin to see our effect take shape.

**11.** Duplicate the layer several times to add density to the effect, link the effect layers only, (in my example these are the 'BOOM' layers), then merge these layers, **Layers palette> Merged Linked**.

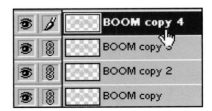

**12.** Now press CTRL/CMD+F, or go to the **Filters** menu and notice Radial Blur at the top of the list. Select this to reapply exactly the same blur as was used before.

> **TIP:** *To re-apply the last filter used, with exactly the same settings, you click CTRL/CMD+F. Experiment with filters, it's amazing the results you can achieve by applying a filter more than once. If you don't like the results there's always the Undo option.*

This is our basic explosion. It's good, but it needs more pizzazz, so let's see what we can do.

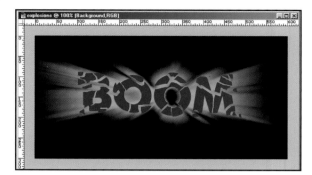

**13.** The explosion has a denser and smoother look to it now. You can fill the background with black to see the effect better.

## Adding sparks

**1.** First, let's make some sparks fly now. Duplicate (**Layer>Duplicate Layer**) the effect layer, mine is called BOOM copy 4.

**2.** Change the blending mode of the new layer to Dissolve, and lower the Opacity to 27%, hopefully now you'll see how the sparks are beginning to take effect.

3. Let's brighten up the sparks; **Image>Adjust>Hue/Saturation**, (CTRL/CMD+U). Lighten the layer to give it more emphasis. In my image I've changed the **Lightness** value to –53.

4. The effect is much more convincing but we can make it better. Let's add a Bevel to make it more 3D. Click on the **Add a layer style** icon at the bottom of the Layers palette, and select **Bevel and Emboss.** Choose the settings as shown in the screen shot.

6. Drag the new layer to the top of the Layers palette, and lower the Opacity to 9% for a subtle effect.

7. Experiment with different colored explosions and sparks for different results. Here is an example with the hue changed on the explosion layer.

5. It's time for the little bit extra again. Let's add a few sparks in front of the type to add more realism. Duplicate your sparks layer.

> **INFO:** *You can add to the effect of movement by adding noise to one of the yellow layers, applying a small Zoom Blur and switching to Hard Light. If you duplicate this layer and place the one on the top at about 50% Opacity, you'll get a real sense of particles flying out from the center. (Thanks to Paul Sinclair for this suggestion.)*

These effects are of course not just limited to being used for text; you could apply these techniques to creating buttons, interfaces, or even backgrounds. But in this chapter I hope that you have seen how a striking graphic element can add a distinctive flavor to your work. The golden rule, as ever, is to use these wild text effects sparingly. An extreme font on a clean background can be impressively eye-catching, but if your work is already busy, then you risk having a cluttered feel. In the next chapter we'll create 3D effects that you'll want to reach out and touch, so pick up your funky red and green 3D glasses, and we'll move on.

# Chapter 8
# Faux 3D

Photoshop is really a 2D photo manipulation tool, but what happens when you manipulate the manipulator? You can fool the viewer into seeing the third dimension. In this chapter I am going to demonstrate my techniques for creating 3D objects.

Any 3D illustration created entirely on a computer must begin with primitives. Primitives means the basic shape families; cubes, cylinders, spheres, and cones. These shapes are the building blocks for more complex shapes. You can add them together, mix and match them, intersect and carve them out from each other to form all kinds of 3D objects.

I am going to show you how to create your own primitives and dress them up a bit in this chapter. It's really important that you think as you work, or you will miss the whole point of this book. I am hoping to equip you with skills that go beyond the tutorials you are currently working on.

## 1: The cube

We are going to build a cube and then I will show you how to put photos on the surfaces to create your own photo cubes. The cube is an important building block for 3D. We will be making extensive use of the **Free Transform** tool in this tutorial. In fact you will use almost every aspect of this tool during this project.

1.  Create a new blank document of 600x600 pixels at 72 dpi and RGB color space.

2.  Create a new layer and call it 'side 1'.

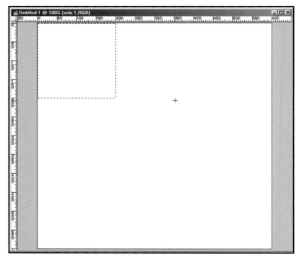

*To make things easier, you could create guides to help keep things aligned. To create a guide: First show rulers by pressing CTRL/CMD+R. Now click your mouse on a ruler and drag into the document, you will notice that a guide has been created, continue dragging until you reach your desired location and then release the mouse. Guides were a handy utility introduced in Photoshop 5. Another good thing about guides are the fact that the transformations can snap to the guides allowing ease of use.*

4.  Fill with a black to white Linear Gradient.

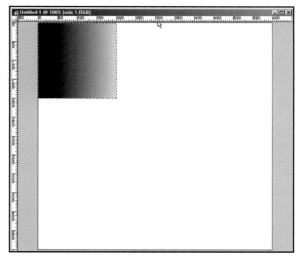

3.  Using the **Rectangular Marquee** tool, draw a selection of 200X200 pixels. Hold down the SHIFT key while dragging to draw a perfect square.

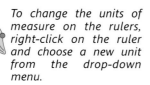

*To change the units of measure on the rulers, right-click on the ruler and choose a new unit from the drop-down menu.*

5.  Deselect (CTRL/CMD+D) and move the square to the right-center of the image. We now have the foundation for our cube.

    Although a cube has six sides, you can only view three sides at a time, so we are going to create three sides that fit together. The Free Transform tool is our key to distorting the square to become a side of the cube.

6. Press CTRL/CMD+T to enter free transform mode. You will see a box and nine handles called nodes. The center handle sets the center point for the transformations and the four corner points are for rotation, proportional scaling, and distortion. The four middle points are for scaling and skewing.

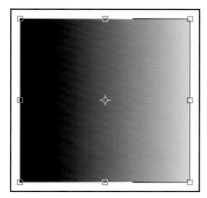

7. We want to distort the side at an angle. Right-click, or Control click on the Mac, and you will see a context sensitive menu. Choose Skew.

8. Drag the right middle handle and watch your square distort.

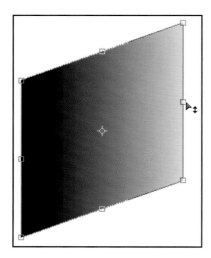

You now have it at an angle, but it still looks like it lacks something. It looks strange. That's because in the real world everything has per-spective, meaning that the further away a section of the object is from the viewer, the smaller it appears. For example when you look at a long fence, it appears to diminish into the horizon. The technical term for this is vanishing point.

9. Fortunately Photoshop comes with its own little perspective control. Right-click/CTRL-click again and, this time, choose Perspective.

10. Click and drag the top right corner node. Notice as you drag, the opposite corner reflects the change. Drag it down just a little bit until you have a believable perspective.

Now it seems the square is looking more like a rectangle, another illusion of 3D. When perspective comes into play it effects the perceived proportions of an image. That is the reason, I sometimes prefer to "eyeball" an image rather than just rely on technical measurements. The image must not just be technically correct; it must also look correct.

11. Right-click/CTRL-click and choose Scale. Drag the right middle node to the left to give us the correct proportions.

12. Press ENTER/RETURN to apply the transformations. We now have the right side of the cube.

Now, let's make the left side. Fortunately you don't have to go through all those steps again.

13. Duplicate the side 1 layer, by dragging the thumbnail to the new layer icon or press CTRL/CMD+J. Rename the new layer as 'side 2'.

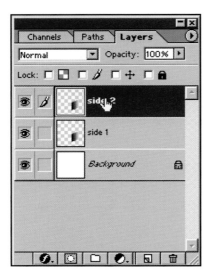

14. Press CTRL/CMD+T to once again enter the free transform mode, right-click/CTRL-click and choose Flip Horizontal.

15. Click anywhere inside the box and drag the left side until it fits nice and snug against the right side. Hold the SHIFT key while dragging to keep the baselines aligned. Press ENTER/RETURN to apply the transformation.

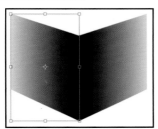

Great! We now have two sides; we just need the top to finish the effect.

16. Create a new layer and call it 'top'. Using the same technique as before, draw another square and fill it with the same gradient we used before, except applied at a different angle.

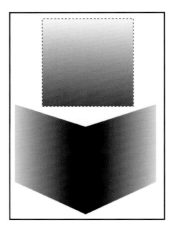

17. Press CTRL/CMD+T for the free transform mode again, right-click/CTRL-click and select Distort.

18. We are going to distort the top into shape. Don't worry this is not as difficult as it may seem. Drag the bottom right corner of the top to touch the top right of the sides.

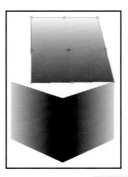

*For precision movement, select a node and nudge with your keyboard arrow keys.*

**19.** Next, drag the bottom left corner to match with the middle point of the sides. (If you wanted to create a box with an open lid, you can see how you could do it here)

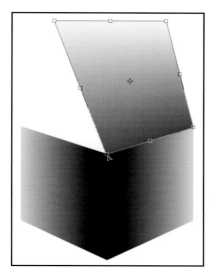

**20.** Now take the top left of the lid and drag it to match the top left of the sides.

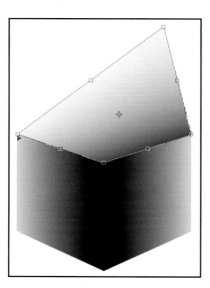

**21.** Last but not least, drag the remaining point to the center to create a diamond and press Enter/Return. You now have a completed cube.

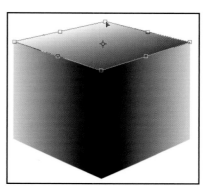

Congratulations, you have now finished your first 3D object in Photoshop. If your cube's proportions don't quite look correct, you could link the sides together and use the Free Transform tool to tweak it into shape. For some more modifications read on.

## 2: Colorizing multiple layers at once

Here is an easy way to colorize our cube, which consists of three layers, without flattening the image.

1.  With the 'top' layer selected, click on the little black and white circle in the Layers palette. This is the adjustment layer control. In the drop-down menu, which will appear, select **Hue/Saturation.** (We will take an extensive look at Hue/Saturation in the Creative Colorizing chapter)

2.  Click the Colorize box in the Hue/Saturation control panel. Slide the Hue slider to 121, and the Saturation to around 25. You will now see a green tint to the entire image. Since this is an adjustment layer, it is non-destructive, meaning that you can go back and change the settings at any time.

Here is our cube set against a colored background so you can see it better.

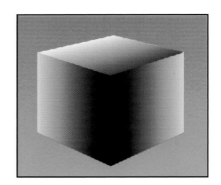

> The adjustment layer will colorize every layer beneath it. Fortunately every adjustment layer comes equipped with a mask. This is the second thumbnail to the right. To "knock out" the color, select the layer mask by clicking on it. Now make a selection around the areas where you want to preserve the original color, and fill the selection on the layer mask with black. Bingo! The areas that are masked black will be ignored by the adjustment effect.

## 3: Adding pictures to the cube

We can add pictures to the cube by distorting them to fit using the same method. Notice that when I add a picture to the cube it also takes on the green tint? This is because the adjustment layer effects all the layers underneath it and the cube is below the adjustment layer.

There are two ways to fix this: either move the new layers above the adjustment layer, or hide the adjustment layer by clicking the eye icon on the Hue/Saturation layer. I chose the second option because there will be no further need for the green tint, since I want to add colored pictures to all three visible faces of the cube.

Now I am going to show you step-by-step how to attach a picture to a face of the cube.

1. Open a new picture in Photoshop (your favorite holiday snapshots would work great) and drag the picture into the cube document.

2. Enter Free Transform again and this time, scale the image to the height of the cube. (Hold down the SHIFT key to maintain the correct proportions).

3. Place the left side of the image snugly against the center of the cube.

4. Still in free transform, right-click to choose Distort.

5. Drag the top right to match the right top corner.

6. Drag the bottom left to match the right bottom corner.

7. Add the top image and distort it in the same way and place against a suitable background. There you have a picture cube. Perfect for all those special occasions.

You could use this technique to create mock product box shots and really impress your clients! I have also used this technique for advertising pieces. Remember, you don't have to have all the sides of an equal width, experiment.

## 4: The cylinder

Now, let's take a look at the cylinder. This shape is useful for creating pipes, cans, barrels and much more. In this tutorial you will learn how to use different selection modes.

1. Create a new blank document of 600x600 pixels at 72 dpi and RGB color space. Create a new layer and draw a rectangle with the Marquee tool.

   We want to create a rounded bottom to the cylinder and add some dimension to it.

2. With the Marquee tool still selected, choose **Add to Selection** from the top toolbar.

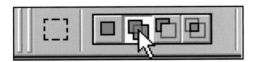

3. Choose the Elliptical marquee tool and begin to draw an oval starting from the left.

*To move a selection while drawing, hold down the SPACEBAR on the keyboard.*

4. Move the ellipse until it is positioned on the bottom.

5. Release the mouse button and we have a nice rounded bottom.

6. Now choose the Linear Gradient tool. Gradients form the backbone of cylinder effects. Choose the default copper gradient from the library.

7. Drag horizontally from left to right to create the cylinder gradient. So far it's looking good but we will need to create an oval for the top too.

*Holding down the SHIFT key while applying a gradient will enable you to apply a perfect vertical or horizontal gradient.*

8. Press CTRL/CMD+D to deselect.

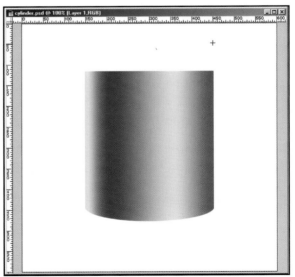

9. This time we will want to create a new selection, so change the selection mode back to the regular mode New Selection.

10. Draw another oval over the top of the cylinder.

11. We will want to fill the whole selection with a new gradient to give the impression of looking at the cylinder from a slightly elevated position. Keep the same copper gradient and keep it set for linear. This time begin to drag from further left and drag the gradient tool past the right to disperse the gradient differently to the last one.

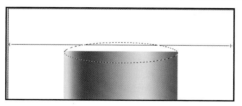

There! We now have a realistic cylinder

I modified it here by adjusting the curves: **Image>Adjust>Curves**. This gives a titanium look to the cylinder. If you wanted you could use an adjustment layer to achieve this effect.

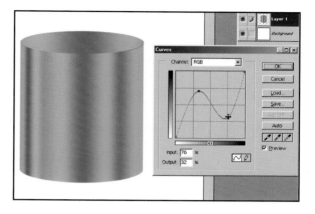

Experiment with your own gradients and create all kinds of cylinders and pipes.

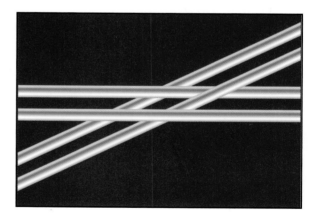

## 5: Creating the sphere

Now it's time to break away from those straight lines. The sphere we are going to create here is an orb that has a silvery sheen to it. We will accomplish this through the use of gradients, blurs, layers, and a reflection map.

1. Begin with a 600x600 canvas in RGB mode at 72 dpi. Save this as a .psd and call it sphere.psd. Create a new layer, name it 'sphere', and draw a circular selection with the Elliptical Marquee tool.

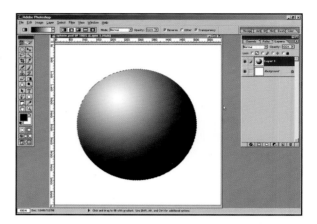

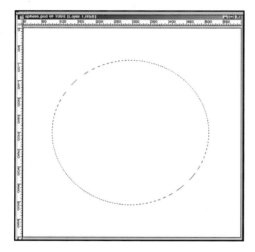

2. To form a basic sphere, select the Gradient tool. Choose black to white and **Radial Gradient**. Start about three quarters of the way to the top left and drag down to the bottom right of the circle and release to apply the gradient. Don't deselect yet.

*If the gradient appears to be going the opposite way, check the **Reverse** option in the top toolbar.*

Here is the basic sphere, now to dress it up a bit. The first thing we want to do is add a spectrum of color. This will create an interesting color effect that will add a great deal of depth.

3. With the Radial Gradient still selected, choose the **Spectrum Gradient**.

4. Create a new layer and call it 'color'. With the selection still active apply the Spectrum Gradient.

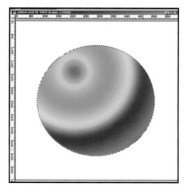

**5.** Let's alter the gradient to make it more natural. With the selection still active, apply **Filter>Blur>Radial Blur** with the following settings:

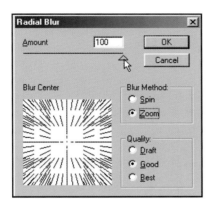

**6.** Press OK to apply the blur, which will spread the colors a bit.

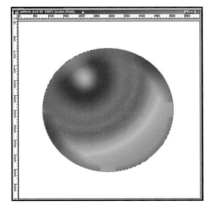

**7.** Now to soften the colors, apply **Filter>Blur>Gaussian Blur**, here I used a setting of 47.7

The gradient is now looking nice and soft, so let's blend it into the sphere.

**8.** In the Layers palette, on the color layer, set the blending mode to Overlay and 83% Opacity.

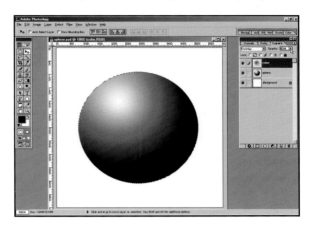

Now we need to look at creating some good reflections to make our orb appear more realistic. A great way to do this is to use a photograph and blur it.

**9.** To do this drag any image to your document, (we have used the dunes image from the **Program files > Adobe >Photoshop > Samples > Dune** folder on your hard drive.) Drag the image into your working document and it will appear as a new layer, make sure it fills the window and name the new layer 'reflection'. Move the layer to the top. We will now create what I call a reflection map.

**10.** Load the selection of the circle. With the reflection layer active, CRTL/CMD+click on the sphere layer.

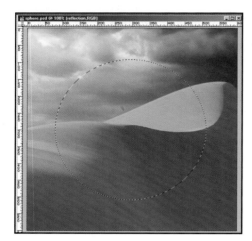

**11.** Let's add a distortion to the image to match the contour of the sphere. Go to **Filter>Distort>Spherize** and set the amount to the maximum of 100.

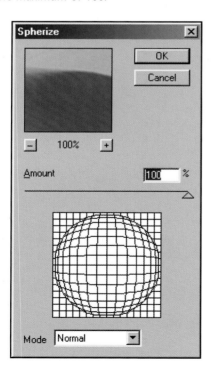

**12.** Click OK and the area inside the selection will be distorted. Press CTRL/CMD+F to repeat the filter.

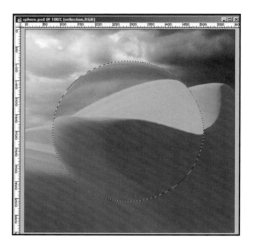

**13.** Let's get rid of the background. Invert the selection by **Select>Inverse** (CTRL/CMD+SHIFT+I) and press DELETE.

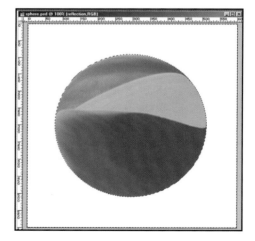

**14.** Invert your selection again (CTRL/CMD+SHIFT+I). Because we want the image to be just a hint of a reflection we will want to remove some of the definition of the photo. Go to **Filter>Blur>Gaussian Blur** and enter a setting of 8.6.

**15.** Deselect the image by pressing CTRL/CMD+D or by clicking away from the image.

16. Let's blend our reflection with the rest of the sphere so to begin with, switch the layer mode to hard light. This makes portions of the top image semi-transparent and allows the attributes of the top layer to be blended with the rest of the image.

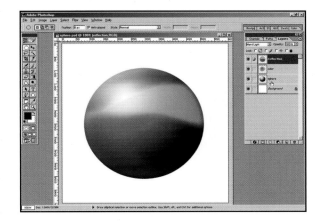

17. Drag the reflection layer below the color layer and drop the Opacity to 63%. That makes it look much better!

    Let's add some ambient reflection. Ambient is the resident light in an atmosphere.

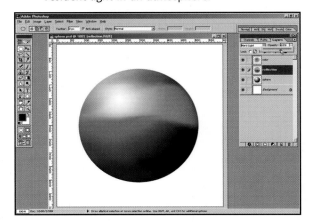

We are going to add a soft reflection to the bottom of the sphere. We will make a soft edged selection smaller than the image and fill it with a white to transparent gradient, this is a great method for creating highlights and simulating a reflective surface.

18. Load the selection again. We will shrink the selection slightly. Create a new layer called 'highlight' and contract the selection using **Select>Modify>Contract** with a setting of 4.

19. Now we will soften the edge using **Select>Feather** and make it 3 pixels.

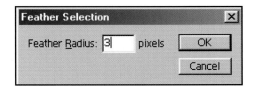

20. Set the foreground color to white and choose the Foreground to Transparent Linear Gradient.

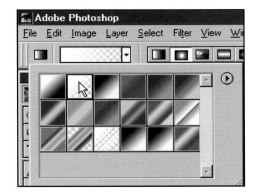

21. Drag the gradient tool from the bottom to three quarters of the way up the sphere.

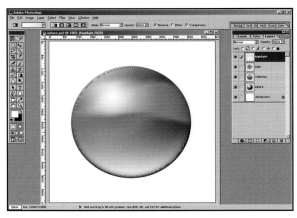

22. Switch to Lighten mode and drop the Opacity to 54%. Deselect the image, CTRL/CMD+D or just click away from the selection with any marquee tool active.

    We are now going to add a spectral highlight to set off the sphere.

23. Create a new layer called 'top highlight'.

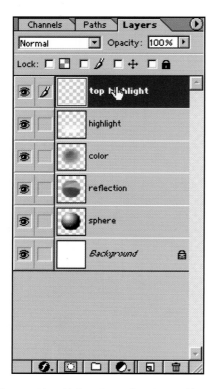

24. Choose the **Airbrush** tool, select white as your color and 45 pixels soft brush in Normal mode with a pressure of 32%.

25. Paint a small oval on the top left of the sphere. We are almost done now. There are just a couple of small tweaks to make it look a bit better.

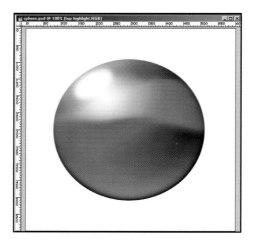

You can see there is a line that is too sharp around the bottom highlight. Let's soften it up.

26. Choose the highlight layer and apply a Gaussian Blur of 7 pixels.

    In this particular image the reflection is too uniform to get the effect we are after, so this next step is completely optional, as the image you are using for the reflection map may already look great.

27. Select the reflection layer and apply **Filter>Blur>Radial Blur**: Select Spin and a setting of 85.

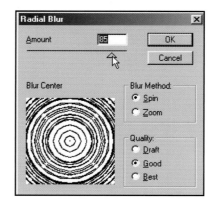

There we have the result: a sphere that is a little out of the ordinary. Try experimenting with the settings to produce different results.

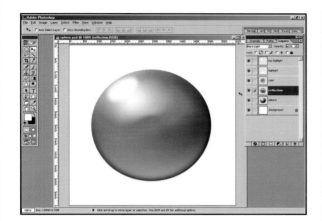

Here is the sphere presented with a reflection on a glassy surface. You will learn how to create reflections like this in the next chapter.

You're making good progress. You have now learned how to create cubes, cylinders, and spheres. Now let's progress on to creating a cone.

## 6: The cone

Our final 3D primitive object, to complete our collection, is going to be the cone.

1.  As standard practice in this chapter, we'll begin with a new blank document of 600x600 pixels at 72 dpi and RGB color space. Create a new layer, and call it 'cone'. Save the document as `cone.psd`.

2.  Draw a rectangular selection. Just like we did in the cylinder tutorial, fill with a copper linear gradient.

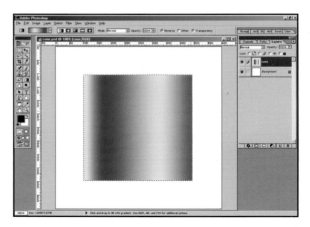

We are going to make our cylinder into a cone in one transformation using the Free Transform tool again.

**3.** Don't worry if you didn't figure it out, here is what you need to do. Press CTRL/CMD+T to enter the Free Transform mode.

**4.** Right-click/CTRL+click and select Perspective.

**5.** Drag one of the top corners into the middle and press the ENTER/RETURN key, and there you have a cone.

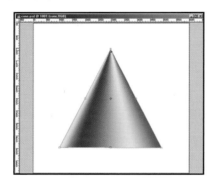

**6.** We want to round the bottom to give a more 3D appearance to the cone so with the Elliptical Marquee tool, draw an oval around the bottom of the cone.

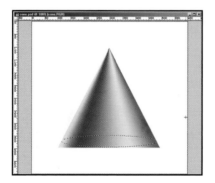

**7.** Let's invert the selection using **Select>Inverse**. Select a large eraser and begin to erase the bottom corners.

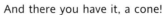
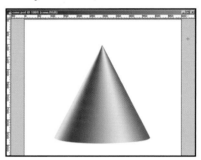

And there you have it, a cone!

Here is an illustration where I used these same techniques. Going through the image is beyond the scope of this book, but I wanted to give you an idea of what is possible with a bit of experimentation and patience.

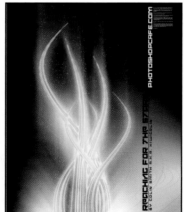

Congratulations, you have just completed several 3D objects in Photoshop. Who said it couldn't be done? It's amazing what Photoshop can do when you break the rules a little bit. Combine these effects to make all kinds of objects and 3D art that your friends would swear you used a 3D program to create.

# Chapter 9
# Creative Colorizing

A big part of design involves color. Color can portray mood, stimulate emotion, and make a powerful statement. Never underestimate the impact of color. For example, blues are the coolest of colors and yellows suggest warmth. We can change the overall impact of a piece of work by simply changing the color. Sometimes we may want to change the color of an entire image, other times we may want to merely change a portion of an image for impact. In this chapter we are going to look at some colorizing tricks. We will start by unlocking the power of the **Hue/Saturation** tool and finish with some tricks involving the layer blending modes.

## Tricks with Hue/Saturation

This is one of my favorite tools and has a lot of hidden potential. We are going to look at a few different uses for this tool that should help you to develop plenty of creative ideas. I rarely open Photoshop without using this feature at some time. Its great for both minor tweaks and for radical color changes to an image.

Let's start by looking at the **Hue/Saturation** dialog box:

Most of the controls are self-explanatory. I have labeled the basic commands and their uses here. The most notable ones are the **Hue slider** and the **Colorize** box. In the course of this chapter we will cover every aspect of this powerful little factory plug-in.

### 1: Creating a monochromatic image

Let's look at a really quick and simple effect here. We will take a color image and convert it to the trendy monotone effect. Monotones are images that consist of one color in different tones. This effect is very popular in web-design and also looks great in print.

1.  Begin with a color image in **RGB** mode.

2.  **Image>Adjust>Hue/Saturation** to open the Hue/Saturation dialog box, (CTRL/CMD+U).

3.  Check the **Colorize** box and adjust the Hue slider until you get a color you like.

4.  Here you have the final image. This is a great way to begin a collage, as the monotones blend well without a lot of distracting color to make the image appear too busy.

## 2: From black and white to monotone

The procedure for this effect is almost the same as the last image.

1. Begin with a grayscale image.

2. Before any color can be added to this image, we will need to convert it to RGB, **Image>Mode>RGB Color**. This adds color channels so that Photoshop has somewhere to store the color information.

3. CTRL/CMD+U to open **Hue/Saturation**. Check the Colorize box and adjust the Hue slider. This time, increase the Saturation to add more intensity to the color.

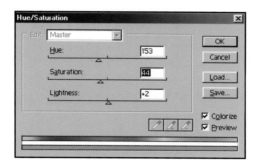

4. And the result... black and white no more!

## 3: Colorizing one portion of an image

This tip will show you how to take an image, convert it to grayscale, and then reapply full color to selected portions of an image. This will help draw the eye to the important part of an image and reduce distraction from the background.

1. Begin with your color image.

2. To remove the color from your image, go to **Image>Adjust>Desaturate** or use the shortcut SHIFT+CTRL/CMD+U.

3. Choose the **History Brush** tool (Y).

4. In the **History** palette, click the box to the left of the state before the Desaturate state.

> The history brush came along in Photoshop 5 and is a very useful little creature. This allows you to selectively paint back portions of the image during a determined number of states. In plain words, you can paint it back how it was.

5. Choose a soft brush from the **Brushes** palette, (this is found on the History Brush options bar).

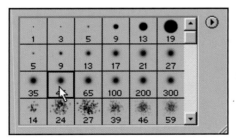

> Use the [ and ] keys to change the size of a brush. Hold down the Shift key at the same time to change the softness.

6. Now, for the fun part, begin to paint back the color portions of your image.

7. Keep painting until you have covered the entire portion of the image that you want to restore color to. Don't worry if you go over the edges a little bit, we're going to clear that up next.

8. Zoom up close to your image to see the stray areas where you have gone over the lines.

**9.** Click in the square to the left of the Desaturate state in the History palette.

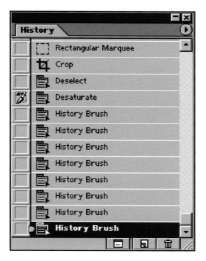

*Hold down the Spacebar to navigate around the image, this will temporarily switch to the Hand tool.*

**10.** Now choose a smaller brush, we'll be effectively painting back the grayscale. So paint all around the edges of your image to clean it up.

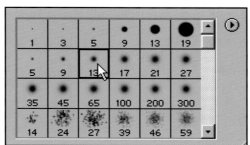

Notice how the motorcycle really pops now. This is a great way to draw attention to portions of an image.

You could use this technique for many creative purposes. One application could be to draw attention to certain individuals in a group photo. Experiment and come up with lots of your own ideas.

## 4: Color shifting

There is a little known feature in the Hue/Saturation dialog box that allows you to easily recolor portions of an image. This is a very powerful and natural looking effect, and it works by selecting a color and then shifting the hue.

1. Here we have an image of a woman with a blue shawl. We want to change the color of the shawl to green without affecting the rest of the image.

2. Again, click CRTL/CMD+U to open the Hue/Saturation dialog. In the Edit menu you will notice a drop-down menu. As a starting point, choose the color that is the closest to the color you want to shift. In this case we chose blue.

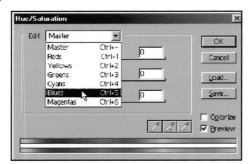

3. Choose the **Eyedropper** tool (T) and click it on the image to sample the color. You will notice the color sliders are changing on the bottom of the palette.

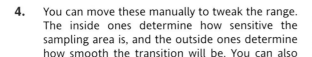

4. You can move these manually to tweak the range. The inside ones determine how sensitive the sampling area is, and the outside ones determine how smooth the transition will be. You can also use these to tweak your selection **after** you have shifted the color to get a smooth effect.

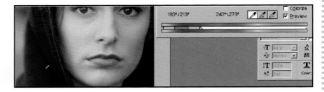

5. Time to shift the color: Move the **Hue** slider and watch your blue change color just like magic.

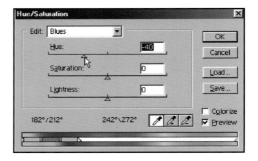

Here is the image with the color shifted next to the original. Could you tell which was the original if I showed you both?

Occasionally you will have some unwanted color shift in areas that you wanted to leave original. You can easily use the history brush to retouch unwanted color shifts. The technique is the same as the previous tutorial.

This is a great effect for creating sales design. You've got the right style, but wrong color? No need for a photo re-shoot, just head for the Hue/Saturation box!

## 5: Colorizing a black and white photo

Have you ever seen any old hand tinted family photographs? You know the ones, where Uncle Fred has bright pink cheeks, and Auntie Vera's blonde locks are painted yellow? Well, with Photoshop we can transform black and white pictures into really believable color.

The technique we're going to look at now is simplicity itself; we're only going to use two tools; the Eyedropper; and the Airbrush tool. This is so easy Auntie Vera herself could manage it. Obviously the key to realistic colorization is in careful sampling, so to add realism you could add more colors than we have in this tutorial. I'm hoping you'll be amazed at the results you receive.

1.  Open your black and white photo in Photoshop, I'll be working on a portrait as skin tones are some of the hardest colors to match realistically. I recommend you work on a portrait too, have you got an old high school picture that you'd like to see in glorious Technicolor?

2.  The secret to natural color is to use a reference image. Rather than guess the colors, we are going to sample them from another image. Open a color photo of a similar subject to the one you want to colorize.

3.  Click I to select the **Eyedropper** tool.

4.  In the toolbar option, change the settings to 5 by 5 Average, this will give you a more even sample of the colors.

5.  Using the Eyedropper, find a good skin tone color from the color image and click on it. The foreground color will change to match the sampled color. Now return to your black and white image, if the foreground color is gray then your image is probably in grayscale color mode, so change this to RGB by going to **Image>Mode>RGB Color**.

9. Select the **Airbrush** tool (J) and a large soft brush.

10. Create a new layer (CTRL/CMD+ SHIFT+ N) and call it 'color'. Switch the layer blending mode to Color. We are now ready to begin colorizing the image.

*The Color blending mode is perfect because it affects nothing but the color. The tonal qualities of the image are entirely unaffected.*

11. Paint over all the exposed skin with the large brush. For more accuracy, zoom in close and use a smaller brush around the edges.

12. See how the color blending mode only affects the color and keeps all the details including shadows and highlights.

13. Now let's do the lips. Create a new layer, sample a good color from the color picture and paint them in.

14. Whoops, it looks like he's wearing lipstick now, it's easy to overdo the color on lips, so always be careful. To soften this effect I'll run a 4.8 pixel Gaussian Blur (**Filters>Blur>Gaussian Blur**).

**15.** Now it looks a bit better. We will touch them up some more later.

**16.** Sample the brown from the hair, and paint over the hair and eyebrows.

**17.** Sample a light blue color from the color picture. We are going to use this to paint the shirt on our picture. You can take color from anywhere it doesn't have to be from the same object.

**18.** Now for the tie, let's sample the red from the book spine.

**19.** Painting over the tie produces a nice result. I also painted over the frames of the glasses with the same red color.

**20.** This next step is very subtle, but makes a big difference to the image. Nothing attracts the visual attention more than the eyes. Sample the color from one of the eyes.

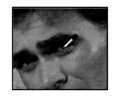

**21.** Paint the eyes in the sampled color. See how it makes the image come alive.

**22.** The last thing we will color is the background. I've chosen the blue/gray color from the spine of a book. Paint it into the background to finish the color effect.

**23.** Almost finished, let's do a couple of little tweaks to clean it up and make the image more presentable.

I'm still not happy with the way the lips look. Lips are probably the most difficult part of the face to colorize. Too little color and they are washed out, too much and we risk a clown-like effect. In addition, we need to consider the transition between the lips and the surrounding skin tone, which has to be as subtle as possible.

**24.** Choose the **Blur** tool from the tools palette, rub it around the lips a little bit to soften the transition.

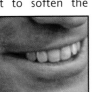

**25.** Finally we want to clean up the white areas. With all the painting it's easy to get some color in these areas by mistake. Select white as your foreground color. Zoom in nice and close and paint over the teeth.

**26.** Finally paint over the whites of the eyes.

Well done! You have colorized a whole photograph. Here is the finished image. It would be very difficult to tell that this wasn't originally a color photo.

Notice the Layers palette. All the color is on a separate layer so that it doesn't affect the original. If you wanted to touch up any part of the image, you could sample that color and paint over the color layer.

Here is the color layer by itself so you can see what you have done.

Once again, here is the finished image next to the original black and white so you can compare the two. I wish I knew about this procedure a few years ago, it would have saved me a lot of time and produced better results than the way I used to do it. If you take your time you can produce very realistic effects.

I hope you gleaned a lot of useful information from this chapter. You now have enough colorizing skills under your belt to really make your images stand out. You should never have to bear with bad color again. Try these techniques on some of your own images; modify them to come up with some interesting variations of your own. The sky is the limit.

# Chapter 10
# Web tricks

Photoshop has long been used as a tool for preparing images for the Internet. Since the release of ImageReady 3, the sister program that ships with Photoshop 6, Adobe has made it easier to integrate your Photoshop images with web projects. This handy little program, which you can access by clicking the **Jump to ImageReady** icon, right at the bottom of the Tools palette, comes equipped with lots of web-friendly features. These include better slicing, easier animations, and weighted optimization. ImageReady makes it easy to create Image maps and rollovers too. We'll cover all of these terms in this chapter, but for more details on Photoshop and the web see Foundation Photoshop, also published by friends of ED.

## 1: Different types of buttons for the web

Buttons are tempting little devices that say, "Press me and see what happens." Every designer should have a few buttons up their sleeve. We'll now look at a few great button styles, once you've learnt these techniques, you can use them to create an endless array of buttons.

## OSX button

The first button we will look at is the much wanted gel button. This is similar to the Apple Mac OSX look. There are tons of ways to create this effect, in my opinion this is the quickest and easiest method.

1.  Start with a new document of 150 x 100 pixels at 72ppi. RGB mode. In reality, you would probably make your document a little smaller, but we are going to do it slightly larger to really see what is going on. Of course you can always reduce the size later. Create a new layer and call it 'button'.

2.  Select the **Rounded Rectangular** tool. Click the **Fill pixels** button, the third option from the left at the top, so we draw pixels and not a path. For Radius, choose 30 pixels.

3.  Drag the tool on your document. You should now have a nice pill shape. This tool is a great addition in Photoshop 6.

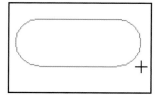

4.  We're now going to use the **Gradient** tool to fill in the shape, so choose a dark blue for the foreground and a light blue/cyan for the background.

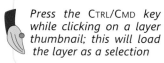

5.  Make the selection around the pill active.

*Press the CTRL/CMD key while clicking on a layer thumbnail; this will load the layer as a selection*

6.  Choose the Gradient tool, Foreground to Background and Linear. Fill with the blue gradient from top to bottom.

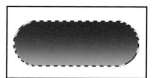

7.  With the selection still active and the Gradient tool still selected, choose the Foreground to Transparent gradient. Set white as the foreground color.

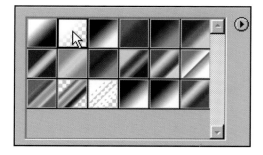

8.  Create a new layer and call it 'highlight'. Apply the gradient as shown. The top third should have a white gradient. Press CRTL/CMD+D to deselect.

9. Press CTRL/CMD+T for the Free Transform mode. Use the Scale and Perspective controls to shrink the gradient slightly. Bring the top down just a hair and the sides in a bit. This will form the basis of our highlight.

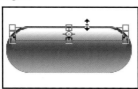

*When a node is active, you can nudge it by using the arrow keys on the keyboard.*

10. Add a 1.5 pixel Gaussian Blur to soften the effect. We now have our button with a highlight on it.

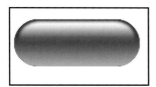

If you look at the OSX buttons, you will see that they seem to have a light glow in the bottom center. Let's add that little bit of glow.

11. Create a new layer called 'lower highlight'.

12. Select the Elliptical Marquee tool. In the top tool bar enter 5 as the Feather to soften the edges.

*Make sure you reset the Feather to 0 after you have applied this effect otherwise all your selections will be feathered. It's easy to forget this.*

13. Draw an oval on the bottom half of the button.

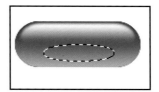

14. Fill with white and deselect.

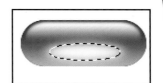

*To fill with fore-ground color press ALT+BACKSPACE/OP+ DEL. To fill with background press CTRL/CMD+DEL.*

15. Change the layer Blending mode to Overlay and reduce the Opacity to 68%. Reposition the highlight if necessary.

16. Now let's add a Drop Shadow. On the gel buttons, the drop shadow tends to be more of a bluish glow. Select the button layer and add a Layer style. Choose Drop Shadow and change the color to cyan. Drop the Opacity down to 50% and adjust the Distance, Angle, and Size as shown below:

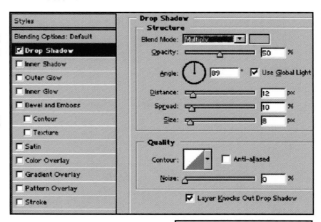

All we need to do now is add some text to our completed button.

17. Create your text in black using a sans serif font like Futura or Arial. I am starting with the 'home' text. Drag the text layer under the highlight layers so that the reflections will be above the text. This produces an effect of the text being in the glass.

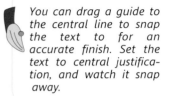

*You can drag a guide to the central line to snap the text to for an accurate finish. Set the text to central justification, and watch it snap away.*

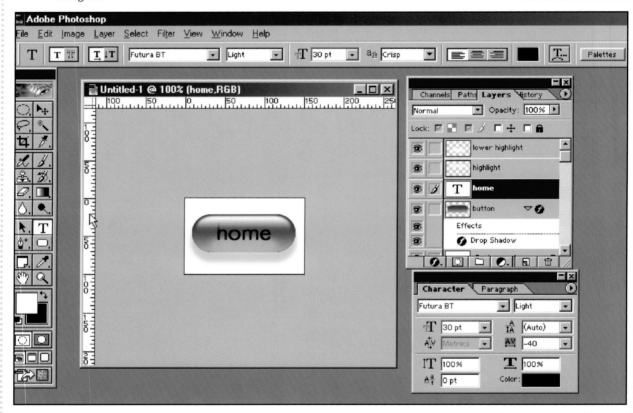

And now for that little bit extra: Add a Drop Shadow to the text. This adds to the depth of the effect.

*If the edges don't look too clean try this:* **Layer>Matting>Defringe** *and try a setting of 1 pixel.*

Have fun with the gel buttons and remember you can use any color you choose and any shape too.

## Round glassy button

This next button is also very popular for web design. We are going to create a round glassy button.

1. Start with a new document of 150 x 150 pixels at 72ppi. RGB mode. As we said in the last section, you will probably want it a little smaller, but we are going to do it larger so you can see what is going on. Create a new layer and call it 'button'.

2. Using the Elliptical Marquee tool, draw a circle. Remember, to draw a perfect circle, hold down the SHIFT key as you drag the selection, and hold down the ALT/OPTION key to draw from the center.

3. Choose a light green for the foreground color and a dark green for the background color. Select the Radial Gradient tool and choose Foreground to Background. Apply a gradient in a similar way to how we did it in the 3D Sphere chapter. Don't deselect yet.

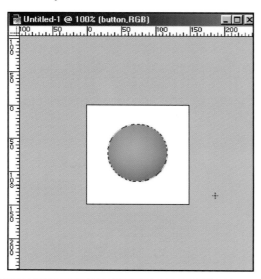

4. Now we have a rounded button. Let's add our highlights to get the glassy look.

5. Create a new layer and call it 'highlight'.

6. Set the foreground color to white and change to a Linear Gradient of Foreground to Transparent. Apply the gradient to the top part of the circle and then deselect.

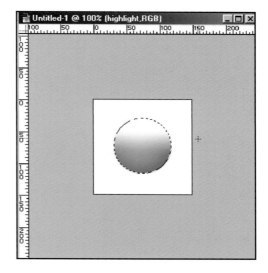

7. Press CTRL/CMD+T for the Free Transform mode. Scale the highlight so that it is a bit smaller than the circle. Press the ENTER/RETURN key to apply the transformation.

8. Duplicate the highlight layer by dragging the layer to the new layer icon.

**167**

**9.** Using Free Transform, flip the highlight copy vertically and drag to the bottom.

> Holding down shift whilst dragging constrains the movement to 45-degree increments.

**10.** Apply a 4.6 pixel Gaussian Blur to the bottom highlight to soften the effect.

**11.** Switch to Overlay mode to give the highlight a really translucent look.

**12.** Let's soften the top highlight too. Select the highlight layer and choose a 1.1 pixel Gaussian Blur. We chose a smaller blur because we wanted to keep the highlight pretty sharp and give a really good glassy feel.

**13.** Add some text to the button using a black sans serif font for a nice clean look.

**14.** Make sure that the text layer is positioned beneath the highlights. Here is our button. The last thing to do is add a small Drop Shadow.

**15.** Apply a green Drop Shadow to the button layer.

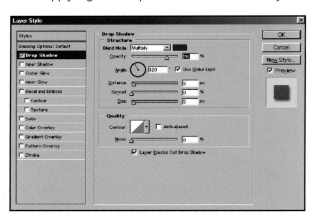

Here is our finished button. Use this on your web pages and even in your print work for special effects.

## Specialty metallic hexagonal buttons

The next button that we will create is more of a custom button. We will walk through the creation of this with a few variations. The variations will provide a good learning experience and a glimpse into the creative process and how you can get drastically different results from minor tweaks.

1. Once again, start with a new document of 150x150 pixels at 72ppi. RGB mode. This time select black for the background color. Reset the default foreground/background colors by pressing the D key.

2. Create a new layer and call it 'texture'. We are going to fill it with a brushed metal. Apply the copper gradient diagonally to this layer.

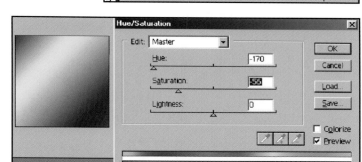

3. Adjust the Hue/Saturation (CTRL/CMD+U) to a hint of blue for a true silvery effect.

4. To create the brushed texture: Add noise, **Filter>Noise>Add Noise** set to 5 %.

5. Add a blur to the noise to get the brushed feel through **Filters>Blur>Motion Blur** with the following settings:

6. Create a new layer to use to make our button. Call it "shape".

7. Choose the **Polygon Shape** tool and select 6 for the number of sides. Also select Create Filled Region from the top left three options.

8. Drag out a hexagon and release the mouse to draw the shape.

> Holding down the SHIFT key will constrain the baseline of the shape to 45-degree angles.

9. Make sure the texture layer is active and then CTRL/CMD+click on the shape thumbnail. This will load the selection of the shape. So you should see this:

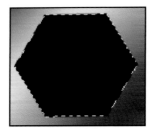

10. We want to move the selected texture to its own layer so press CTRL/CMD+SHIFT+J to move the selection to a new layer.

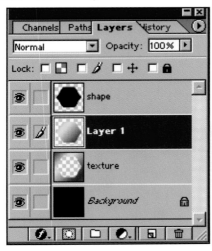

11. Hide the shape layer and the texture layer by clicking on the eye icon and you should now see the shape and the background.

12. To add some 3D depth, apply a Bevel and Emboss Layer style. For Style choose Pillow Emboss.

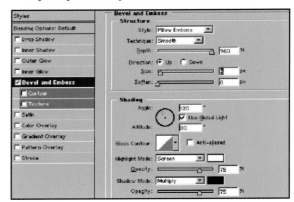

If we show the texture layer again, you should see our texture with our shape chiseled out in it.

Finally, add some text to the shape. You could finish right here or continue for some variations. Save your file now in case you want to return to this stage later.

## Variations

For our first variation, we will emboss the type and make the button more shiny.

1.  CTRL/CMD+click on the type layer to load the text as a selection.

2.  With the text selected, highlight the new shape layer 1 and hide the text layer. You should now see the shape with a selection for the text.

3.  Press the DELETE key for an instant bevel to the text. What happened? We just deleted part of the shape and the layer style was automatically applied to the new edges.

4.  Next, let's enhance the metal for a more shiny look. Go to **Image>Adjust>Curves** and create a curve similar to what is seen in the screen shot.

CTRL/CMD+M *opens the curves dialog box*

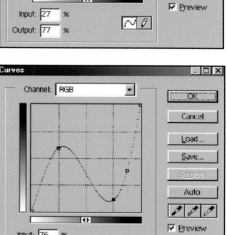

5.  Click OK and apply the curve a second time, choose settings that will compliment the first application of the curves.

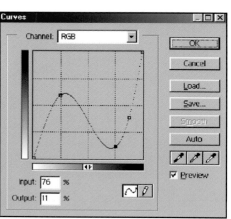

6. Notice there is some color shift. You may like the effect it gives, if not open the Hue/Saturation box and click Colorize, slide the Hue to blue and it will be all one color again.

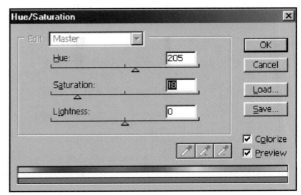

7. Hide the texture layer and we will make another variation. Apply an Outer Glow using lime green.

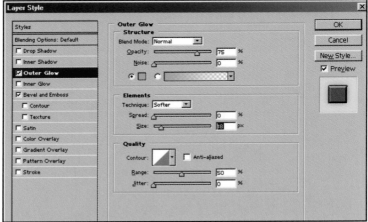

We now have a different look with basically the same button.

Here is the button duplicated a few times with some different text on them and used as an interface.

You could create a navigation interface by adding a glow around the hexagon shapes and placing some type on them.

Another variation would be to use **Free Transform>Perspective** to create an interface. Be sure you group all the layers that you want transformed before applying the transformation.

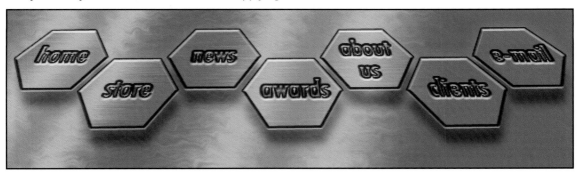

## 2: Multiple rollovers

Rollovers are now integral to every modern, attractive web site. A rollover is an event that happens on a website when a mouse passes over a certain area of a web page. The most common event is when your mouse crosses over an image; it switches to a different image. This creates the impression of a button lighting up or being pushed down. This makes it almost irresistible for the visitor to not press the button and explore the website.

In this chapter I am not just going to show you how to create rollovers, I am going to teach you how to create multiple rollovers. These are the same as rollovers except they have the additional fun of another part of the image changing at the same time. These are sometimes called remote rollovers. We are going to be using ImageReady for this functionality. What will amaze you is just how easy it is with ImageReady 3.

We are going to go through three sections:
- Preparing the images in Photoshop
- Slicing and serving in ImageReady
- Testing in ImageReady and exporting to a web browser

Without any further delay, let's dive in.

## Preparing the images in Photoshop

1. Create a gel button like the one at the beginning of this chapter but this time make it green instead of blue. Make it about 150X40 pixels in size.

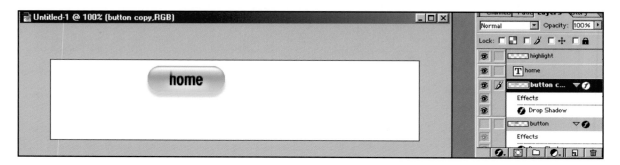

2. Open the interface provided for download on the friends of ED web site (rollover demo.psd). This was created using the techniques you have learned in this book. We will even build an interface from scratch in the first Design Project. By hiding the button layer in the gel button we get a neutral colored button because of the highlight layers. In order to have rollovers you must have a layer you can show/hide to create the effect. Here is our interface with all the buttons in their neutral state and another with them activated.

3. Now we want to create some text that we will use for our remote rollover.

4. Create a new Layer set and call it 'rollover text'. Layer sets are great to help you keep all your layers organized. Click the new folder icon in the Layers palette. These sets are new in Photoshop 6 and allow you to collapse or expand their view in the Layers palette and also group layers for ease of view and navigation.

5. Add some text to the image in the screen I prepared on the interface. This is what you will see in the Layers palette.

6. Keep adding text until you have a message for all four buttons. Keeping each line of text on a separate layer. It's a good idea to hide each layer as you create it, so you can see what you are doing.

Notice that the layers 3 down, 2 down, 1 down, and home down are hidden.

Here is the same image with all the button layers showing. See how it looks and notice that all the layers 3 down, 2 down, 1 down, and home down are now shown in the Layers palette. This is basically how rollovers work. We are now going to use ImageReady to automate this process.

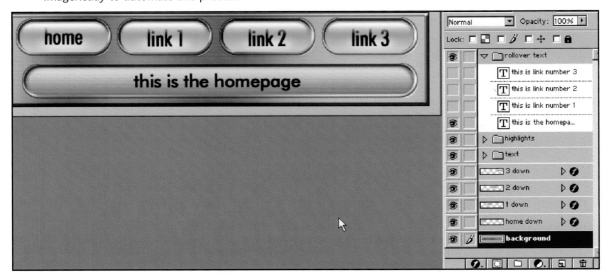

7. Save the image to your hard drive.

8. On the bottom of the toolbar, there is a button that will launch ImageReady and load your image.

9. Click this button and wait. It may take a minute or two for ImageReady to launch and build the file.

## Slicing and serving in ImageReady

Here is your image launched in ImageReady, all ready for you to prepare for service on the web.

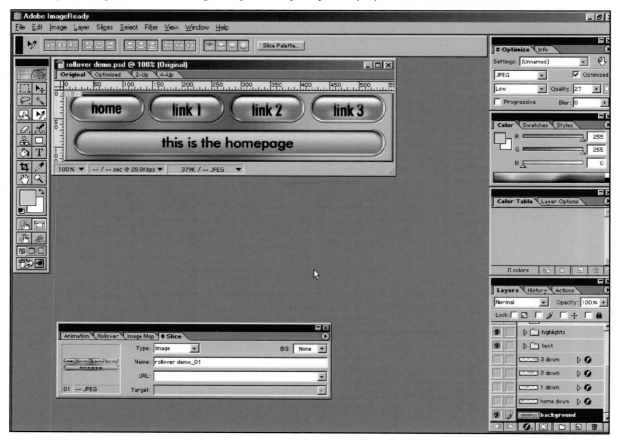

For ImageReady to know which part of the image will be effected we need to create slices. Slicing breaks the image into different pieces like a jigsaw puzzle. These will be reassembled on the web page by the use of automatically generated tables which are invisible and seamless. This allows for a seamless image that is efficient in loading because you can optimize each slice separately from each other.

1. Select the **Slice** tool from the toolbar

2. Starting from the top left, drag the Slice tool around the first button. The Slice tool acts a lot like the Marquee tool in its feel.

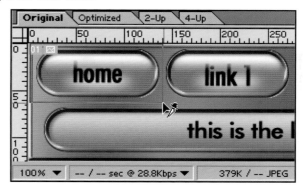

3. You will see a small blue box appear in the corner with the number 01. This indicates that a slice has been defined for the area.

4. Continue adding slices for each of the buttons. The last slice will always be automatically generated. Your image should now be divided into five slices - one for each button and one for the text window.

*Ensure that your slices border each other exactly or pointless extra slices will be created that will only make things more complex when it is time to put them all together again.*

5. Before we do anything else, hide the rollover text for the home link. We want everything to be totally neutral at this point.

6. Now, we're going to add the links for each button. Choose the **Slice Select** tool and select slice 01 or the home button.

   In the Slice palette, type in a link of home.html.

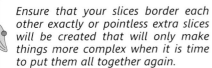

7. Select each button and add links until you have a link for each button.

8. Now select the home button again and select the Rollover palette. Notice it says Normal – this is what the image looks like when there is no mouse activity.

9. Press the **New State** button, the first on the left at the bottom of the Rollover palette.

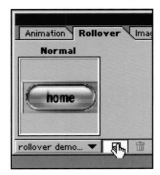

A new state will now be added called Over. This is what the image will look like when the mouse is over the slice that contains this button.

Whatever you hide or show in the Layers palette while the Over state is selected is what will be seen in the web browser when the mouse rolls over the slice. It is much easier to put both states in the same image (by means of layers) rather than have separate images for each state.

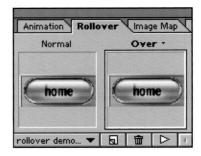

10. In the Layers palette, show the rollover text for the home button. You will see the text in the image window.

11. Now also show the colored button for the home button. Notice how we now have color in the button and the text is showing. You have just created a rollover; I hope you found it nice and easy.

Also, the previews in the Rollover palette will reflect the new rollover state.

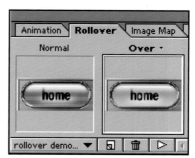

12. Select slice 02 or the link 1 button. In the Slices palette add a new state just like before. Show the button for link 1 and also show the text. You should now see that link 1 and its text are displayed in your image window. Again, in the Slices palette you should see your Normal and Over states.

Keep repeating these steps for the last two buttons. We are now ready to test our rollovers and see how they work.

## Testing in ImageReady and exporting to a web browser

In the toolbar there is a button that allows us to test out rollovers from within ImageReady. Click this button.

As you roll your mouse over the image, you'll see the buttons interact with the cursor. Make sure that each slice changes to the correct image and that they all restore correctly when the mouse moves out of the target area. If things don't work quite right, go back to the Slices palette and make your corrections by showing and hiding the correct images. When you have finished testing the rollovers, switch off the rollover preview by clicking the button again.

Once you have all the rollovers working correctly, we can proceed to the next step. We are going to export the images, the html and JavaScript code will be written by ImageReady. The good news is that you don't need to know any programming at all!

Before we export the images, we want to optimize them. Optimization is where we find a happy medium between image quality and file size. We want to make the images as small as possible for faster download speeds but we want to keep the quality the best we can for sharper images.

1.  Select each slice using the Slice Select tool and then change the settings in the Optimize palette. Change the Image window to the Optimized view by clicking on the tab and then experiment with the quality slider until you find a good balance, if you are using a JPEG. If you are getting better results with GIFs then you will instead be adding and subtracting colors from the image. Repeat this step for each slice.

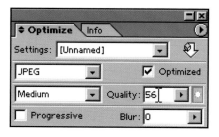

For images with gradients and photos, JPG's work best. For large areas of solid color, repeating patterns, and text, gifs usually work the best. You will be able to see the file size in the bottom of the image window.

2.  When you have optimized every slice it's time to export your webpage.

3.  Go to **File>Save Optimized As** and create a folder on your hard drive where you want the website to be exported to. In the Save as Type field ensure that HTML and Images (default) is selected and, in the **Slices** field choose **All Slices**. Click the Save button and your code and images will be generated.

You will find that ImageReady will create a document in HTML and a folder called Images. Inside the images folder will be all the sliced images from your document. This is a mini website in itself and will be fully functional.

Let's take a closer look at the **Save Optimized As** dialog box options:

■ The **Save as type** field has three options available:
**HTML and Images**: This will generate both the code and the images.
**Images Only**: This will generate the images but not affect the code.
**HTML Only**: This will generate the code only and not affect the images.

■ The **Slices** field has two options available:
**All Slices**: This will export the entire image as sequential slices.
**Selected Slices:** This will only export the slice you are working on, everything else will remain unchanged. This is the best option for making modifications to your work later on.

3.  Navigate to the html document on your hard drive. Double-click on the thumbnail to launch your page in your favorite web browser.

images      rollover-dem...

Your page will now be loaded in the browser with all the images and rollovers intact. Test it by rolling your mouse over each button and watch it come to life. You should also see the text appear in the window beneath the buttons.

Congratulations! You have now created a webpage with multiple remote rollovers. This will really impress your friends and clients and it wasn't as hard as you though it would be was it? I love ImageReady for this type of functionality. Even if you do know JavaScript, it saves a lot of time to let ImageReady write some of your code for you. I have also found the code to be reliable across different browsers and platforms. In fact the rollovers at www.photoshopcafe.com were created the very way I have just shown you.

## 3: Animated rollovers

In this tutorial we are going beyond the remote rollover. We will incorporate what you've just learned, but we will have the additional attraction of an animation. When your mouse rolls over the button, the button will light up and the doors will slide open. We are going to create the slices and rollovers in ImageReady. Then we are going to create an animation also in ImageReady. Lastly I will show you a work around to switch the static rollover image for a cool animated one.

The components we will be working with are the interface, a highlighted version of the button, and two doors, each on its own layer.

Begin by opening your interface in ImageReady. The source file is available for download at the friends of ED web site, it's called `animated rollover before.psd`. The finished rollover is also supplied for you to play with.

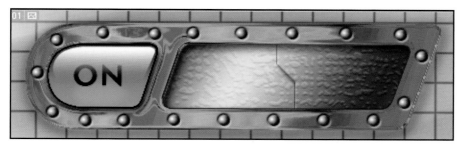

1.  Using the Slice tool. Make a slice around the button.

2. Make a second slice around the door area. Notice that all the other slices are automatically generated.

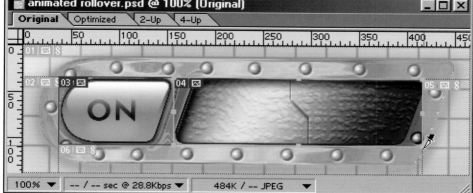

3. Using the Slice Selection tool, choose the button that is slice 03.

4. In the Slice palette, assign a link under URL.

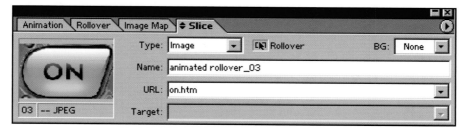

5. Let's create the rollover, switch to the Rollover palette and click on the new state button. The Over state is now added.

6. Show the 'button lit' layer, this will give the impression of the button glowing.

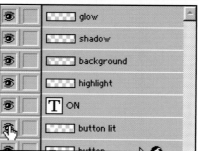

Giving the result:

On the Layers palette, there are two layers called door right and door left. These are the doors that we will animate soon.

7. Open the Animation palette. Click on the duplicate frame button to add a new frame.

8. With the new frame selected (Frame 2), select the 'door left' layer.

   **Important**: At this point make sure you change to the **Move** tool on the toolbar or your slices will move instead of your layers.

9. Using the arrow keys on your keyboard, tap the left key until the door is slid all the way to the left.

*Hold the Shift key to nudge the image in increments of 10 pixels instead of 1 pixel to save time.*

10. Select the door right layer.

11. Use the right arrow key and move the door all the way to the right. We now have the ending frame of the doors open.

Looking in the Animation palette, you will see two frames. Frame 1 is the image with the doors fully closed, whilst Frame 2 is the image with the doors fully open.

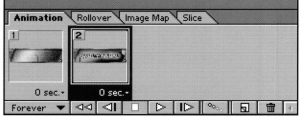

12. For a smooth animation, we will need to create some in-between frames of the doors opening. The good news is that ImageReady can create them for you; it's called **tweening** or **in-betweening**. Click the little arrow in the top right of the Animation palette and choose Tween.

13. You will see this window pop up. Choose 4 for the number of frames to add. Leave all the other settings as the default settings. Click OK.

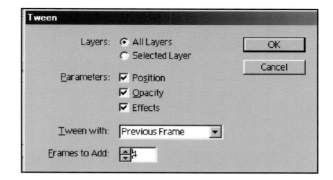

The four frames are now generated automatically. We now have a total of six frames for a very smooth animation.

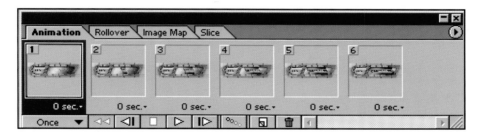

14. Press the Play button to test the animation. Press Stop when you are done.

You may notice that the animation keeps repeating, or looping as it's called. In a lot of cases this is good. In this case however, we don't want it to loop, we want the doors to open once and then remain open. If your animation is looping, go to the button in the bottom left and change the looping from Forever to Once.

15. Click the Play button to test the animation again. The doors should slide open and then stay open.

## Optimizing the slices

Now that the animation is working, it's time to output the page.

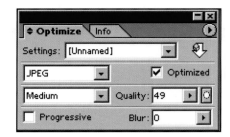

1.  Choose a jpeg for all the slices except for the door slice (04).

2.  Select slice 04 (the doors).

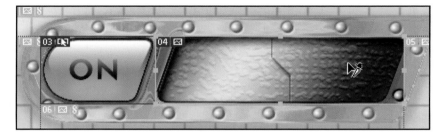

3.  In the Optimize palette, change this slice to a gif. We made it a gif because only gifs can be animated.

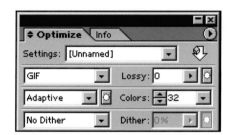

4.  We will now output the document just like we did in the last tutorial so select **File>Save Optimized As**.

5.  Create a new folder and export the new page to that location. Save as type: HTML and Images should be selected as well as All Slices. Click Save to generate the code and sliced images.

6.  We are now ready to launch our new animated remote rollover. Go to your saved folder and find the animated-rollover HTML document. Launch it in your favorite web browser to view.

As your mouse goes over the button, the button glows and the doors slide open. I'm sure your brain is thinking of lots of uses for this trick now. You can really spice up your web pages with animated rollovers and stand out from the crowd.

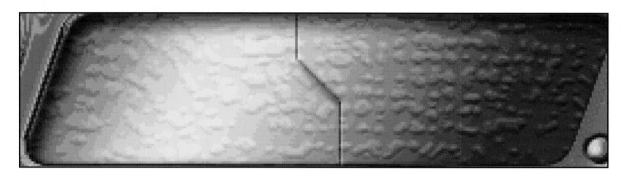

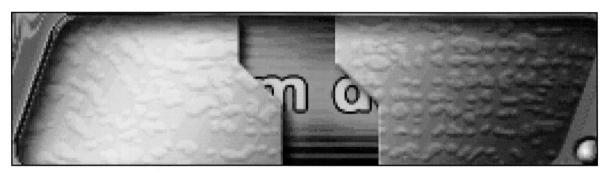

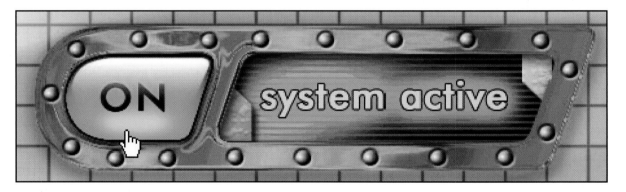

I hope you have enjoyed this chapter. You have learned some advanced interactivity for your Photoshop images on the web and for multimedia purposes. You have also learned some of the useful features of ImageReady. The techniques aren't really that hard to master, and once you have got to grips with them you'll be able to produce some stunning web pages.

# Chapter 11
# Lines and grids

Lately the tech trend has hit graphics. Everywhere we look the graphics are boasting the high-tech scanline and grid look. These effects are relatively simple to create and most are based on the use of patterns. We are going to begin with the creation of the simple but useful TV scanline and then take it to a grid then go crazy and distort it, twist it, and map it. This chapter will be a lot of fun and after this primer, your images will never be the same again.

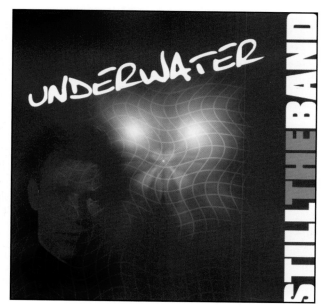

## Scanlines

This is a highly popular effect and it certainly won't hurt you to learn it. This is the effect that creates those thin lines that run through your image and make it appear like it's on TV.

### 1: Creating the scanline pattern

1.  Begin with a new document with a white back-ground. Make it 2 pixels wide and 6 high with 72ppi resolution and RGB Color. If you want a thicker line, then make the height larger as this is the dimension that dictates the thickness of the line. We are going to create our repeating pattern used for the scanline here.

2.  Since the document is tiny, zoom in (CTRL/CMD++) until it's large enough to work with.

3.  Using the **Rectangular Marquee** tool, select the top half of the docu-ment and fill with black.

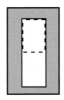

4.  Select the entire document by press-ing CTRL/CMD+A.

5.  Let's save it as a pattern so go to **Edit>Define Pattern.** The following dialog box will pop up. Name the new pattern 'scanline'. We are saving our selection to the Pattern library in Photoshop so we will be able to access this in the future to be used as a repeating pattern.

6.  Close the document and you have now created your pattern for use anytime in Photoshop.

## 2: Applying the scanline

1. Open a new image in Photoshop.

2. Create a new layer and call it "scanline".

3. Select **Edit>Fill** to open the fill box and choose Pattern for Contents.

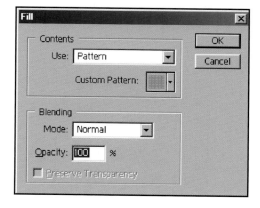

> Press SHIFT+BACKSPACE/SHIFT+DEL *to open the fill dialog box.*

4. Click in the pattern thumbnail to reveal all your patterns. Select the "scanline" pattern we just created.

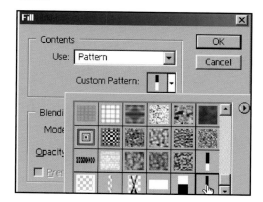

5. Click OK and your document will be filled with the scanlines as a repeating pattern.

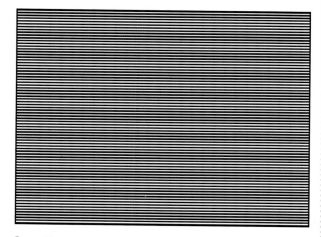

6. Oh No! Our picture has gone. Not to fear, Layer Blending Modes to the rescue. Change the mode to Screen in the Layers palette.

Now you can see our image showing through the lines. The screen mode makes the black lines transparent.

7. Drop the Opacity to allow some of the image to show through the white lines for a smoother result.

Here we have our image with the scanlines applied.

Another way we could do this is to apply the Overlay mode. This makes the white lines invisible and causes the black to show. This creates the same effect but darker and works best on lighter images.

The image below shows our image but with Overlay mode applied instead of changing the Opacity:

There we go. That wasn't nearly as difficult as you thought it might be. You will notice that everyone is using scanlines, you will see them on TV commercials, magazine ads, video games, web sites, and product packaging to name a few places.

# The grid

Now that we have learned the principles of patterns from using scanlines, we will create a grid. Grids can be used in similar ways to scanlines and may even be combined for effect. We are going to create the basic grid first and then we are going to look at some advanced creative options that will open up whole new worlds to your design.

## 3: Creating the pattern

1.  Make a new document that is 20 x 20 pixels and has a transparent background.

2.  Zoom up, CTRL/CMD++, larger on the document so you can see what is happening.

3.  Select all by pressing CTRL/CMD+A or **Select>All**. You should now see the selection around the entire canvas area.

4.  We are now going to create an outline around the box so click **on Edit>Stroke**. For Width use 1 pixel, Location as Center, and Color as white. Click OK. This will give us a thin border around the entire canvas. This is going to be our grid pattern so don't deselect.

5.  Go to **Edit>Define Pattern** and name it "grid".

We have created our grid pattern all ready for use later. You can close this document now, as we are finished with it. You won't need to save it as the pattern is already saved in the Pattern library.

191

## 4: Applying the grid

1. Open an image you want to use for the background. Here is one of the stock photographs that I altered the coloring of with the addition of a couple of layers, some clouds, motion blur, hue/saturation, and a lens flare.

2. Create a new layer and call it "grid" (such creative names).

3. Go to **Edit>Fill** and choose Pattern. Navigate to our new grid pattern.

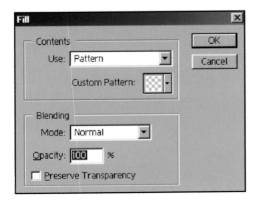

4. Here is our picture with the grid applied to it.

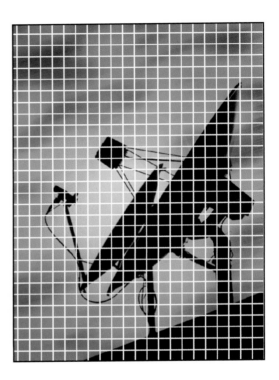

5. Switch to Overlay mode and lower the Opacity to 65% for a better blend.

Ahhh, much better. It's always important to make sure our effects blend well with the images and are not just "stuck there". You will find that I make extensive use of Layer Blending Modes as they make all the difference. If you want to know more about them, there is a section on them and two chapters on Layers in Foundation Photoshop, also by friends of ED.

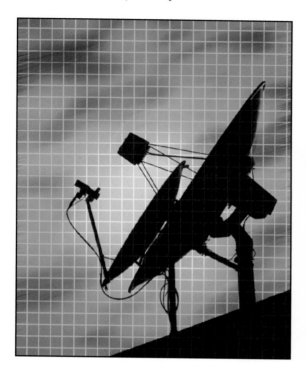

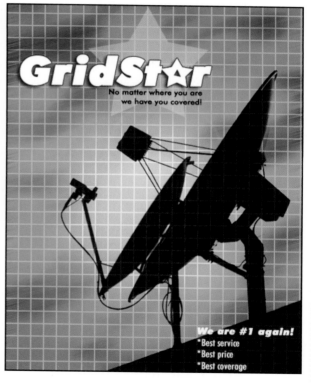

If you were to add a little bit of type, you could use this image as a cover for a brochure or flyer.

## 5: Perspective grid

We are now going to look at the first variation of the grid. In this section we will create a perspective grid that fades off into the distance. This effect is great to accentuate distance.

1. Begin with a picture. Here is another stock photo that I modified. This time I duplicated the layer, inverted it, and changed the Layer Blending Mode to produce an interesting effect.

2. Create a new layer and name it 'grid', again.

3. Go to **Edit>Fill** and use the grid pattern.

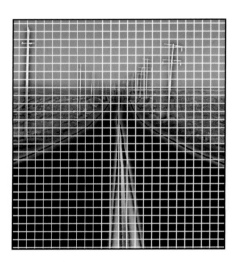

4. Zoom out of the image so that the pasteboard is visible, I zoomed out to 50% here. The reason will be obvious in a moment.

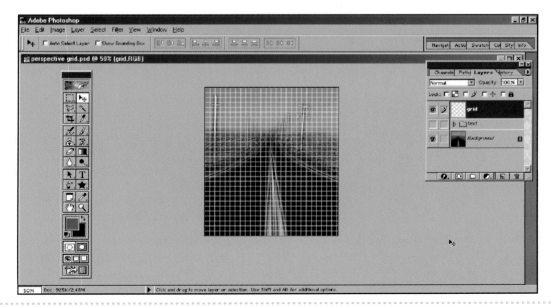

5. Press CTRL/CMD+T for Free Transform mode. Right-click and choose Perspective.

6. Drag out the bottom corners until the angle matches the perspective in the image.

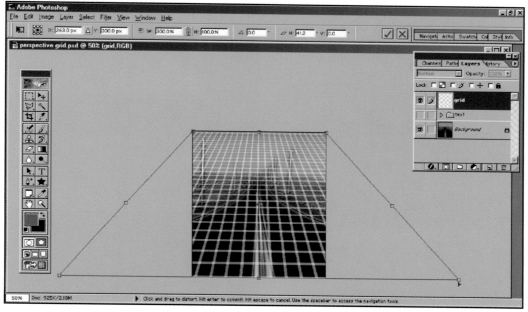

7. Don't apply the effect just yet, right-click and choose Scale.

8. Drag the top down until it fits on the horizon. You may have to go back and forth between the Perspective and Scale a few times to get the angle just right.

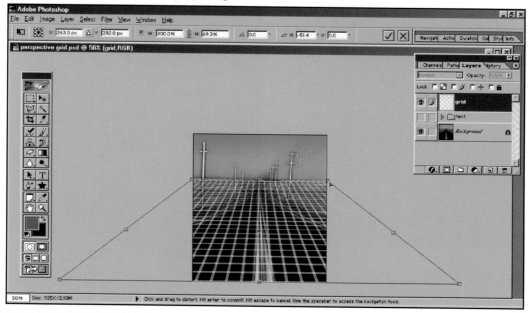

**9.** Press the ENTER/RETURN key to apply the effect.

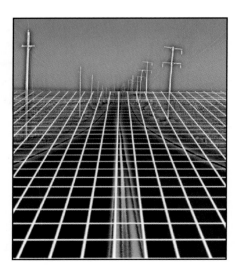

**10.** Now for the sky, duplicate the grid layer.

**11.** Go to Free Transform mode (CTRL/CMD+T), right-click, and choose Flip Vertical. Drag into position. You now have two grids flowing with the perspective and meeting along the horizon of the image.

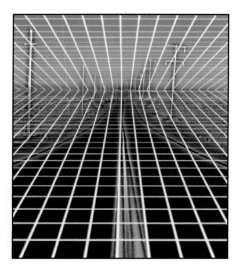

**12.** On the top grid layer, add a Layer Mask.

This is what you should see in the Layers palette.

**13.** Using a black to white Linear Gradient, start at the horizon line and drag up about half way and the grid will fade.

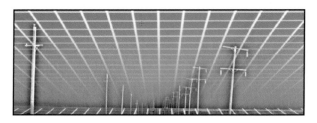

**14.** Now add a Layer Mask to the bottom grid and drag the gradient through the bottom grid.

We now have the top and bottom grids fading into the distance.

Here we have the finished grid faded into the image, a nice effect indeed.

15. Drop the Opacity down by about 50% to blend the grid into the image better.

16. Change the top grid to Overlay mode.

You could use this as a cover for an annual report.

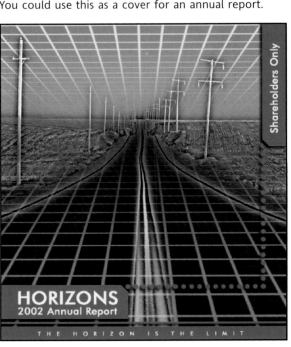

## 6: Distorted wave grid

Are you ready to dive into something a bit more wild and creative now? We are going to create a wavy grid. This effect is a lot of fun and has many artistic uses.

1. Begin with a new image. This is one I made with the cloud filters, lens flare, radial blur, and a lot of layer trickery. The image is 600X600 and 72 dpi.

2. Create a new layer and name it (yeah you got the picture by now) 'grid'.

3. Go to **Edit>Fill** and fill with our grid pattern.

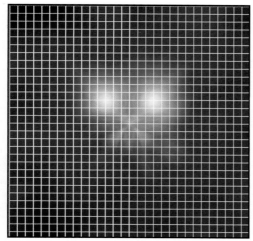

4. Zoom out to 50% so we can see the pasteboard area.

5. Using Free Transform, drag all the sides of the canvas. The reason we are doing this, is so when we distort the grid, there is plenty of extra space to play with so it doesn't run off the edge of the image.

 *Drag a corner while holding down* Shift+Alt/Option *to enlarge the entire layer from the center proportionally.*

6. Press Enter/Return to apply the transformation.

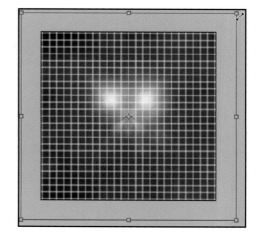

7. Time to apply the effect. First go to **Filter>Distort>Wave**. Choose similar settings to what you see here. The important steps are to reduce the horizontal and vertical scale and reduce the number of generators.

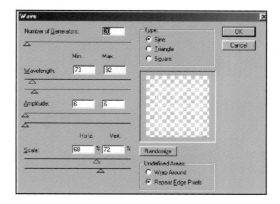

8. Click OK and you have a distorted grid.

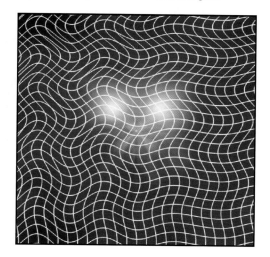

9. Change to Overlay mode and lower the Opacity to 73% to blend in the grid. Here is the result of the layer adjustment, big difference? Got to love those blending modes. I do!

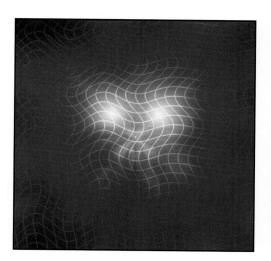

10. Let's fade part of the image. Add a Layer Mask to the grid layer and run a black to white Linear Gradient diagonally. The result shows a nice fade effect to our image.

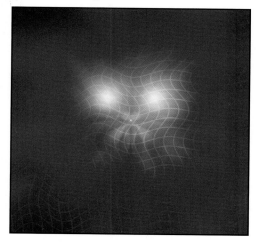

Here I turned it into a CD cover by adding a little bit of text and my picture.

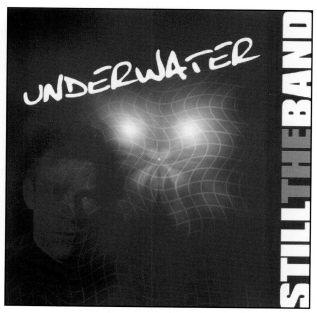

You could try applying different types of effects to the grid to get all kinds of wild and fun results. Don't be afraid to try anything, that's how you learn.

## Displaced grid

This is the last effect we will be doing with the grid and this is the most advanced as well as the coolest. We are going to wrap a grid around an object, with it hugging all the curves. We will achieve this by the use of a displacement map. I chose a piece of fabric to use for this exercise.

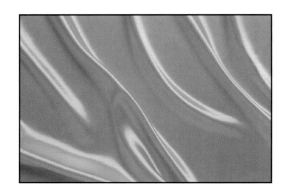

## 7: Creating the map

1. Open the Channels palette.

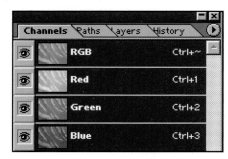

2. Click on each channel in turn and look for the channel with the most contrast. In this case it looks like it's the green channel.

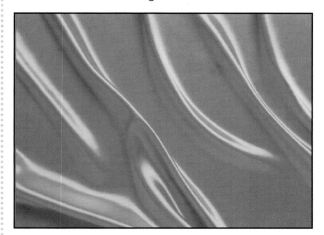

3. Right-click on the channel name and choose Duplicate Channel from the pop up menu.

4. Under Document select New. The channel will now be created as a new document.

5. Add a slight Gaussian Blur to soften the details a little bit.

6. Now save this image as a .psd on your hard disk. Call it map.psd. Close the map.psd document, as we will use this later.

## Applying the map

1. Click on RGB in the Channel palette of the original document to display all the channels again.

2. Create a new layer and name it 'grid'.

3. Go to **Edit>Fill** and choose our grid. Zoom out so we can see the pasteboard area.

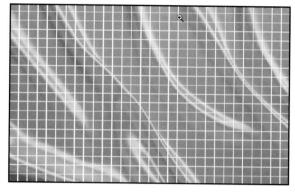

4. Using Free Transform, enlarge the grid a small bit.

5. Let's apply the effect so select **Filter>Distort>Displace**, which will open this dialog box. Default settings will do the job just fine. You will notice there are two options called Stretch to Fit or Tile. This is useful if the document size is different than the image map size. With Stretch to Fit, it will resize the map to the size of the page. Checking the Tile option will retain the size of the map and repeat it on the page.

6. A dialog box will pop up looking for an image to use as a displacement map. Use our map.psd. Like magic the grid will wrap around the cloth!

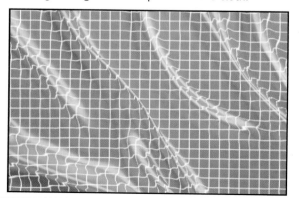

7. Invert the color of the grid (CTRL/CMD+I) for a better effect with this color.

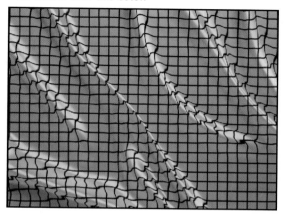

You could apply some text to finish it off. Use the same displacement map for the text.

## 8: Crystals

This has been one of the most popular effects lately. It seems like everyone wants to design those crazy abstract shard crystals. This is how you do it:

1. Begin with a new image as the background, 800X600 RGB will work fine, create a new layer, and call it "crystals". I've used a bright blue background, but this is just personal preference.

2. Choose the **Polygon Lasso** tool. This is the backbone of the entire effect.

3. Begin clicking to form your shards. When you have drawn all the lines click on the start point, you will see a little circle indicating you are at the start/finish point.

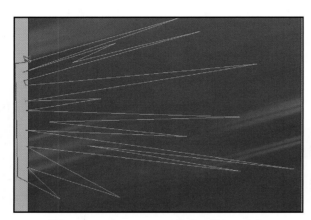

When you close your path it will turn into a selection.

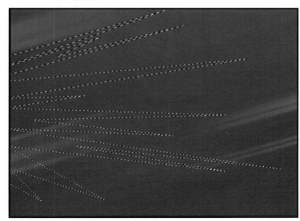

4. Fill with white.

5. Let's add some shading so go to **Select>Modify>Contract** and enter 5.

6. Next, enter 4 into the Feather Selection (**Select>Feather**). You will now see an inner selection

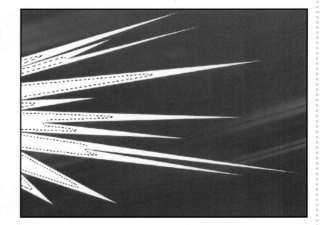

7. Choose a light blue color and fill the shards with the light blue.

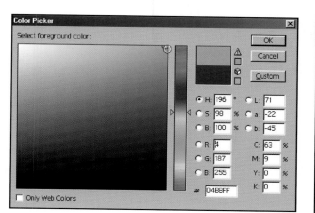

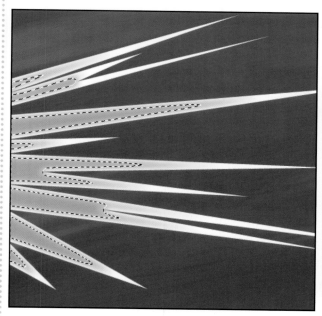

8. Deselect and add a Bevel Layer Style with the following settings:

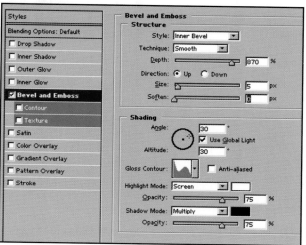

9. In the Blending Options section, reduce the Fill Opacity to give it a semi-transparent look.

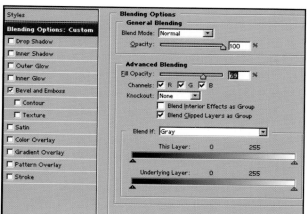

**10.** Click OK and this is what you should see.

**11.** Duplicate the crystals layer and change the top crystals layer to Soft Light Blending Mode.

**12.** Change the bottom one to Hard Light.

**13.** Go back to the Layer Styles and add an Outer Glow to both crystal layers as below:

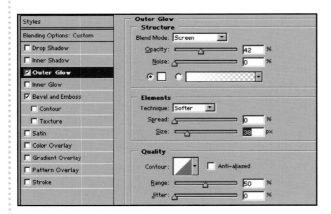

**14.** Reposition the layers so they overlap each other and there you have your crystals.

Try different shapes and bevel types and sizes for different results. Here is one I did previously.

I'm sure you will find that this chapter will open up all kinds of creative doors for your design and art. Start to experiment and apply these effects to your work and you will never have to have a boring image again. This chapter has taught you how to apply effects and patterns and really give your images that high tech look.

# Chapter 12
# One hit wonders

Some of the best songs written came from bands that happened to come across a magic formula that produced a hit single, and then disappeared without a trace. If they ever produced an album it had that one great song on it, then lots of boring filler. The purpose of this book is to get right to the good stuff and avoid all the boring filler. This chapter will look at some great effects that don't really need an entire chapter on each one. I'll present these effects one at a time, show you how to create them and use them, and then move on to the next one and allow you to use your own creative license in modifying and abusing these techniques.

## 1: Graffiti

Ever wanted to do something crazy, like painting a slogan on a national monument? You can be sure you would be hauled off to jail for it. Here's your chance to venture into tagging in the comfort of your own home. It's safe, easy, and moreover, it's legal. I'll show you how to add a graffiti effect to your type and then blend it into an image in a realistic fashion.

1.   Create a new document of 600x200 pixels in RGB mode.

2.   Add some text in a graffiti style scrawl. I used the font TagsXtreme at 60 points. This font can be found at: www.pizzadude.dk, another good source of free fonts is www.1001freefonts.com.

3.   I also increased the letter spacing (kerning) to 50 to allow the font to breathe a bit, as the standard kerning was a bit too tight.

**Info**: *When the text is rasterized, Photoshop no longer sees it as a font, but as a series of shapes, which are therefore editable.*

4. Convert the text layer to a regular layer by right-clicking on the layer name and selecting Rasterize Layer. This step will enable us to add a gradient to our text.

5. Now choose the **Gradient** tool, and open up the **Gradient Editor** by clicking in the gradient window on the Options bar. We're going to mix up a custom gradient like the one shown here. For more info on gradients see Chapter 6.

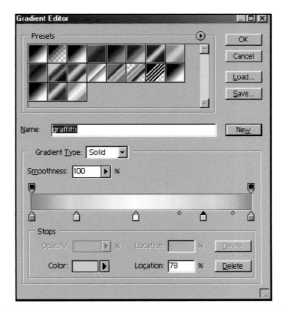

6. Load the text as a selection. CTRL/CMD+click on the layer thumbnail to do this.

7. Select the **Linear Gradient** from the Options bar, and apply the gradient to the text from top to bottom. Don't deselect yet.

8. We are now going to apply a soft gray outline to the text. Create a new layer (CTRL/CMD+N) and call it 'stroke'.

9. Go to **Edit>Stroke** and apply a 3px stroke in light gray, with a setting of **Outside**.

10. Click OK and deselect (CTRL/CMD+D).

11. We will want to soften the gray now, to better represent a sprayed on effect. Select **Filter>Blur>Gaussian Blur** and enter a setting of 0.7 for just a little softening.

12. Now we want to merge the text and the outline together. With the stroke layer still active, click on the box between the thumbnail and the eye icon on the text layer. You should see an icon of a chain. This indicates that the layers are linked.

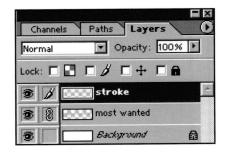

13. Click the arrow on the top right of the Layers palette and choose **Merge Linked** from the drop-down menu. The merged layers will take on the attributes and name of the top most merged layer. Notice it's now called 'stroke'.

14. We are now going to add a black outline; so start by loading the stroke layer as a selection, (CTRL/CMD+click).

15. **Edit>Stroke** adds a 2 pixel black stroke. Again choose the Outside setting.

16. We now have a double outline around our text. Deselect (CTRL/CMD+D) and let's move on to creating a shadow.

17. Duplicate the stroke layer. Load the layer as a selection and fill with black.

**TIP** *A quick way to fill with black: Press D to set the colors to the default black and white, then press ALT/OPTION+DELETE to fill with foreground color.*

18. Move the black layer below the text to the left and down a bit to give a nice tag style shadow. There we go, we have now created a graffiti style effect. Let's look at applying it to images in a couple of ways.

19. Here we have our effect over a background. We merged the two graffiti layers to create this effect.

20. Experiment with the layer blending modes to find the best match for your particular image. In this case I changed it to Hard Light mode. You will have to merge the two graffiti layers before applying layer blending modes.

21. Here is another example of our text on a metal grate effect. You can download this background image, which was also created in Photoshop, from the friends of ED web site www.friendsofed.com/code.

22. This time Overlay mode yielded the most realistic results.

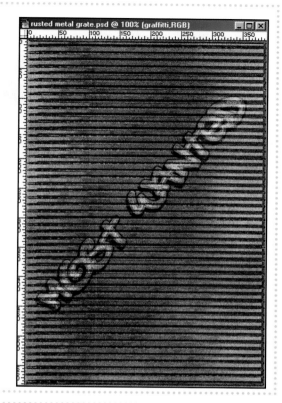

Have fun with this effect and remember; **do** try this effect at home.

## 2: Reflections

Let's take a look at reflections. We will be creating realistic reflections on glass and water. This technique comes in handy in a lot of places, in artwork and photo manipulation and it's also a great effect just for fun. There are two ways of doing it. The first is for an image on a layer and the second way I will show you is for a flattened photo.

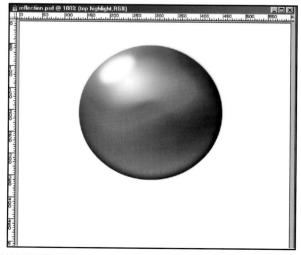

1. Let's begin with our sphere that we created in the last chapter. Of course you can apply this effect to any image. Reposition the sphere so that it sits above the middle of the image.

2. This layer should be called 'sphere', so if this is not already the case, rename the layer by going to **Layer>Layer Properties**, or access Layer Properties via the Layers palette drop-down menu.

3. Create a new layer; name it 'background color' and fill with a gradient.

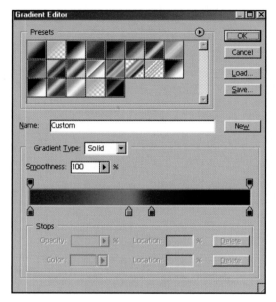

4. Drag the gradient below the sphere. You are now ready to begin the reflection effect. In order to create a convincing reflection we'll duplicate the sphere, flip it, move it, and then fade it.

5. So, the first thing we need to do is duplicate the sphere. Drag the sphere thumbnail into the **New Layer** icon on the Layers palette. A new layer will be created called 'sphere copy'. This will become our reflection.

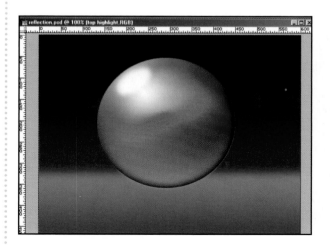

6. To flip the sphere on its y-axis, go to **Edit>Transform>Flip Vertical**, or click CTRL/CMD+T, right-click to get the Free Transform menu, and select Flip Vertical.

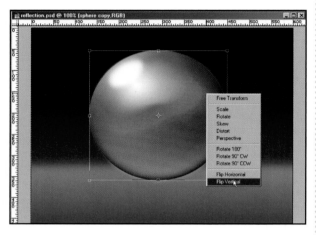

7. Move the new layer until the top is just touching the bottom of the original sphere.

> **TIP** *Holding down the* SHIFT *key constrains this movement to purely vertical.*

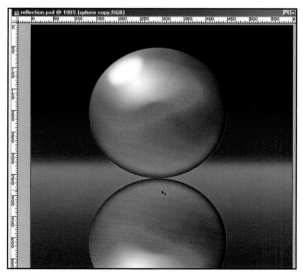

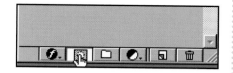

8. The reflected image looks good, now we want to fade it a little bit to get an effect of depth. To achieve this effect, we'll use a layer mask. With the sphere copy layer active, press the **Add Layer Mask** icon.

9. You'll now see a layer mask attached to the reflection layer.

10. Select a Black to White Linear gradient and apply it on the layer mask. Drag from the top of the reflected sphere to the bottom of the document. (Check the Reverse box in the Option bar if the gradients are working in reverse for you.) You should have a bottom-faded effect like seen here.

**INFO:** *The layer mask is a useful utility that affects a layer's transparency in this way: When the mask is filled with white, the layer is opaque, when it is filled with black it is transparent. The different shades of gray will give the image different transparency properties; hence the gradient will produce a smooth transparency blend.*

11. Reapply the gradient until you are satisfied with the result. Click on the layer thumbnail to turn off the mask editing, you should now see the brush icon displayed again. Its important to do this before going on to the next step, otherwise you'll just blur the mask itself rather than the image.

12. Let's tweak it a little to add that extra little something to turn a good image into a great image. Add a 10-pixel motion blur at -90 degrees, **Filter>Blur>Motion Blur**.

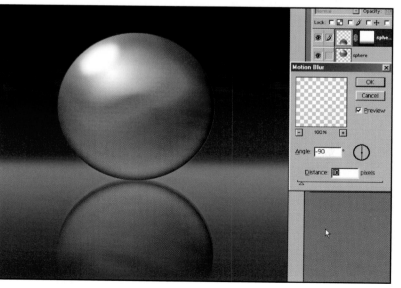

13. We have a pretty good glassy reflection now. What if we don't want glass, but rather liquid? We'll now take this image and add some ripples to it. Before we do this save your completed work as `reflection.psd`.

14. In order to get a consistent ripple we'll have to merge all the layers that will make up the background. With the sphere copy layer still active, link the background color layer by clicking the box to the left of the thumbnail. You will see the little chain icon appear.

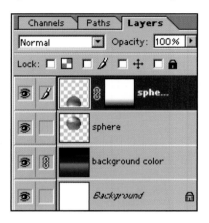

15. Select Merge Linked from the Layers menu and this is what you will see.

16. Drag the background layer beneath the sphere layer and our sphere will reappear.

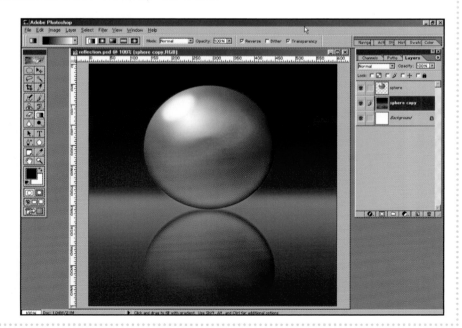

17. To apply the ripple, go to **Filter>Distort>Ocean ripple**. I used a size of 11 and a magnitude of 16.

18. Let's apply a motion blur to the ripple for some realistic looking water. **Filters>Blur>Motion Blur**, set the angle for 0 and the distance for 30 pixels.

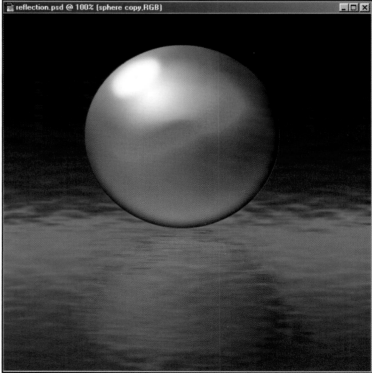

Here is the result of our two-step water process. Save this image, we're going to adapt it a little to create something new.

### 3: Reflections, slight return

1. Our previous sphere is floating just above the water. How about if it was lightly touching the water's surface? Go to the History palette and select the stage where you added the ripple, adjust the size to 13, and the magnitude to 6. We'll have a calmer lake for this one.

2. Make sure that the Background layer is active, and draw an oval around the base of the sphere with the **Elliptical Marquee** tool.

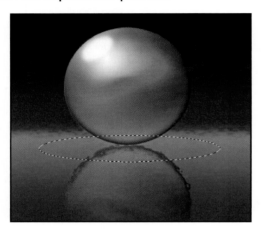

3. Let's feather the selection for a nice soft effect. **S e l e c t > F e a t h e r** (ALT/OPTION+CTRL/CMD+D) and add a setting of 10 pixels.

4. We will now use the **Polar Coordinates** filter. This is a useful little filter designed to re-map pixels from straight to circular and back. It also works on selections as you can see here. **Filters>Distort>Polar Coordinates**; choose **Rectangular to Polar** and click OK, then deselect (CTRL/CMD+D).

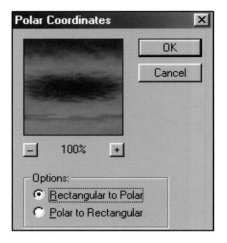

5. Congratulations, you have now added a very cool ripple. It's amazing what you can do with a little tweak and a bit of imagination.

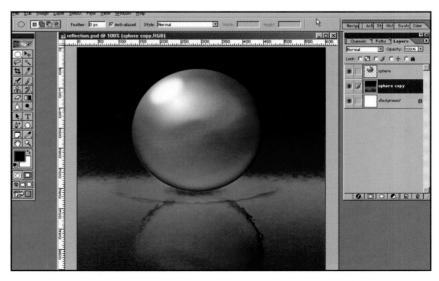

We have now created two types of reflections with an object. Let's quickly look at the different approach we would use with a photo.

## 4: Reflecting a photo

The principles are pretty much the same when it comes to reflecting photos. There is a slightly different approach, so we will move quickly over ground already covered and look at the differences in more detail.

1.  Open up a photographic image of your choice.

> **TIP** *If the photo simply consists of a background layer then you can convert this into a regular, editable layer by double-clicking on the word* **Background**. *You will be prompted to enter a new name, so name your layer and click OK.*

2.  Now we need to increase the canvas size, so we have room to apply our effect, **Image>Canvas Size**. Double the original height and on Anchor click the top center square. This will add the new canvas underneath the original image.

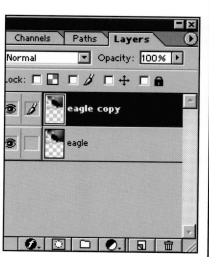

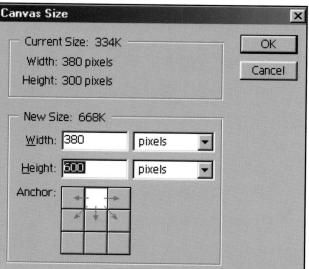

3.  Duplicate the image layer, and then flip the new, duplicated layer vertically. You remember how to flip vertically don't you? CTRL/CMD+T to Free Transform, and then right-click/CTRL+click to access the menu.

4. Reposition the duplicated layer so that it mirrors the original layer, and apply a motion blur to the duplicated layer. I used a 10-pixel blur at an angle of −90 degrees.

5. Click CTRL/CMD+T to select Free Transform, now using the middle top and bottom handles, scale the bottom image vertically so that the image protrudes slightly off the canvas.

6. While still in Free Transform mode, right-click/CTRL-click and select Perspective. The effect we are trying to create is of the reflection spreading slightly as it hits the water. To do this, we'll pull the bottom of the image outwards a little. This is a subtle effect; so don't go too crazy with it. When you are happy, click ENTER/RETURN to apply the transformation.

7. Now let's fade like we did for the reflected sphere. Apply a layer mask to the duplicated layer by clicking on the **Add Layer Mask** icon at the bottom of the Layers palette.

8. Zoom out on the image to change the view size and show more of the canvas. Select a Linear, Foreground to Background gradient; remember this is selected by clicking in the Gradient window of the Options bar. Starting about halfway up the reflected layer, drag all the way down and off the canvas to fade the image into transparency at the bottom.

9. We will want to fill the transparent area with some color to finish off the effect. Create a new layer and call it, 'background'. Drag the new layer to the bottom of the Layers palette.

10. Choose a light blue color in the foreground color picker, and using the **Paint Bucket** tool (G) fill the background layer with the light blue color to complete the glassy, reflected effect.

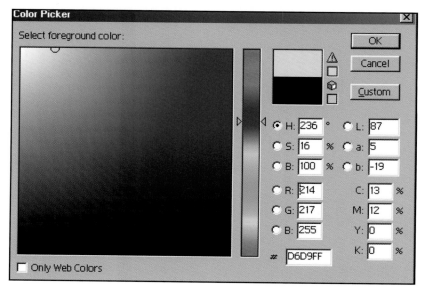

11.  To get the watery reflection, apply the Ripple filter (Size: Medium, Amount: 100%) to the reflected layer.

Our finished image should look something like this.

Hopefully, you've learnt a few new tricks in this chapter, as well as making some great effects, we've also covered a few tips, such as how effective blending modes can be for solving problems that some might attempt to solve the hard way – for example, trying to manually remove the black from around the lightning. Experiment with these effects and create your own. I may have called these techniques one hit wonders, but they'll prove useful to you time and time again. Put the various effects together in different combinations and you'll be amazed at the results.

# Chapter 13
# Collage secrets

In this chapter we are going to take a lot of the elements that you learned in the last six chapters and begin to put them together to produce artwork. We are going to build a wallpaper type composition. These types of images are popular as splash pages for web sites, backgrounds for images, and building blocks for posters. (When I first showed people how to create these effects at my web site, www.photoshopcafe.com, the response was overwhelming.) Collaging is one of the most fun things you can do in Photoshop, and you can easily achieve stunning results by following a few simple techniques. The pace of this chapter will be a little faster than before because we don't want to re-cover too much ground that was explained in detail earlier on in the book.

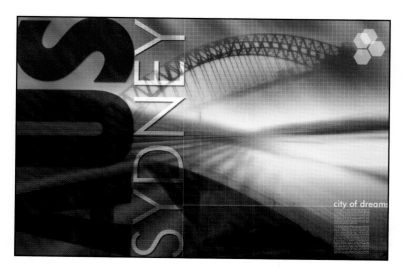

## 1: Splash page collage

### Creating the colored background

**1.** Begin by opening `Waterfall.tif`, which can be found in the Samples folder that loads with Photoshop 6. If you cannot find this image it's not a big problem, you can use any image as a starting point for this exercise. In any case, we are about to alter the image beyond all recognition.

> **INFO:** *If you are using* `Waterfall.tif`, *you may notice that this is a* **16 bit per channel** *image. This is a very high-resolution image, and very few filters will work on it. You will need to convert it to 8 bits, by going to* **Image>Mode>8 Bits/Channel**.

**2.** The first thing we will need to do, is remove most of the detail of the image. Apply a large Gaussian Blur to the image.

**3.** To create a soft, flowing feel we will now apply a Motion Blur, **Filter>Blur>Motion Blur**. Set the Angle to 40 degrees, and the Distance to 166 pixels.

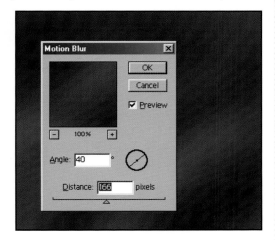

**4.** Now we will change the color. CTRL/CMD+U for the Hue/Saturation menu. Don't click on the Colorize box this time. Adjust the Hue slider until you get a color you like. I went for a purple tint.

We basically have the base for our colored background now. You will notice that it looks nothing like the original already.

**5.** We are now going to create some vibrant colors by using layers and blending modes. Duplicate the background layer, and apply a lens flare to the layer, **Filter>Render>Lens Flare**.

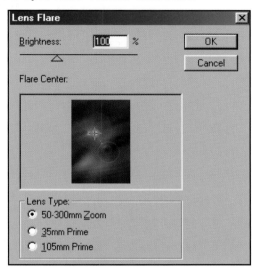

Here is the result. We already have something very celestial looking.

**6.** Let's soften that a little, so go to **Filter>Blur>Radial Blur**, set it for 100 and select the Zoom Blur Method.

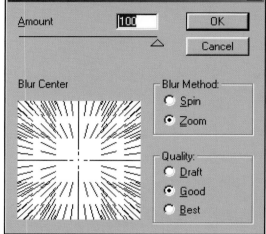

**7.** Change to Screen mode to blend the two layers together. The color is already beginning to come through, and the depth is now really building up.

**8.** Duplicate the layer again, this time change the layer blending to **Color Dodge** mode. We want a really soft effect, so apply the **Radial Blur** again about 10 –15 times.

**TIP:** *To do this quickly keep pressing* CTRL/CMD+F *to reapply the last filter used.*

See how the image just keeps getting more powerful as we add layers.

9. The last step of this four-layer color effect is to duplicate the layer again, and change it to **Soft Light** mode.

10. The combination of these four layers produces some stunning color effects. Merge the four layers into one background layer.

## Stylizing the background

1. Let's add some of the effects we learned earlier on, starting with scanlines we covered in Chapter 11. Create a new scanlines layer and name it as such.

2. Fill with the scanlines pattern. Change to **Overlay** mode and reduce the Opacity to 17%. Click on the **Add a mask** icon at the bottom of the Layers palette, to add a layer mask.

3. Apply a Black to White, Linear Gradient to the layer mask to fade the scanlines out on half of the image.

Here is the result so far.

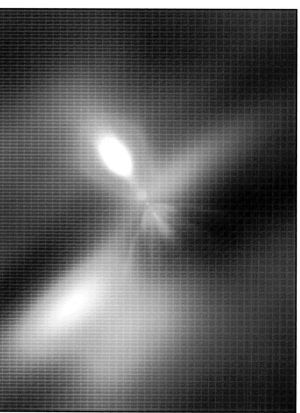

4. Create a new layer and call it, 'grid'. Fill this layer with the grid pattern we created in Chapter 13. Change to Overlay mode and lower the Opacity to 19%.

5. Let's rotate our image 90 degrees, **Image>Rotate Canvas>90° CW**. This will change the orientation for a computer desktop.

6. Apply a layer mask to the grid layer, and apply the gradient again; make it slightly diagonal revealing the bottom right the most.

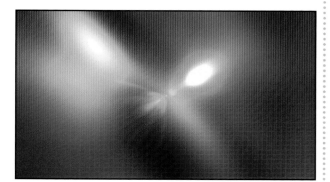

## Adding a point of focus

Any good design should have a point of focus. This is the dominant part of the image that draws the eye. You may choose to feature a product if you are doing advertising design. Just for fun we have used the sphere that we created in Chapter 10. The source file is included for download at the friends of ED web site. It's called `Sphere.psd`.

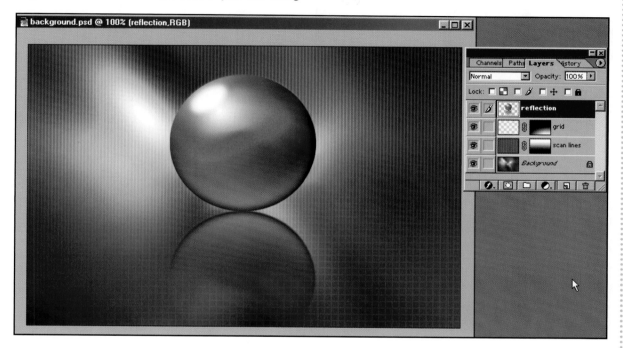

## Fonts

One of the secrets to good layout is type. Choosing the correct typeface will make or break an image. You'll see that I've used a plain font that doesn't fight for attention within the image, the colors I've chosen are the simplest: black and white, with no effects at all. This creates a contrast with the highly colored image. Contrast is crucial to good design.

Since we are using soft curves, sharp lines, and a clean, modern feel to our design, a matching typeface like Futura will work perfectly. Here I've used contrasting fonts together. If you are going to mix fonts, it's a good idea to use very different fonts; the fat, extended typeface fits really well with the thin condensed font.

Both are from the Futura family, if you don't have the Futura font, you'll find that Arial is similar, and just about every computer has it loaded as a default font.

> *INFO: This book is all about effects, and we've covered all of our favorites in these pages, but don't be tempted to add effects just for the sake of it. Clean images are more powerful because they don't confuse the eye.*

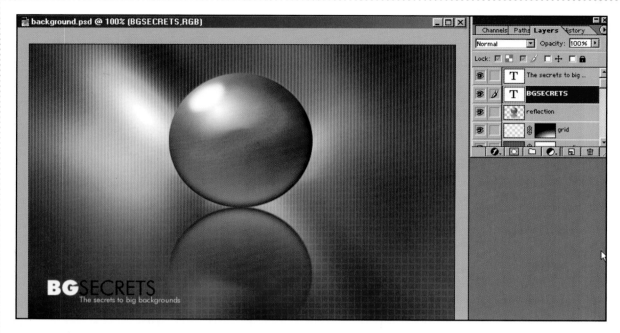

1.  Let's make the grid wavy; remember we covered this in Chapter 13. Select the grid layer, and go to **Filter>Distort>Wave**.

2.  Use the default settings in the Wave dialog box, or experiment with your own.

3.  Here is the image with the wavy grid. Move the grid if you need to hide any edges.

## Shaping things up

This is a simple little effect that adds a lot to a layout. We are going to add a few little hexagons.

1. Create a new layer and name it: 'shapes'. Set white as your foreground color.

2. Choose the **Polygon** tool, (U). Change the Sides to 6 and select the **Create filled region** option.

3. Drag out a small hexagon shape. As soon as you release the mouse button the shape will be filled with white. Hold down the SHIFT key while dragging to keep the hexagon at a straight angle.

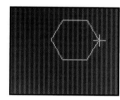

4. Lower the Opacity to 32%. We are going to create semi-transparent shapes with solid borders.

5. Create a new layer and name it, 'outline'. Load the selection from the 'shapes' layer by CTRL/CMD clicking on the shapes thumbnail.

6. Making sure the outline layer is active, add a 1 pixel Stroke (**Edit>Stroke**) to the shape. Here is the desired result:

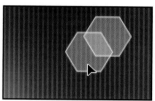

7. Merge the shape and outline layers together.

8. Duplicate the shape layer and arrange in a pattern.

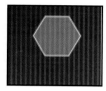

> **TIP:** *To make a duplicate of a layer, hold down the ALT/OPTION key and drag the object. You'll notice a double arrow; this indicates you are dragging a copy.*

9. Keep duplicating the shapes until you have built up a little cluster.

BG SECRETS
The secrets to big backgrounds

229

## Adding lines for effect

We are now going to create some single pixel lines for effect. Lines are a useful design trick, used to guide the eye around an image. They can be creative and strategic at the same time.

1. Create some more type, and rotate it.

2. Create a new layer and call it, 'lines'.

3. Select the **Single Row Marquee** tool; this tool is great for making thin lines, as it selects only 1 pixel tall.

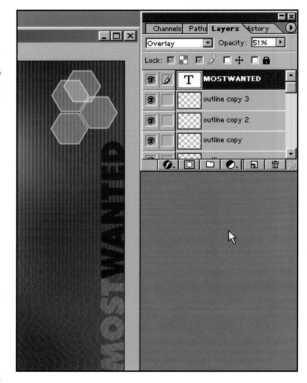

4. Drag the selection to the bottom of the type. Fill with white and deselect. Notice how this draws a really clean line.

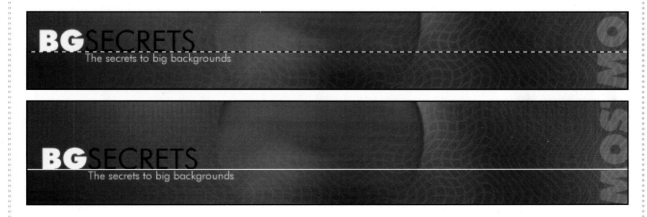

**5.** Add another line to the right side, switch to the **Single Column Marquee** tool, which selects areas just one pixel wide, and fill. The only drawback with this method is that it draws lines across the full page. The solution is to make a selection around the areas you want to delete with the Rectangular Marquee tool.

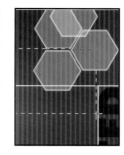

**6.** Press the DELETE key to clear unwanted portions.

## Tiny text

A recent trend is to take a section of text and reduce its size to the extent that it is too tiny to read. This is a great technique that can add a lot of interest; it really makes the design look technical.

1. Open a text editor (for example Word, or Apple Text) or a web browser, and load some text into it. Select a portion of text and CTRL/CMD+C to copy it to the clipboard.

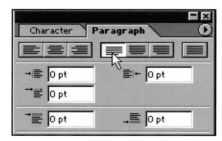

2. In Photoshop select the **Type** tool and choose a small, condensed font. I am using Futura BT.

3. In the Paragraph palette, choose the **Justify last left** alignment option.

4. Make a text box for the paragraph text, by clicking and dragging the Type tool. Place the cursor inside the box and paste the text, CTRL/CMD+V.

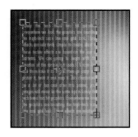

5. You could make it even smaller if you so desire, by dragging the corner of the text box.

Here is the final background collage. The possibilities are endless. Once again, my advice is to experiment as much as possible. You can come up with endless variations. The purpose of this book is not only to show you some cool examples but to open up new doors of possibilities to your imagination.

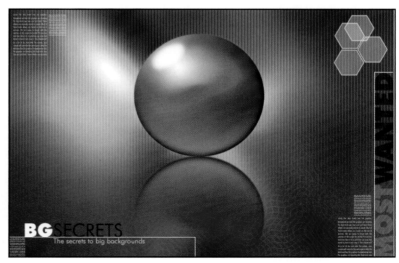

## 2: Advanced collaging techniques with photos

We have just looked at creating background collages. Now, we are going to do something a little different, but along a similar approach. We are going to create a high-resolution collage using photographs. These photos are at 300 dpi, which is printing resolution.

The photos that we'll use for this image are located on the friends of ED web site, they are: `Australia 1.tif`, `Australia 2.tif`, and `Australia 3.tif`. Open all three images in Photoshop. We are going to create a composition out of the pictures that could be used as the front of a travel brochure or a postcard. I have entitled this composition, 'City Of Dreams'.

1. We will be using the image of the steps as our base for the collage. Save this document as, `collage.psd`, and convert the background layer to a regular layer by double-clicking on its name. Call this new layer, 'steps'.

2. Drag the image of the Opera House into the base image. Now do the same with the Sydney Harbor Bridge.

3. You should now have three layers. Rename the last two, 'bridge' and 'opera house' accordingly.

4. Now that all the important images are in one document, close all other documents in Photoshop, to optimize its performance. Let's begin collaging.

5. Hide the bridge and opera house layers. Select the steps layer. Apply a 100 Radial Blur, **Filter>Blur>Radial Blur**, and choose the Zoom Blur Method. I love the result this filter has on the image.

## Blending images

1. Show and select the opera house layer. Transform the image( CTRL/CMD+T). Flip horizontal, resize, and position the image into the bottom right side.

2. Add a layer mask and select it.

3. Using a soft Airbrush set to black, begin to paint around the image. You will notice that black will paint away the image. This is the functionality of a layer mask. When you paint black, the image will disappear, when you paint white, you will paint the image back in.

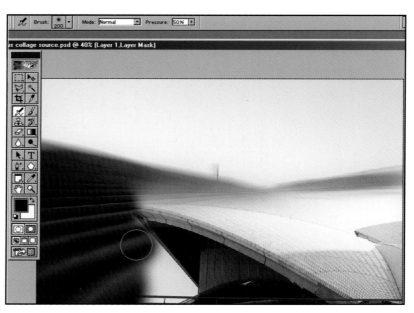

4. Continue painting until you have painted away all the excess, and are only left with the shape of the opera house.

5. To complete the blending effect, change the layer blending mode to Overlay and lower the Opacity to 80%. See how smoothly the images blend together:

6. The only drawback is that we have lost some detail in the opera house image. We can enhance the tones in the image to bring back some detail using **Image>Adjust>Levels** (CTRL/CMD+L). Adjust as shown in the screenshot.

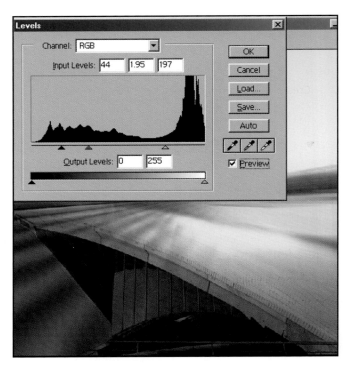

7. Notice that there is a lot of boring white sky in the steps layer. Apply a layer mask, then using the Linear Gradient tool, White to Black, apply the gradient to fade the steps to transparent.

Your image should look like this. We are going to create some interesting sky effects to put underneath the image.

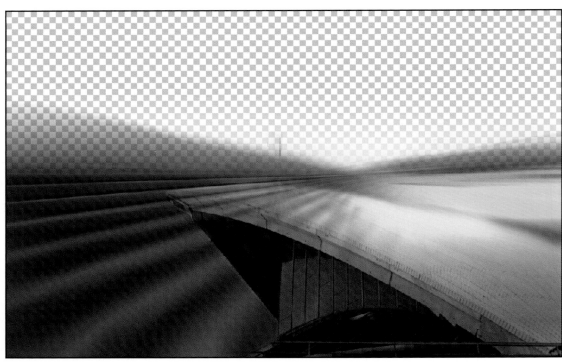

8. Set the foreground to blue, and the background to white.

9. Create a new layer, move it to the bottom, and apply the clouds filter (**Filter>Render>Clouds**) to the new layer.

10. Add a large motion blur to the clouds, so the texture complements the steps. Go to **Filters>Blur>Motion Blur** and use a setting of 426 pixels, and angle of –50 degrees.

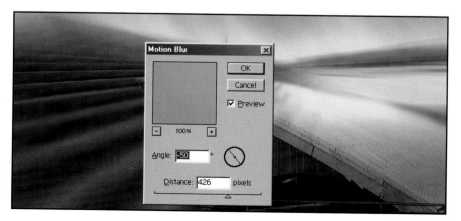

**11.** Show and select the bridge layer. Press CTRL/CMD+T to rotate and scale the bridge until it is at an angle. Press ENTER/RETURN to apply the transformation.

**12.** Now we need to blend the bridge into the rest of the image. We are going to use a combination of the gradient and airbrush method. Apply a layer mask to the bridge layer.

**13.** Use a gradient to blend the bottom of the bridge in to the image. It's important to apply the gradient first, and then touch up with the airbrush, otherwise the gradient will undo all the airbrush work.

**14.** Take a large soft airbrush and paint away the top of the bridge.

15. Drag the bridge layer underneath the steps layer, and switch to Luminosity mode. This will make the bridge take on the color attributes of the blue background layer and provide a smoother blend without getting too busy with the color.

Here is the result so far. We have finished blending the objects; the next step is to affect the color.

*This is one of the potential traps of collaging; don't allow the colors to clash with each other.*

## Pulling the composition together with color

1. Make a duplicate layer of the steps and bring it to the top. Change to Overlay mode. We are going to use this as a color layer to help simplify the colors in the composition.

2. Go to **Image>Adjust>Hue/Saturation**, (CTRL/CMD+U), and click the Colorize option. Crank the Saturation all the way to the right for maximum color depth, increase the Lightness a little bit, and change the Hue until you get a nice warm orange color. I like the way the cool blue of the sky contrasts with the warm orange.

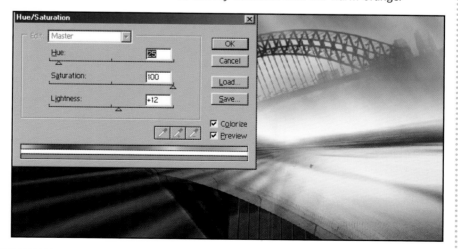

3. I think we need to strengthen the blue to properly contrast the orange. Click **Image>Adjust>Levels**, (CTRL/CMD+L). Move the shadow (left) slider to the right, this will darken the blue. Move the mid tone slider to the right also, this will deepen the blue.

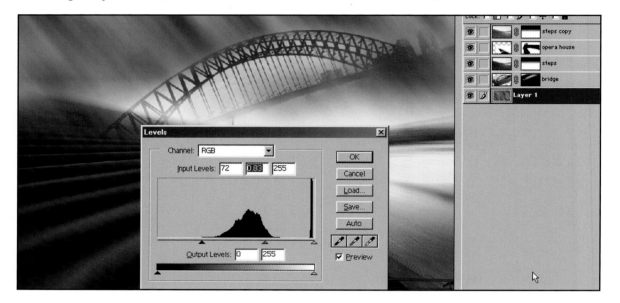

## Creating a composite layer

We are now going to take all the images from all the layers and place them all together in one layer without flattening the image. This is called a composite layer.

1. Create a new layer at the top of the layers stack and name it, 'composite'.

2. In the Layers menu, select Merge Visible, but hold down the ALT/OPTION key as you click it and instead of the layers being flattened a composite layer will be created. This is a very useful trick indeed!

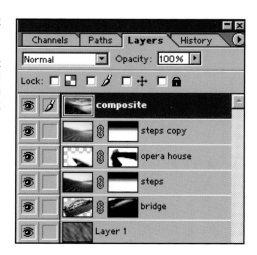

Here is our collage so far, with the composite layer on top. In order to soften our collage, we are going to blur this and blend it with the image underneath.

3.  Apply a 7 pixel Gaussian Blur (**Filter> Blur>Gaussian Blur**) to the composite layer, and reduce the Opacity to 50%. See how this helps to smoothen the blending without sacrificing image detail.

## Adding decorative elements

**1.** Create a new layer called, 'scanlines'. Apply our scanline pattern that we created in an earlier chapter. Change to Screen mode and lower the Opacity to 25%.

**2.** Apply a layer mask and apply a linear gradient to fade out the scan lines from the right of the image.

**3.** Let's add a grid. Create a new layer and name it, 'grid'. Fill with our grid pattern, change to Overlay mode and reduce the opacity to 30%.

**4.** Apply a layer mask, and using the linear gradient, fade the grid to the left.

**5.** Now let's create some type, type the letters AUS in black with a large, bold font. Type the word Sydney in white, using a thin font, make it the same width as the AUS and move it underneath.

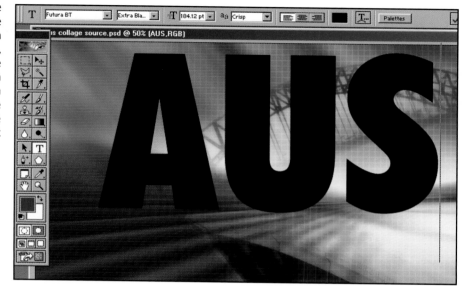

**6.** Link the two text layers together.

**7.** Rotate, and if necessary scale down, the text and place it to the hard left, notice that the linked layers will be transformed together.

**8.** Change the Sydney text layer to Overlay mode. This allows the color to bleed through from underneath.

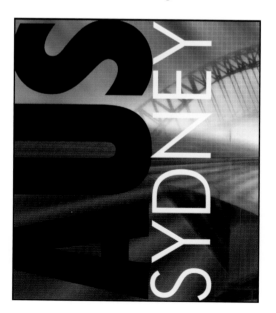

**9.** Lower the Opacity of the AUS layer to 65%, to let some of the image beneath show through.

Last touch for the text is to apply a default Drop Shadow layer style to both type layers. This helps readability.

## Adding lines

**1.** Create a new layer and name it, 'lines'. Using the Single Row Marquee Tool, select and fill with white, just like we did in the previous tutorial. Select the unwanted areas and delete the excess lines.

**2.** Here are the lines added to the page, this really helps break up the image.

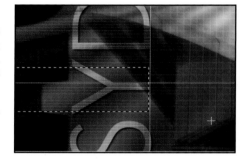

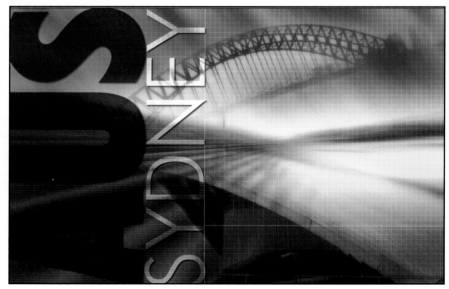

## Selective colorizing with adjustment layers

1. Make a selection around the bottom right of the image. We're going to recolor this section.

**INFO:** *One of the good things about adjustment layers is that they affect all the layers underneath them, so the colorizing will be consistent.*

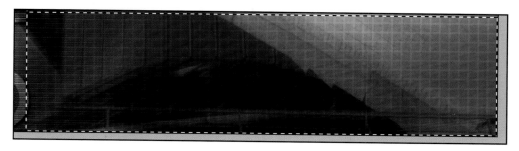

2. In the Layers palette click on the little button which is a half white and half black circle. Choose Hue/Saturation.

3. Click Colorize and change the hue to a gray/blue color. Set the Hue slider to 207, the Saturation to 35, and the Lightness to −5.

4. You will see that an adjustment layer has been created for you. Move this layer under the 'lines' layer so that the color of the lines is not changed.

## Adding shapes

1. How could a collage be complete without a few of those cute little shapes? Create a new layer and name it, 'shapes'.

2. Select the Polygon Shape tool, set the Sides to 6 and the mode to **Create filled region**.

3. Draw a small hexagon and lower the Opacity to 60%.

4. Duplicate the shape a few times and arrange in a pattern.

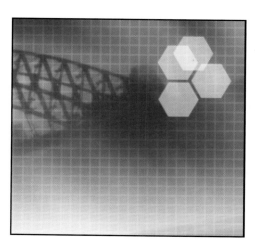

245

## Finishing touches

1. Let's add a bit more type. Choose the same font we used for the word Sydney. This time make it smaller like 10 points.

2. Type the words, 'city of dreams' all in lowercase, move this to the far right and perch it right on the line.

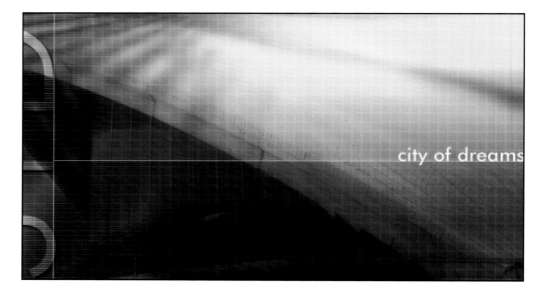

3. Our last task is to add some of the infamous **tiny text**. Choose the same font we have just used but lower the size to 1.5 points

4. Finish some text and copy it to the pasteboard. With the Type tool selected, drag a text box and paste our paragraph text in it.

**5.** If you need more text, just keep pasting the same text. It should be so small no-one can read it anyway, but watch everyone try! It's fun.

Phew! We have finally done it!

The collage is complete. Give yourself a pat on the back. These techniques you've just learned will stand you in good stead for years to come. It has taken me many moons to develop the techniques that I use. That's the beauty of books; you have the chance to assimilate someone else's knowledge in a short space of time.

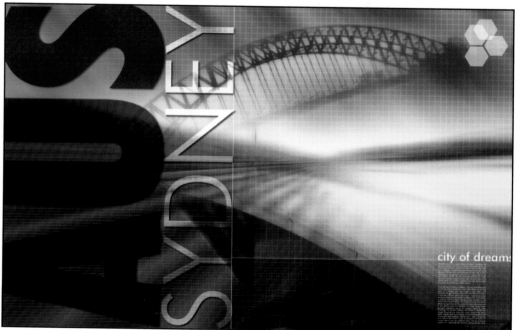

In this chapter we have covered a few real-world design techniques from composition to typography, taking in new trends along the way such as tiny text. I hope you have found the collages a good springboard to your own designs, we will continue to explore more real-world design issues over the next few chapters. Al and I will join forces to create three different projects. By now you've probably noticed that Al and I have different styles. Al is very heavily into layer styles, and gadgets and I am more into the layers, and channels. It's going to be fun, so see you next chapter.

# Design project 1
# Web page interface

Collaboration is very common in the design community, and it often leads to innovative results as each person will have their own take on a situation. Al and I are going to come together in these next three chapters and work with you on some real world projects. This should be interesting to see what we come up with. You will learn different ways of applying effects already covered and discover some new ones. You will also get a peek inside our minds to see how we think and see two different approaches coming together in harmony (hopefully).

The first project we are going to work on is designing a web page interface. We are going to show you how to build it in Photoshop. If you wanted to add some interactive features, then check out the techniques covered in Chapter 10.

## 1: Creating the interface

1. Begin with a new document. I made this one 1200X800, with a resolution of 100 ppi and RGB color. This is a lot bigger than you would use for a web page normally, but I wanted you to really see what is going on. When you are finished you can reduce the finished document to half the size. This is a technique employed by some interface designers as it allows you to create some very fine detail.

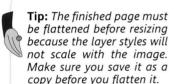

**Tip:** *The finished page must be flattened before resizing because the layer styles will not scale with the image. Make sure you save it as a copy before you flatten it.*

2. Press CTRL/CMD+R to view the Rulers and then drag out some guides to help with the sizing of the interface, like below:

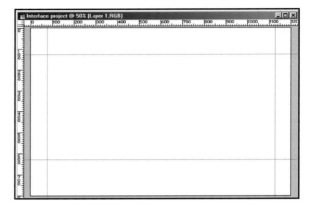

## Smooth rounded corners

We are going to create the outline shape with rounded corners.

1. Create a new layer (SHIFT+CTRL/CMD+N) and call it 'base', this will be our outside box.

2. Choose the **Rounded Rectangle** tool and set the radius for 40px.

3. Choose black as the foreground color, press D to reset the default colors. Draw the shape to fit within the guides. CTRL/CMD+click in the layer thumbnail to load the shape as a selection

4. Create a new layer and call it 'inside base'. This will be the inside box for our interface and will have a different shape than the outside.

5. We are creating a smaller box for the inside so with the new layer active and the selection still turned on, **Select>Modify>Contract** the selection and enter 25.

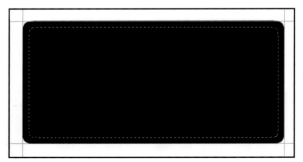

6. Open the Channels palette and click on the new channel button. Our selection will be loaded into alpha 1. Fill (**Edit>Fill**) with white.

**Tip:** *Press SHIFT+BACKSPACE/DELETE to open the fill dialog box and choose white under the Use menu.*

7. Here is our shape in the channel. Deselect (CTRL/CMD+D).

8. We want this shape to bulge a little bit. Go to **Filter>Distort>Pinch**. Choose an amount of -14%.

9. Click OK and see how our shape looks now.

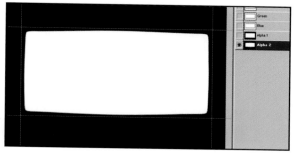

10. Load the channel as a selection by CTRL/CMD+clicking on the channel's thumbnail.

11. Go back to the Layers palette and choose the inside base layer. Fill (SHIFT+BACKSPACE/DELETE) with white, then deselect.

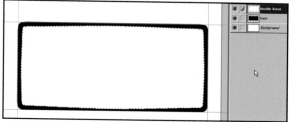

## Adding extra shapes

Now we are going to add some shapes. We are going to use these shapes to cut holes in our interface.

1. Create a new layer called 'cutout'.

2. Draw a rectangle with the **Rectangular Marquee** tool and fill (**Edit>Fill**) with black.

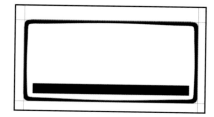

3. Select the **Rounded Rectangle** tool and choose a setting of 20.

4. Draw a rounded rectangular shape on the same 'cutout' layer, this will become our screen later on.

5.  Using the **Elliptical Marquee** tool, draw a circle and fill it with black.

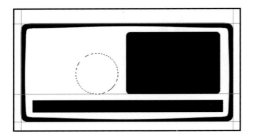

6.  Create a duplicate circle the easy way: Without deselecting, hold down the ALT/OPTION key and click and drag a copy of the circle. Deselect.

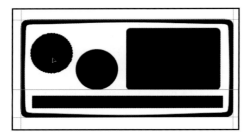

7.  Use the **Polygon Lasso** tool to join the circles.

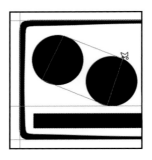

> **INFO:** *To use this tool, just click and when you click again a line will be drawn between the two points. When you click back on the start point a little circle will be displayed signaling you are about to complete your selection.*

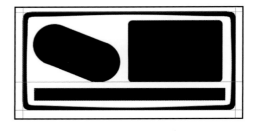

8.  Fill (**Edit>Fill**) the selection with black.

## Rounding the corners

1.  Load the entire layer as a selection by CTRL/CMD+clicking on the layer thumbnail. You will see the marching ants to indicate a selection is active.

2.  Create a new channel in the Channels palette. It will be called 'alpha 2' because there is a selection, the selected areas are automatically filled with white. Press CTRL/CMD+D to deselect.

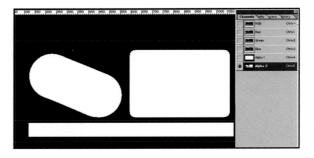

3.  Apply a Gaussian Blur to soften the edges (**Filter>Blur>Gaussian Blur**) with a setting of 10.

4.  We will now sharpen the edges again, using the **Levels** tool (**Image>Adjust>Levels**). Slide the three triangles until they are together. This effect is created by squeezing the tonal range of the channel.

**Tip:** *The placement of the arrows determines the size of the shapes. The further left the arrows meet the larger the shapes will be.*

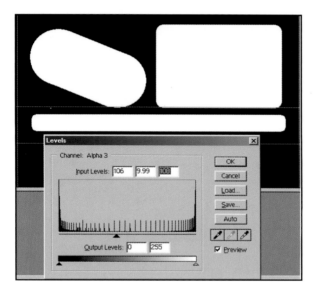

5. We now want to combine our shape with the inside base image that is on 'alpha 1' channel. To do this, make alpha 1 active and CTRL/CMD+click on the 'alpha 2' thumbnail. You should see a selection like this:

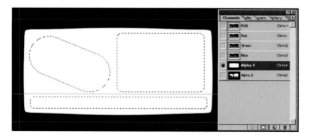

6. Press the DELETE key to cut out the selections and create your template.

7. Deselect your channel. We are now going to create a bump map, so we can combine it with the lighting effects to produce some 3D effects. As a good practice leave your template channel intact in case we need to use it later. So make a duplicate of the channel for us to work on. The new channel will be called 'alpha 1 copy'.

8. By blurring the channel it will rearrange the grayscale pixels around the edges and give us the base for a 3D texture. Select **Filter>Blur>Gaussian Blur** and enter a setting of 7.3.

9. Let's create our shape layer. Create a new layer and name it 'shape'.

10. Load the selection from the 'base' layer. While the 'shape' layer is active, CTRL/CMD+click on the 'base' layer thumbnail

11. Fill (SHIFT+BACKSPACE/DELETE) the selection with 50% gray in the 'shape' layer.

12. Deselect. Let's get the 3D look with the lighting effects now. Go to **Filter>Render>Lighting Effects**. Load the 'alpha 1' channel as our Texture Channel and duplicate the settings as you see here.

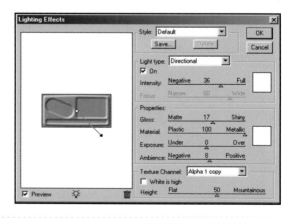

Here is the effect applied to the 'shape' layer:

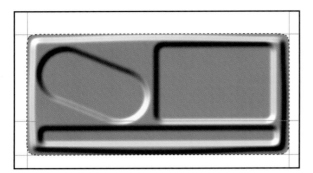

13. Let's trim up the faceplate now. With the 'shape' layer active, load the selection (CTRL/CMD+click) from the 'inside base' layer. Invert the selection (CTRL/CMD+SHIFT+I) and press DELETE.

14. Now let's do the same steps to cut out the shapes from the inside. With the 'shape' layer active, load the selection from the 'cutout' layer. Press DELETE to remove the unwanted portions of the faceplate ('shape' layer) and deselect. Here is the base for the interface.

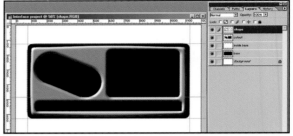

Let's hand it over to Al now to see what he will do with it.

## 2: Enhancing the faceplate

It looks like Colin has a great start on what appears to be a car stereo. Time to give this slab a face-lift! What better way to do that? You guessed it. Time to open up the Layer Styles.

1. To get this moving, I'm starting with a Bevel. Take a look at the edges of the faceplate. Most car stereos have a stark edge around the perimeter. The Bevel and Emboss Layer Styles settings have a feature called **Contour** that will handle this nicely.

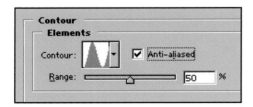

2. When applying the Contour, use the 'Ring' preset found in the default contours set. Now we can set the rest of the standard bevel values.

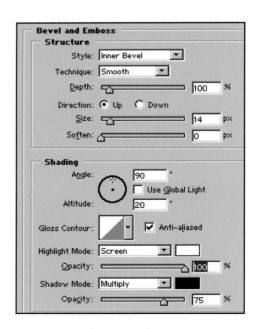

The edges of the interface now appear to be pinched, with a light metallic sheen thanks to the Bevel and the application of the Ring Contour.

3.  Let's apply some character to the face. Duplicate the layer we have been working on (the 'shape' layer). Let's call this new layer 'texture-iface'.

4.  First, let's tweak the Bevel settings just a bit. These might change from time to time as we begin applying settings, because we want them to blend well together and that is hard to do the first time out of the gate.

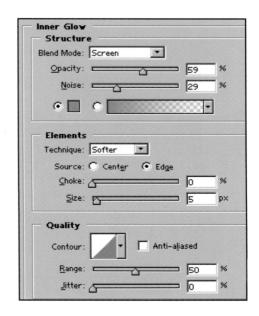

So how do we increase the realistic feel of the faceplate? You may be considering finding some cool texture image to overlay on the stereo, but in reality we need only apply an Inner Glow.

An inner glow? How could that possibly help us texture the interface? Check this out.

5.  Bring up the Inner Glow options in the Layer Styles. Choose a tan/brown, set the mode to Screen (it should be there already by default). Now bump up the noise and increase the size, but decrease the opacity.

## 3: LED

Let's step away from the faceplate for a bit, and play with what will be the display. When Colin approached me with this style of interface, he also sent an example of a real stereo to get inspiration from. That stereo had a very interesting display, as seen in the capture here.

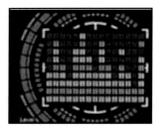

What catches my eye in the example is the chopped double ring around the central display. After a nanosecond of thought, I realized this would be remarkably easy to recreate in just a few steps.

I don't really want to mess with the entire interface and all its layers, so to create the effect I'll do it in a new document and cut/paste it back into the interface.

1. To begin, I'll create a new image (CTRL/CMD+N) that is 5X5 inches with a resolution of 100 dpi, is RGB and transparent. We won't need a background, so all of our work can be done in a single layer.

2. Select the Rectangular Marquee tool. In the Marquee Options bar, click the **Add to Selection** button.

3. Create two long, thin rectangular horizontal selections. Make the lower one slightly wider and longer than the one above. Fill both with black so you have two black lines covering nearly the entire width of the new image.

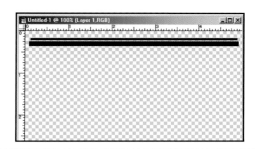

4. Make a narrow vertical selection crossing both lines vertically just inside the left hand side of the marks. Delete the selection so that a space appears. Using the SHIFT+RIGHT ARROW, move the tool and repeat. Do this until the lines are divided across the page.

I've shown you how to do it this way or we could have used a pattern, which Colin prefers.

5. We want these two lines to be just above center. If you were to divide the document vertically, move the lines so that there is about 30% of the images blank space above the lines, 70% below.

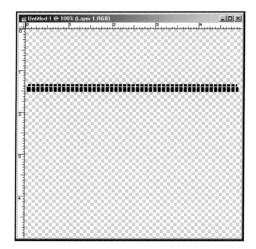

6. Go to **Filter>Distort>Polar Coordinates**. Select Rectangular to Polar and click OK.

7. Take a look at the other image. If your circle appears too small for the display (or too large) go to **Edit>Transform> Scale** and resize it accordingly.

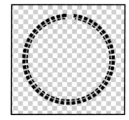

8. Make a selection around the circle and copy it (CTRL/CMD+C).

9.  Go back to the interface image. Create a new layer above the texture layer and paste the circle into the interface.

10. Move the circle into the display area. I am going to make this visible by applying a simple Color Overlay in the Layer Styles for this layer.

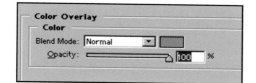

11. Now to chop the circle in two. Using the Rectangular Marquee tool, select the right half of the circle. Go to **Layer>New>Layer via Cut** (SHIFT+CTRL/CMD+J).

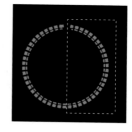

12. Using the arrow keys, move the right half to the right, separating the two portions so we can place the graphical equalizer between the two halves.

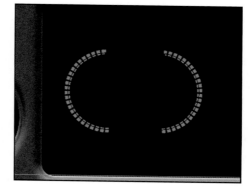

Now let's send it back to Colin and see what other goodies he can come up with!

## 4: Adding buttons to the display

I love the texture and the beginnings of the display. I think we will add two things before we give it back to Al. Let's create a row of buttons and a spectrum analyzer in the display.

Before we do anything, let's do a little housework. We are going to organize the layers into layer sets for ease of getting around. A friend told me that organized people are just too lazy to look for things. That's a different way of looking at things, but in this case we will make it a bit easier to find our layers.

1.  I renamed the two display layers as 'LED L' and 'LED R'. We are going to group them together into a layer set. We will use this set as a sub folder for all the images used on the display, this will help keep them all together.

2.  With LED L active, click the **Link Layer** box on the LED R layer. You will see the little chain indicating the two layers are linked.

3.  In the drop-down menu in the Layers palette, select **New Set from linked.** A dialog box will pop up asking for a name for the new set. Name it 'display'. Click OK and you will see a new folder in the Layers palette that contains the LED layers.

You can click on the little arrow to expand and collapse the set.

4. Now, let's create the buttons. First create a new layer set and call it 'buttons'. We will keep all the images pertaining to the buttons in this set.

5. Within the 'buttons' layer set, create a new layer and call it 'bottom buttons'. This is where we will make our frame for the buttons. We will want to select the hole in the bottom of the faceplate.

*Here is a great little trick for making selections really fast. With the 'bottom buttons' layer still active, choose the **Magic Wand** tool. In the tool bar click on **Use All Layers**. This will make the Magic Wand treat the Photoshop document as an entire document and ignore what layer is active at the time.*

Click inside the space in the bottom area with the Magic Wand and notice it makes a selection even though that layer isn't active? This is a great time saver.

6. Fill the selection in the bottom buttons with 50% gray (**Edit>Fill>50% Gray**). There we go, we have the beginnings of the place where we will make our buttons.

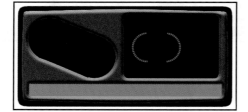

Let's apply a layer style to the area. Rather than create a new one this time, let's use the one that Al created for the 'shape' layer. We can just drag and drop a layer style from any layer to any other layer and that effect will be duplicated on the new layer.

7. Click on the word Effects in the 'shape' layer.

8. Drag and drop it on the 'bottom buttons' layer and the layer style will be reproduced.

Here is what it looks like:

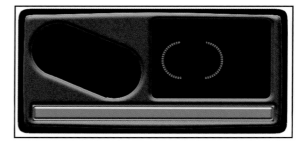

Let's take advantage of the flexibility of layer styles to create our buttons.

9. Duplicate the 'bottom buttons' layer. We will modify this new layer and use it for the buttons by cutting it up a bit and using the layer styles.

10. Drag out some guides to give us an idea of where our buttons will go. We are going to create four buttons.

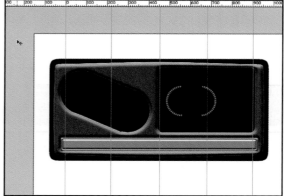

11. Make a selection with the Rectangular Marquee tool, make the selection cut into the top of our panel.

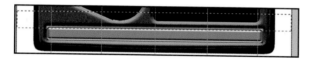

12. Press the DELETE key to cut the top off the layer. You will notice that the layer style automatically adapts to the new edge. This is what we are going to be taking advantage of.

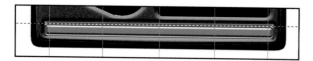

13. Make a selection that cuts into the bottom of the layer and press DELETE.

14. Do the same thing for the left and right edges.

Note: We could have achieved the same result by just scaling the layer, but I want you to get used to the selecting and deleting method too.

15. Now we want to separate the thin bar into four segments that will become buttons. Make a thin rectangular selection at the middle of the second guide.

16. Press DELETE to separate the two sections and don't deselect. Rather, use the arrow keys on your keyboard to move the selection over to the

next guide. If you hold down the SHIFT key, the selection will move faster.

17. When the selection is at the next guide, press the DELETE key once again.

18. Repeat one more time to complete the button separation.

19. Do you think the bevels are too big on the buttons? Well here is a neat trick:

> **TIP:** *Right-click on the layer style symbol at the bottom of the Layers palette and you will see an option called **Scale Layer Effects**, click this. You will now be faced with a new dialog box. As you change the settings, all the effects on any selected layer will be scaled proportionally. This is a tool I use all the time.*

Drop the Scale down to 60% and notice the difference we have on our buttons. The shape is looking good, so let's make the buttons look like buttons.

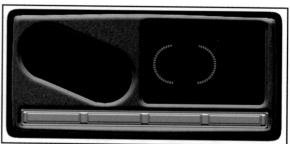

20. Open the Layer Styles box on the 'buttons' layer by double-clicking on the 'f' symbol. Choose Gradient Overlay and make a new gradient as seen below.

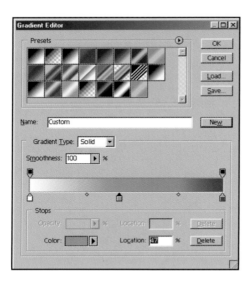

21. Then use the settings as shown here. Make the Scale 64%.

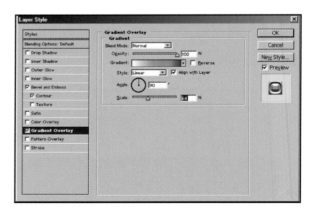

22. Click OK to apply the layer style and watch the buttons come to life.

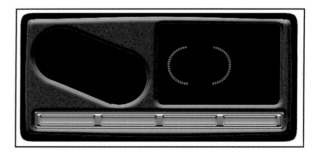

23. To finish off the buttons, add some text. Make sure all these new layers are created in the 'buttons' layer set to stay organized.

## 5: Creating the spectrum analyzer meter

Al did such a wonderful job of the circle in the display. Let's finish off the meter.

1. Create a new layer and name it 'meter'.

2. Using the Elliptical Marquee tool, make a selection just a bit smaller than the ring.

Remember to hold the SPACEBAR down to move the selection as you draw it.

3. Fill the selection with black. Don't deselect yet.

4. Let's make our little squares. Open the fill dialog box again but this time choose Pattern and select the grid pattern that we created in Chapter 13. Click OK. You will see our selection filled with a grid. Let's make them squares.

5. Press CTRL/CMD+I to invert the selection. If your result doesn't look anything like this and the grid disappears, then you forgot to fill with black before you applied the grid.

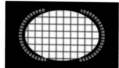

6. Remember when we used the blur and levels to soften the corners of the interface in the channels? We are going to use the same technique to turn the grid into squares. Apply a 2.4 pixel Gaussian blur (**Filter>Blur>Gaussian blur**).

7. Now adjust the Levels (CTRL/CMD+L) to sharpen the edges and create squares.

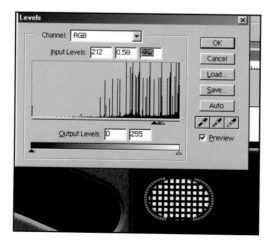

8. Next step is to add some color. Press CTRL/CMD+U to open the Hue/Saturation dialog box. Click Colorize and use similar settings as shown here. To add color to white, you will need to lower the Lightness a little. The mastery of this tool is a real balancing act. Deselect when you have finished.

We have all our little squares now and they look good except they are all the same color. Let's change the top part top make it look more lively.

9. Using the Rectangular Marquee tool, select the top two rows.

>  **TIP:** *Once you have made your initial selection, if you hold down the SHIFT key and drag out the marquee tool, the new selection will be added to the existing one.*

10. Hold down the Shift key and begin adding to the selection.

We should have a selection that cuts the top of the graph and includes partial columns of squares like so:

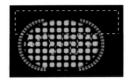

11. Open the Hue/Saturation again and dim the colors on the selected dots. Click OK and deselect (CTRL/CMD+D).

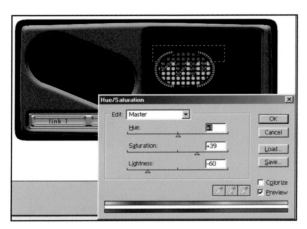

12. Lastly, just to add some stronger contrast, apply the levels command (**Image>Adjust>Levels**). Move the Highlights slider to the left a little to brighten up the highlights. Also move the mid tones to the right slightly to tighten up the image. Click OK.

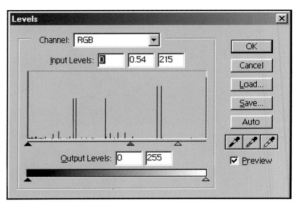

Here is the image now. It's time to give it back to Al to see what wild and wonderful ideas he has.

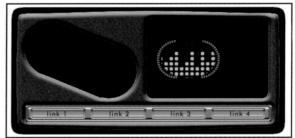

## 6: The tuner and volume dials

It appears that Colin has overlooked something in his product development. Every stereo needs a tuner and volume control. Let's create some dials to handle these important tasks.

1. For this portion, I'll again create a new layer, called 'dial', and, with the Elliptical Marquee, make a circular selection in what, to me, appears to have been created for the purpose of mounting our audio controls.

**TIP:** *To make perfect circles, hold down the SHIFT key while drawing with the elliptical marquee.*

2. We are going to be working with styles, so fill (SHIFT+BACKSPACE/DELETE) the selection with 50% gray to have pixel information in the layer to apply the style settings to.

3. I generally always start with a Bevel. As we learned on a few occasions in previous chapters, applying a bevel and then a contour to the bevel gives us an excellent edge, especially on faux-metal objects.

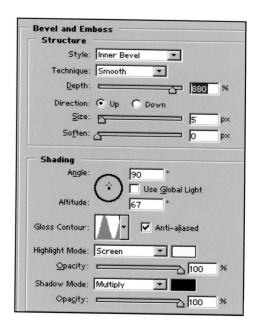

For the reflections on a radial dial, Photoshop gives us half the tools we need, but for effect we will need to build a gradient (as seen in Chapter 6).

4. Go to Gradient Overlay and change the Style to Angle. Click inside the Gradient window, to bring up the Gradient Editor and make a custom gradient for use on the dials. Take a look at the mixture of whites, grays, and blacks that I set in the example.

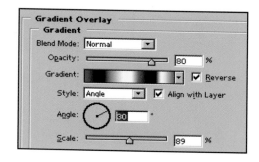

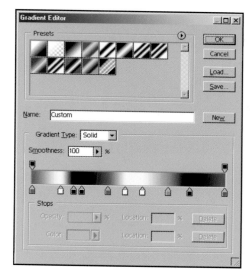

5. Next, duplicate the 'dial' layer and move the new dial into position.

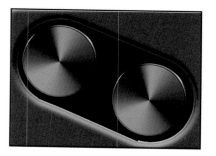

6. For a bit of variation between the two dials, access the Gradient Overlay for the duplicate dial layer, again open the Gradient Editor, and simply move my Color Stops a bit. Add an extra stop with a little blue as well.

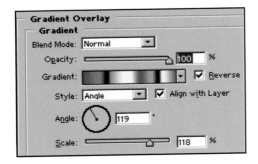

7. Let's add a bit of color to the area the dials are mounted on. To do this go to the cutout layer and, with the Magic Wand, select the black portion behind the dials.

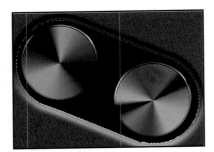

8. Create a new layer just above the 'cutout' layer and name it 'behind dials'. Now change the foreground color to a dark blue, background

to black, and fill the selection with a Foreground to Background Linear Gradient.

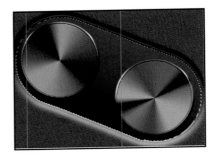

9. Give the gradient layer an Inner Shadow to give the illusion of being recessed.

10. I don't want to do much else to this, except maybe apply a Drop Shadow to the dials.

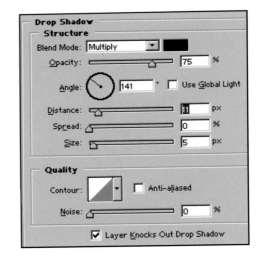

Now let's send it back to Colin for the finishing touches!

## 7: Button enhancements

Nice dials Al! They put my buttons to shame now. I guess I had better enhance them a little.

1. Activate the top 'bottom buttons' layer where we created the buttons.

2. I'm sure you remember what happened when we cut selections out of a layer style. We are going to do that a little more. This time take the Polygon Lasso tool and make triangular selections around the edges of the buttons and delete the excess.

3. Keep trimming the edges to give the buttons an angular look. Make a circular selection around the middle.

4. Press DELETE to get an interesting variation. Here are our buttons now, much better I think.

The bar that the buttons sit on feels too bright, so let's change the color.

5. Switch to the bottom 'bottom buttons' layer, which is the bar.

6. Open the Layer Style palette and add a Color Overlay. Use a similar color to the iface body.

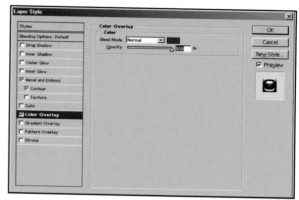

Ahh! That's much nicer.

7. While we are on quick layer styles, add a Drop Shadow to the 'base' layer. Just use the default Drop Shadow layer style and increase the Size to 38. It's amazing what a little drop shadow can do.

8. Let's put a few finishing touches on it now. We will begin by creating a simple text logo. Add the letter M in a gold color and a sans serif font. I used Futura medium here. Arial will work if you don't have that font.

9. Duplicate the M layer. Rotate it 180 degrees (**Edit>Transform>Rotate 180⁰**) so it now becomes a W.

10. Change the color of the M to blue.

11. Add a 1 pixel white outline to both type layers using the Stroke layer style.

12. Drag the text so the letters are sitting on top of one another.

13. Link the two layers and scale them down a bit as logos aren't supposed to be huge.

14. Add some more text in a small white clean typeface to complete our logo.

15. Add a few more pieces of text around the interface to dress it up a bit. I will leave it up to your creativity to add whatever type pleases you. All the fonts I used here are from the Futura family. This is a simple font that is similar to Arial or Helvetica.

## 8: Adding a glassy reflection to the display

1. Let's add a soft reflection to the display to make it look like it had a glass/plastic cover on it. Load the selection from the 'cutout' layer.

   Notice that there is more selected than we want? We could have used our "select all layers magic wand" technique that we used earlier in this chapter, but let's do it a different way so you can learn a new skill.

2. Hold down the ALT/OPTION key and draw around the unwanted selections with the Rectangular Marquee tool. The ALT/OPTION key will cause it to subtract from the selection.

You should only have the area around the screen selected now.

3. Create a new layer and name it 'highlight'.

4. Choose white as the foreground color and apply a Foreground to Transparent gradient to the selection just like we did for the glassy buttons in Chapter 12.

5. Shrink the gradient. Press CTRL/CMD+T for free transform and move the bottom two thirds of the way up. Pull the sides and top in just slightly and press the RETURN/ENTER key.

6. Soften the gradient a little more by applying a blur. Go to **Filter>Blur>Gaussian Blur** and use a Radius of 3 pixels.

7. Finally drop the Opacity down on the 'highlight' layer to 56%.

8. The very last thing we will do to the interface is create a few little highlights so make a new layer and call it 'top highlight'.

9. With a small white soft Airbrush (10 pixels and 50% pressure) dab a few highlights to the display and buttons.

10. Apply a 3.5 pixel Gaussian Blur (**Filter> Blur>Gaussian Blur**) to the 'highlights' layer to soften it up.

Finally here is the finished product. I know it was a lot of steps, but you have learned a lot of things in this chapter and it was fun writing it.

I hope you had fun doing this and you have lots of new ideas springing out of this project. You can modify these techniques and create interfaces for websites and CD ROMs or even just for fun. Look at the interfaces around you. Take note of these things and glean ideas from them that you can use in your designs. The whole world is a gallery, you just have to open your eyes and look.

This wraps up our first design project. Al is going to be kicking off the second project, which will be a movie poster.

# Design project 2
# Movie poster

Have you ever rented a movie just because you loved the cool graphics on the poster but then realized that you have picked a dud, and endured two hours of the worst acting ever committed to celluloid? I'm a sucker for those high-kitsch, low quality B-list horrors, and for this project I've decided we should develop a movie poster that looks enticing, yet reeks of bad taste.

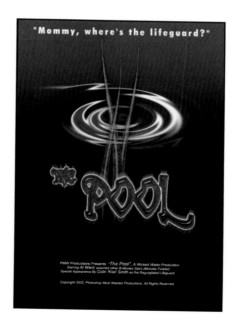

## 1: Creating the background

1. To start the project, I'll create a new image (CTRL/CMD+N) roughly the size of a small poster, 14X20 inches, with a resolution of 150 dpi, and RGB. I'll start with a transparent background and fill it shortly.

2. To be suitably spooky, we need a black background with a hint of blood. Select a black foreground, and a reddish-brown background. Then select a Foreground to Background, Linear Gradient to fill the image. We want the majority to be black, so, starting from the top, apply the gradient vertically to the top third only of the image. As you can see in the screenshot, this results in the background mainly being filled with black, with a wash of brown at the top.

3. My thought is to have an aquatic theme, maybe a creature lurking in a pool of some sort. I'll create a new layer (SHIFT+CTRL/CMD+N) and call it, 'ripples'.

4. To apply ripples to the image, I'll change my foreground color to white. Select a large, soft Airbrush (J) and spray a few white horizontal lines through the upper center of the ripples layer.

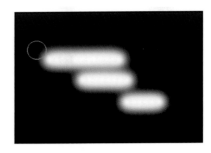

5. Change the foreground to a dark red and paint more lines, being careful to have more white than red.

6. Now, let's apply the Twirl Filter, **Filter>Distort>Twirl**.

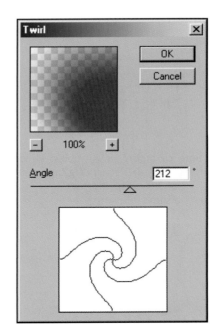

7. For effective ripples, we need to make it wider than it is tall. You can accomplish this by going to **Edit>Transform>Scale** and squeezing it from top to bottom until it flattens out.

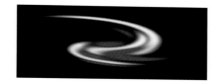

8. Now select the **Elliptical Marquee** tool (M or SHIFT+M), set a Feather radius of 5 and make an oval selection around the swirl.

9. It's time to make some ripples! I'll do that by applying **Filter>Distort>ZigZag**, selecting an Amount of 39% and 5 Ridges. Click CTRL/CMD+F to apply the same filter once more.

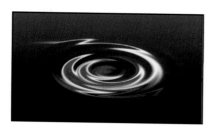

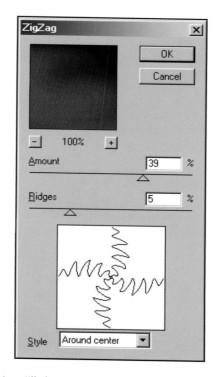

Now I'll throw on a title and some creepy movie message. Don't worry about the font as we're going to send it back to Colin who is going to do some further work with the typed sections.

## 2: Designing the text

This movie poster gives me the chills. I like the colors and realism of it. It looks like something that Tim Burton would produce! I think we need to make a few changes though.

1. Move the title towards the center and make it white to strengthen it and provide a central point of focus for the eye. Also, move the tagline to the top.

2. Put a box around the tagline. Create a new layer (SHIFT+CTRL/CMD+N) and make a rectangular selection around the top of the image.

I think we need something eerie coming out of the water. Like some tentacles, implying that there is something lurking under the surface, sucking down the lifeguard.

3. It's good to keep consistent color whenever possible. Using the **Eyedropper** tool (I), select some of that nice crimson red from the ripple.

4. Now fill our selection with the new color and notice how it provides some balance to our composition without taking away from the title.

### 3: Tentacles

1. Create a new layer (SHIFT+CTRL/CMD+N) called 'tentacles'.

2. We are going to use a technique similar to our cone tutorials in Chapter 8. Choose a green color for your foreground and make a rectangle as shown by making a selection and filling it.

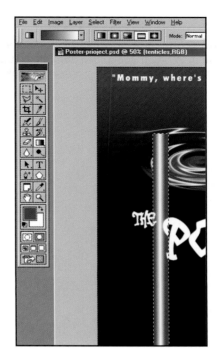

3. With the green as the foreground color and white as the background color, select a Foreground to Background, Reflected gradient. Start from the middle of the rectangle, and drag to the outside until you get your desired gradient. You may have to try it a few times to get it right, don't despair.

4. Now we will turn the cylinder into a cone. Press CTRL/CMD+T for Free Transform mode. CTRL/right-click and select Perspective from the drop-down menu. Drag one of the top corners into the center until you see a nice sharp point formed.

*Hold down the SHIFT key to keep the gradient perfectly horizontal.*

Now we have our cone shape. It looks a bit like a tentacle, but we will need it to curve to get a realistic result.

5. The Shear filter comes to the rescue, **Filter>Distort>Shear**. This filter works by clicking and dragging on the line to create a curve that will be applied to the layer. Click and drag two points in the Shear filter, and look at the result in the preview window. When you're happy click OK to apply.

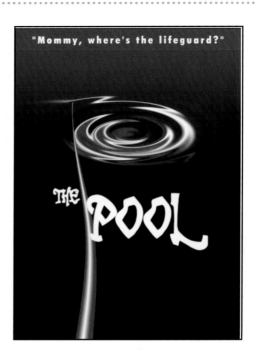

6. Duplicate the tentacle layer twice, arrange, scale, and flip the different layers until you get a nice looking group of three tentacles. You can do all this using the Free Transform tool, CTRL/CMD+T, and then right-click to access the Free Transform menu.

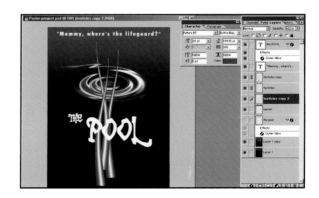

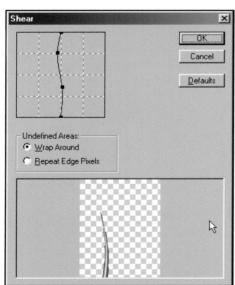

7. We need to link and then merge the tentacle layers so when we modify the layer it will affect them as a group. Select Merge Linked from the Layers menu.

One eerie looking tentacle …

8. Let's fade them into the poster in a smooth way. Add a layer mask to the tentacle layer.

9. Click D to reset the default colors, and apply a Foreground to Background, Linear Gradient to the layer mask, vertically, going upwards in the bottom section of the poster. Change the layer mode to Screen. There we have our tentacles blended into the image a bit smoother. Reposition them to suit your tastes.

10. For a stronger effect, let's duplicate the layer and make the top one have a Color Burn mode, with Opacity set to 100%.

See how adding a second layer and changing its mode produces a different kind of effect.

Ok back to you Al, have fun!

## Enhancing the tentacles

Those tentacles are a nice touch but they need work. Let's see if we can't make them a bit more sinister.

1. Apply a marble Pattern Overlay. We can use the veins in the marble to give the feel of life, and reflections from the surface.

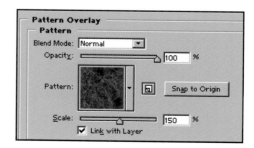

2. Set the Opacity to 60%.

3. Now, on the 'tentacles' layer (not the duplicate), apply a bright green Outer Glow set to Multiply, and a brown Inner Glow set to color Burn.

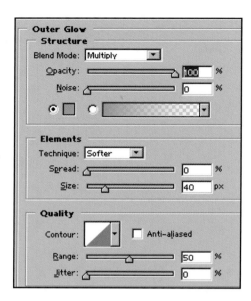

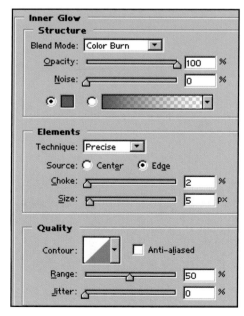

4. We'll add the same marble pattern to this original tentacles layer as we did to the duplicate.

5. Let's add an orange Inner Glow to give it a sick feel.

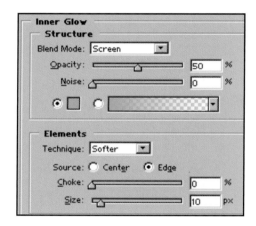

6. How about a dark green Outer Glow?

**7.** Let's go back a few chapters to the Cells layer style we created in Chapter 7 and apply it to the type.

Hey, that fits with our theme pretty well! Let's send it back to Colin again. Take it away!

## 4: Finalizing the poster

Now I think I'm going to modify the words, 'The Pool'.

1. I think we need to modify the settings for our Outer Glow. Change the blend mode to Normal, reduce the Noise, and change the color to white. Also reduce the Size to 10. Then click OK.

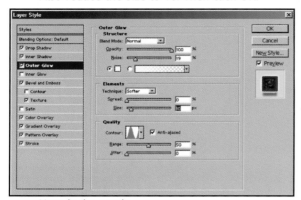

Here is the result.

Now I am going to duplicate the text and add a blur.

2. Duplicate the Pool text layer, and rasterize the type. Right-click/control-click on the layer name and choose Rasterize Layer.

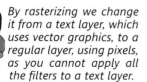

*By rasterizing we change it from a text layer, which uses vector graphics, to a regular layer, using pixels, as you cannot apply all the filters to a text layer.*

We now want to remove the layer styles for the layer we are about to blur. If we blurred it with layer styles, they would still be attached to the image and cause unwanted results. It would look like a huge mess!

3. To remove the layer style from a layer, expand the view if it isn't already. (So you can see the list of effects). Click on the word **Effects** and drag it to the trash can at the bottom of the layers palette.

4. Now to make our blur a little more pronounced it's a good idea to add some noise. This will create streaks in the image as the noise is blurred. Go to **Filter>Noise>Add Noise**, and enter a setting of around 18%. Click OK.

5. We are now ready to apply the blur, **Filter>Blur Motion Blur**, set the Angle to −90 degrees, and the Distance to 58. This will create an interesting blur behind the text.

We are going to put this to rest, but as you know every movie poster needs credits. So without further ado, here they are and here is the final, overall project. I bet you've got your popcorn in hand already!

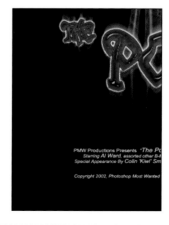

# Design project 3
# Product creation

For this last project, we thought it might be interesting to create a product entirely within Photoshop. The problem with tackling such a project is what could we create that won't take 300 pages to cover? What would incorporate elements of tutorials we've covered thus far, and teach variations on those techniques?

After much pondering, we came up with a simple, yet effective idea, 'How about a nice shiny can?'

It may not sound exciting, but with the techniques that we have learnt over the last few chapters I am sure that we can make an attractive, and realistic can. We'll give it a shot anyway; the challenge is half the fun! If you have read the previous chapters, then the differences between our approaches should be apparent.

## 1: Making the can

1. To start, create a new image and call it 'Ad'. For this project, I'm using an image 8x6 inches, resolution of 100 dpi and RGB. I'm setting the background color to white, but that will change shortly.

2. Nearly every can I've seen is a cylinder of one form or another. Let's create a new layer and call it, 'The Can'. This will be the base for our product image.

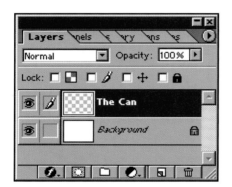

3. I'll start with a rectangular shape made with the **Rectangular Marquee** tool.

4. In chapter 6 we did some work creating custom gradients. Let's create a gradient to fill the can layer. Select the **Gradient** tool, and in the Gradient Options bar click on the Linear Gradient, Normal Mode. Click right inside the gradient example itself (in the Options bar) to bring up the Gradient Editor.

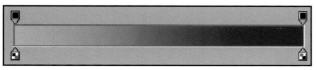

5. We are going to enter several Color Stops, changing their colors to make a gradient fit for a can. Again, if you want to know how to create stops, please see Chapter 6.

6. Fill your selection from left to right with the gradient.

7. We are going to revisit the Shear filter seen in the previous project (the movie poster) to create the curve, or dimension, of the can. Rotate the image counter-clockwise (**Edit>Transform>Rotate 90 CCW**). Deselect (CTRL/CMD+D) and apply **Filter>Distort>Shear**.

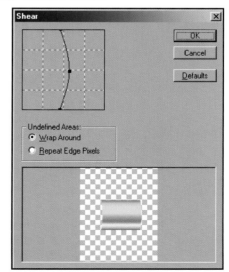

8. Once the filter is applied, rotate the image back to the original position.

9. Duplicate the can layer.

10. With the duplicate selected, go to **Image>Adjust>Desaturate** (SHIFT+CTRL/CMD+U).

11. CTRL/CMD+click the duplicate can layer to make a selection of the can. Go to **Filter>Blur>Gaussian Blur** and set the blur to 30-35 pixels.

12. Now let's apply a curve (CTRL/CMD+M) to the blurred can layer and set the Blending Mode of the layer to Overlay.

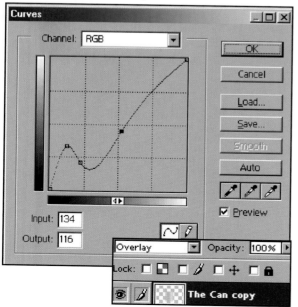

13. Select the original can layer, and create another duplicate. This time place the duplicate beneath the can layer, just above the Background.

14. Flip the second duplicate layer, 'The Can copy 2', vertically (**Edit>Transform>Flip Vertical**) and move the layer so that the lid of the can slides into place.

15. Let's darken up the lid portion. Go to **Image>Adjust>Brightness/Contrast** and set the Brightness to −100, Contrast to +70. Deselect.

16. Go back to the can layer. Create a new layer, and call it 'lip'. We are going to make the seals for the can.

17. Click on the new 'lip' layer and select the **Rectangular Marquee** tool. In the Marquee Options bar, click on the **Add to Selection** icon. Make two selections, one at the top and one at the bottom of the can. Make them a bit wider than the can itself, but not too thick.

18. Fill (**Edit>Fill**) the selections with 50% gray.

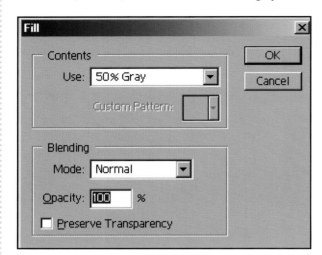

19. Now we need to curve them to match the curve of the can. Deselect the lines, and **Edit> Transform>Rotate>90° CCW**. Run **Filter> Distort>Shear** with the same settings as before. If the curve doesn't quite match, go ahead and run it again. We can do any further corrections with the transform command.

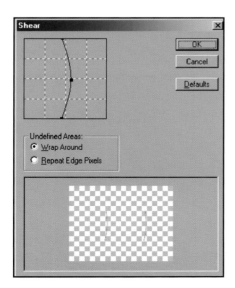

20. Go to **Edit>Transform>Rotate>90°CW**. Use **Edit>Transform>Distort** to fit the lines to the top and bottom curves of the can.

21. That stale gray on the lip layer needs help, so we will go to the Layer Styles. Access the styles for the lip layer, and enter a Bevel that is conducive to metal effects. The main item here is to apply the Gloss Contour in the Shading portion.

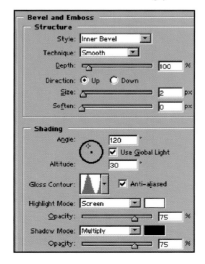

22. We will apply a gradient to this layer also, but will use the Gradient Overlay style to do so. In the Layer Styles pop up, click on the Gradient Overlay. As before we will make a new gradient, so click in the gradient example to bring up the Gradient Editor. Insert 2-3 alternating black and white stops and apply it to the lip layer.

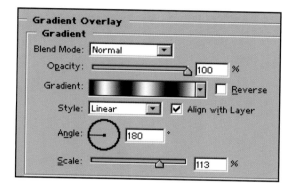

23. To lighten things up and give the lip a nice metallic sheen, go to Inner Shadow and change the color to light gray. Set the Blend Mode to Screen, and increase the Opacity.

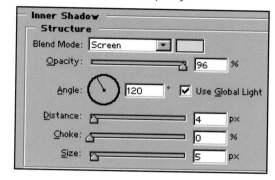

## 2: Applying the label

For this next portion, I've created a fancy little label, which has been provided for you for download at the friends of ED web site; www.friend-sofed.com/code.

1. To begin, open your label and paste it into a new layer in the can image.

2. Select **Edit>Transform>Scale** and move the edges of the label in to match the sides of the can in width. Position the label so it is centered on the can.

3. Let's add just a touch of a Drop Shadow with the Layer Styles. Reduce the Distance to 1 and the size to 1 or 2. Change the angle so the shadow doesn't appear off the side of the can.

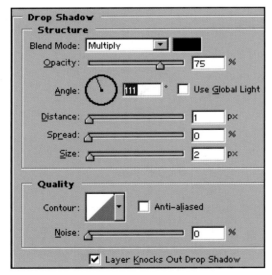

4. The label needs blending into the can a bit, so create a new layer called 'label blending'.

5. We need to create a new gradient, so select the Gradient tool. In the Gradient Options bar, again click in the Gradient example to bring up the Gradient Editor. Insert color stops similar to the ones in the example below.

6. CTRL/CMD+click the label layer to make a selection (stay in the label blending layer), and fill the label blending layer with a Linear Gradient from left to right. Set the Blending mode of the layer to Multiply.

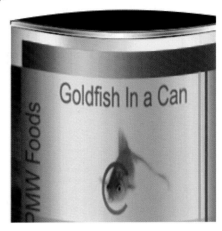

7. Decide on a color scheme for your background. I'm using a gold to brown gradient, so again I'll create the gradient with the Gradient Editor, as I don't want just a foreground to background blend, but would like a third 'midtone' introduced as well. I'm filling my background layer with the Linear Gradient from top to bottom.

8.  Using the **Polygonal Lasso** tool with a Feather setting of 12 pixels, create a rough selection of the background on the right side of the can. Copy the selection from the background and paste it into a new layer (**Layer>New>Layer via Copy** or CTRL/CMD+J). This will help give the illusion that the color of the room is being reflected on the can.

9.  Change the name of the layer to 'background reflection' and set it above the can layer.

10. Let's add a little Noise (**Filter>Noise>Add Noise**) with a setting of 1%, and a Motion Blur (**Filter>Blur>Motion Blur**) with an Angle of 90 and Distance of 33, to blend the reflection and give it a bit of character.

11. If you recall, we have a layer called 'The Can copy' that we ran a blur filter on a few steps ago. CTRL/CMD+click this layer, you should get a rounded, feathered selection. Once you have the selection, go to **Select>Inverse** (SHIFT+CTRL/CMD+I).

12. Create a new layer above the label. Name it 'can blending'. Fill (Edit>Fill) the selection with black.

13. CTRL/CMD+click The Can layer, **Select>Inverse**, and delete the black around the can. Deselect.

14. Let's dress up the background. Create a duplicate of the Background layer. Using the Rectangular Marquee tool, select the top 2/3 of the Background duplicate layer and delete the selection.

15. Select the **Move** tool, and with the arrow keys move the remaining portion of the background down so that a horizon appears behind the can. Deselect.

16. With the Rectangular Marquee tool, with The Can copy 2 layer active select the top 1/3 of the can. Paste this into a new layer behind the can (CTRL/CMD+J).

17. Move it down and to the left so that it rests on the horizon line.

18. In the same layer, click on the Polygonal Lasso tool, ensure the Feather is set to 0. Create a selection leading from the bottom left corner of the can to the left bottom corner of the shadow we just created. Make the selection large enough so that when we fill it, it will look like a complete shadow bisected by the joint of the wall and floor. Fill the selection with black.

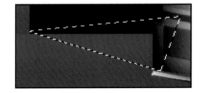

19. Change the Layer Blending mode of the shadow layer to Overlay, and set the Opacity to 70%.

20. Apply a Gaussian Blur (**Filter>Blur>Gaussian Blur**) of 8 to 10 to soften the shadow.

That's about the end of the product tutorial. I wonder what it might look like in an advertisement? Perhaps something like this!

It has been a pleasure to bring these tutorials to you. We hope that, as you worked through the effects found in this book, you started thinking of different ways in which to apply what you've learned. Effects are cool, and tutorials fun, but above all, you've learnt about the process of creating something a little special in Photoshop, using layer styles; layer masks; channels, displacement maps, custom gradients, the free transform menu, and more.

Sometimes, the hardest part of designing is breaking out of the restrictive, 'How did they do that?' mode, and instead thinking 'Hey, I can do that!' With a little bit of imagination, and the knowledge you've gained from this book, you'll be able to go out there and work some real Photoshop magic. Have fun.

# Appendix

## Shortcuts

Throughout this book, you will probably have noticed that we have included different ways of carrying out the same action. An example of this would be:

Create a new layer by selecting **Layer>New Layer** or pressing SHIFT+CTRL/CMD+N.

In this statement, we have told you how to add a new layer to your project by using either the menus (the Layer menu in this case) or a keyboard shortcut. Whenever we have suggested one of these shortcuts, we have given both the PC and Mac version so everyone can use it.

Shortcuts, by definition, will increase your working efficiency, so it's well worth taking the time to learn a few of them. Throughout the book we have shown you a number of different shortcuts whenever we have the chance to use them in the exercises. By now, you'll probably have memorized a few of them through sheer repetition, and by using them in these exercises alone, but you can't be expected to know them all. Here, we have listed all the shortcuts we have shown you. We've grouped dependent on where they are found so let's start with those found by using menus and then we'll look at the ones associated with the tools.

We are not listing every shortcut available with Photoshop just the more commonly used ones.

# MOST WANTED: KEYBOARD SHORTCUTS

## Menus

### FILE

| Menu Listing | Shortcut |
|---|---|
| New | CTRL/CMD+N |
| Open | CTRL/CMD+O |
| Save | CTRL/CMD+S |
| Save As | SHIFT+CTRL/CMD+S |
| Print | CTRL/CMD+P |

### EDIT

| Menu Listing | Shortcut |
|---|---|
| Cut | CTRL/CMD+X |
| Copy | CTRL/CMD+C |
| Paste | CTRL/CMD+V |
| Fill | SHIFT+BACKSPACE/DELETE |
| Fill>Foreground | ALT/OPT+BACKSPACE/DELETE |
| Fill>Background | CTRL/CMD+BACKSPACE/DELETE |
| Free Transform | CTRL/CMD+T |

### IMAGE

| Menu Listing | Shortcut |
|---|---|
| Adjust>Levels | CTRL/CMD+L |
| Adjust>Auto Levels | SHIFT+CTRL/CMD+L |
| Adjust>Curves | CTRL/CMD+M |
| Adjust>Hue Saturation | CTRL/CMD+U |
| Adjust>Desaturate | SHIFT+CTRL/CMD+U |
| Adjust>Invert | CTRL/CMD+I |

### LAYER

| Menu Listing | Shortcut |
|---|---|
| New>Layer | CTRL/CMD+N |
| New>Layer via Copy | CTRL/CMD+J |
| New>Layer via Cut | SHIFT+CTRL/CMD+J |
| Merge Down | CTRL/CMD+E |

### SELECT

| Menu Listing | Shortcut |
|---|---|
| All | CTRL/CMD+A |
| Deselect | CTRL/CMD+D |
| Inverse | SHIFT+CTRL/CMD+I |
| Feather | Alt+Ctrl/Cmd+D |

### FILTER

| Menu Listing | Shortcut |
|---|---|
| Last Filter | CTRL/CMD+F |

### VIEW

| Menu | Listing Shortcut |
|---|---|
| Zoom In | CTRL/CMD++ |
| Zoom Out | CTRL/CMD+- |
| Show/Hide Extras | CTRL/CMD+H |
| Show/Hide Guides | CTRL/CMD+' |
| Show/Hide Rulers | CTRL/CMD+R |

## Tools

| Tool | Button | Shortcut |
|---|---|---|
| Rectangular Marquee | | M OR SHIFT+M |
| Elliptical Marquee | | M OR SHIFT+M |
| Move | | V |
| Lasso | | L OR SHIFT+L |
| Polygonal Lasso | | L OR SHIFT+L |
| Magic Wand | | W |
| Airbrush | | J |
| Paintbrush | | B |
| History Brush | | Y |
| Gradient | | G OR SHIFT+G |
| Paint Bucket | | G OR SHIFT+G |
| Blur | | R OR SHIFT+R |
| Smudge | | R OR SHIFT+R |
| Type | | T |
| Pen | | P |
| Rectangle | | U OR SHIFT+U |
| Rounded Rectangle | | U OR SHIFT+U |
| Ellipse | | U OR SHIFT+U |
| Polygon | | U OR SHIFT+U |
| Line | | U OR SHIFT+U |
| Custom Shape | | U OR SHIFT+U |
| Eyedropper | | I |
| Switch foreground and background colors | | X |
| Default colors | | D |